David A. Collings

The Rubble of Culture

Debris of an Extinct Thought

CCC2 Irreversibility

Series Editors: Tom Cohen and Claire Colebrook

The second phase of 'the Anthropocene,' takes hold as tipping points speculated over in 'Anthropocene 1.0' click into place to retire the speculative bubble of "Anthropocene Talk". Temporalities are dispersed, the memes of 'globalization' revoked. A broad drift into a de facto era of managed extinction events dawns. With this acceleration from the speculative into the material orders, a factor without a means of expression emerges: climate panic.

David A. Collings

The Rubble of Culture

Debris of an Extinct Thought

( )
OPEN HUMANITIES PRESS

London 2023

First edition published by Open Humanities Press 2023

Copyright © 2023 David A. Collings

Print ISBN 978-1-78542-132-7

PDF ISBN 978-1-78542-131-0

( )

OPEN HUMANITIES PRESS

Open Humanities Press is an international, scholar-led open access publishing collective whose mission is to make leading works of contemporary critical thought freely available worldwide. More at http://openhumanitiespress.org

Contents

Preface: In the absence of a future

Today we live in a world whose future is rapidly disappearing. The global environmental crisis, of which the prospect of severe and irreversible climate change is the most obvious signal, threatens to alter beyond recovery the condition of the biosphere on which our various cultures and indeed human life itself depends.

This stunning transformation raises the strong possibility, approaching the likelihood, that humankind itself may disappear. That possibility alone demands careful reflection. While it would be foolish to predict in detail what will actually take place over the coming decades, the process currently under way already reveals that assumptions about the perpetual survival of humankind (however conceived, within or beyond ideological deployments of "the human") which underlie traditional and modern societies alike are no longer credible. Today the premises of the world's cultures, contrary to what they seem to promise, are neither grounded nor enduring, but fragile, transient, and perishable; neither sacred nor secular expectations are secure. As a result, the discourses and practices based on those premises are crumbling; the vast architectures that enable contemporary cultures are now being reduced to rubble.

Accordingly, while one cannot know today the actual course of events in the future, one can know that the possible disappearance of humanity within a century – or mere decades – rather than over the course of a geological expanse of time irreparably harms the foundations of thought. That much is certain. What follows, then, is an attempt to take *that* certainty seriously, to work with the unthinkable thought of what I will call the *terminus*.

While various renditions of global environmental crisis are widely familiar – while studies of the current state of the biosphere, the history of human practices that have contributed to that state and its future, and the technologies and policies we could implement to address the crisis are abundant – those who study the world's cultural legacies have not yet fully engaged with the implications of the terminus for the conditions of thought. Indeed, it is no simple task to do so. A commonplace attitude already reveals the difficulty of the challenge. When people contemplate the possible disappearance of humankind's future, they often respond, in effect, "Well, then, that's it! What is there left to say?" – as if that prospect annihilates the possibility of confronting it, of pondering its import, of thinking it through. Yet the imperative of thought does not disappear in this unprecedented moment; the demand for us to understand our condition does not simply go away when the abyss opens up before us. (On my use of "we" and associated pronouns in this book, see a short essay below.) Nevertheless, insofar as the very ideas we might call upon to interpret that condition are based on premises that no longer hold true, the shattering of culture is not only an object for thought, for it is now the condition of thought itself. To think the rubble of culture, one has little choice but to think *from within* the rubble, to *enact* – as well as to examine – the debris of thought.

What form might be suitable to such a thought? The traditional book with its guiding thesis, its chapters, and its overall conceptual unity implies a coherence that is no longer possible for us. What beckons now is a different procedure – a series of small essays, tentative forays, provisional attempts in which a damaged thought might articulate itself. Such forays will be incomplete and inconsistent, suggesting lines of argument that may fray and collapse in their own right, indeed meditations that may at times diverge from each other or glimpse unsuspected possibilities even within the situation of extinct thought. Distant precedents for this procedure may be found in Benjamin's theses "On the Concept of History" or Adorno's *Minima Moralia*, brilliant instances of how thought takes shape under duress.[1] Yet such works answered to exigencies less dire than those impressed on us today; those models, however acute, can only partially anticipate the form that thought must take in our moment.

What range, what focus, should thought sustain now? If, as I have suggested, the premises on which the world's cultures have typically grounded themselves are now crumbling, thought faces a task of rearticulation on an immense scale. Accordingly, I have set out to do no more than to trace the cracks now appearing in cultural premises most familiar to me. Although those premises have shaped ideas and practices largely in the West, my goal here is not to affirm them once again – to extend still further the hegemony of the West – but rather to discern signs of their dissolution under the sign of the terminus, and on occasion to do so while invoking alternative premises and unsuspected alternatives. (I touched on some relevant themes in an earlier book regarding climate change written for the general public, focusing on the dissonance between the narratives by which we live and the weakening of a future on which those narratives rely, but that book did not address the key questions I take up here.)[2] Moreover, while the concerns I will address – primarily in the underpinnings of Western religious traditions, modern conceptions of history and politics, aspects of modern philosophy, the status of literature, the place of humanity within the biosphere, and the shape of temporality and affect – include many arenas of inquiry, they represent only a fraction of those one must address today. Yet it would be a mistake to suppose that a more valiant effort could provide a comprehensive account of our condition, for there is no "whole" of which we are a part, no foundation on which one might make a fully self-consistent, grounded, or totalizing judgment. These forays are not fragments of a larger argument, but shards in a field of debris whose horizons we cannot see.

1   The extinction of thought

A terminal history. – A leading sign of the difference between previous meditations and our own is the task of conceiving of a *terminal* thought. Recently "late" capitalism has become a term in critical
thinking, much as others have written of a "late" modernity. But the
hour is now later than merely late; we face the prospect of a terminus,
a nonredemptive endpoint to the traditions in which we live. We live
in a *terminal* capitalism, a *terminal* modernity. Taking us well beyond
any instance of lateness or belatedness, as well as beyond any "post-"
condition, the prospect of this terminus demands that we think our
condition otherwise – in terms of its potentially absolute cessation.

A terminal thought is neither the most insightful, the most con-
clusive, nor the best. Nor does it capture the telos of history in the
final cause of ethical action, the Day of Judgment, or the culminating
event that reveals the inner logic of the creation. Nor is it an idea that
sublates all that came before into an absolute perspective. Instead,
it attempts to grasp what it means when the capacity to conceptual-
ize ceases *tout court* – and thus confronts the radical contingency of
thought or its premises within the biosphere.

Would it then apprehend the cancellation of any prospect that history might reach a moment of closure? But as the pivotal work of
Reinhart Koselleck makes clear, modernity itself is premised on the
notion of an open history.[3] That history, liberated from the assumption that human affairs take place within a bounded sphere, cycling
through predictable and known possibilities, now plays out in a temporality with a radically undetermined future, whose contours may
be reshaped *ad infinitum* by collective action, a host of economic and
social developments, or unforeseen events. What confronts thought
today is the cancellation of the idea even of this open history. It does
not follow that history therefore falls back into a bounded, predictable space; rather, history becomes neither bounded nor open, neither
cyclic nor linear, neither knowable nor unknowable. History continues to take place, to be sure, but it loses its shape, its momentum, its
direction, its coherence.

Yet because this terminus arises before us as a consequence of
modernity – as the effect of human action especially in the industrial
era – this radical incoherence reveals what was at play within modernity all along. The terminus, it seems, is not simply a cessation yet
to take place; it is embedded within an open history itself. Evidently,

the sense that the world could break out of temporal bounds relied on an analogous insistence that it break out of environmental limits as well, that the open future could come to pass if modernity could also operate freely in a material scene far more capacious than premodern norms allowed. (Indeed, this conjunction was at least partly evident to advocates for the expansion of capitalism from the start; they pressed for such expansion by dismissing what was already known of its severe costs to the environment.[4]) The terminus has been the underside of an open history as its tacit and devastating counterpart all along: the unbounded future and the prospect of human disappearance have arisen and unfolded together as part of the same process. A heightened existence solicits the arrival of inexistence. Modernity may thus never truly occur; all along it has taken place within the scene of its own future undoing. It is a mirage, a panoply over the abyss, a vanishing carnival.

Thus to think the terminus of history is also to think the collapse of the concept of history itself, the undoing of what we thought history was and is. But because we live within the history that has lost its coherence, our very mode of articulation becomes incoherent as well: from what moment do we speak, on what basis, and to what future? Indeed, what is it to speak, or to write, at this moment? For what purpose – to what end – does one speak at all? Does the heightened existence of thought also solicit its inexistence? Indeed it does: even these words arise from within the scene of their own erasure. The thought of the terminus is already the terminus of thought.

Pile of debris. – If modern history has produced its own undoing, then the concepts that apparently drive it forward – such as enlightenment, liberation, or abundance – crack and fade. In the default of such promises, with the erasure of an open future, that history loses its narrative arc, its justification, its purpose. Yet the events of that history remain in force. No longer a story of progress, no longer the scene of fruitful transformation, its events "take place" – but in what place? Without that narrative arc, without that open future, these events are stranded in a framework that dissolves itself, in a trajectory that undermines any narrative, in a scene without a ground. Accordingly, the collapse of modern temporality leaves behind an array of happenings that lack even the integrity of events – a field of debris.

Do we then find ourselves in the scene Walter Benjamin depicts in his theses "On the Concept of History"? In his ninth thesis, Benjamin reads Paul Klee's *Angelus Novus* as an "angel of history" who, looking back over the past, "sees one single catastrophe, which keeps piling wreckage upon wreckage and hurls it at his feet." The angel, inspired by a redemptive impulse, "would like to stay, awaken the dead, and make whole what has been smashed. But a storm is blowing from Paradise and has got caught in his wings; it is so strong that the angel can no longer close them." As a result, "[t]his storm drives him irresistibly into the future, to which his back is turned, while the pile of debris before him grows toward the sky. What we call progress is *this* storm."[5]

It might seem that the consternation of this angel perfectly captures the horror of our moment, that this passage's demystification of progress speaks exactly to our condition. Before the prospect of a terminus, history cannot progress; its sequence of events merely piles debris on top of debris. In such a condition, the possibility of any redemptive action is barred; no agent, not even an angel, can redeem what is now evidently irredeemable. In this thesis, if not in others, Benjamin abandons the prospect of messianic hope; the angel, incapable of interrupting the wreckage of history, can only witness its accumulation.

But this angel still has the capacity to look back over the totality of this debris: "Where a chain of events appears before *us, he* sees one single catastrophe," the one that keeps hurling "wreckage" at his feet.[6] This angel maintains a perspective denied to those living within history; although the storm of progress holds open his wings, giving him an intimacy with the scene he beholds, he is not caught within that scene but hovers just beyond or above it, witnessing the disaster of which he is not quite a part. But now that what hovers just before and beyond us is history's terminus, not even the fantasy of redemption can remain, nor any wind of progress hold open the angel's wings; the history of which he is the angel dissolves, leaving only a pile of debris reaching up to the sky.

The thought of the terminus shatters Benjamin's angel; the storm sweeps over him, closes his wings, and buries him under still further piles of trash. Henceforth the angel of history finds himself *within* the pile he once witnessed, tossed about in that storm; crushed, denuded, he cannot see the whole, cannot sum up the scene in "one single catastrophe," even if he knows that what surrounds him is something other than a "chain of events." Now a disabled angel, a seer who cannot see, a supernatural figure reduced to a merely finite status, he becomes one more figure within the wreckage, a denizen of the ruins.

The thinker of modern history can have no other fate. She, too, can think only from within the ruins. To think the debris is to enact the debris of thought; the objective is also the subjective genitive. The angel of history can only be a historical angel. Yet this formulation is too confident. Is the field of debris even conceivable as the object of thought? Is this subject truly a subject – or does this shattered subject, finding itself within the wreckage of objects, enact only a fraudulent, mendacious form of thought? Can the thinker truly apprehend what she cannot even conceive?

The extinction of thought. – But why must thought set aside a figure for seeing human history from beyond the terminus? Why shouldn't we be able to incorporate a final perspective on the fate of human-kind into our thinking today? Isn't the thought of the terminus pre-cisely the sort that could enable a magisterial overview of the shape of human history – or at least of its form in recent centuries?

These questions make explicit a confidence that tacitly under-lies several contemporary approaches toward describing the ongo-ing environmental disaster. Consider the current usage of the term "Anthropocene."[7] Names for geological periods refer to bounded units of geological time, which are "decided on fundamental changes in the Earth system, recorded in the rock record."[8] The Anthropocene is no exception: if this term is adopted by geologists, it will refer to a layer whose characteristics a geologist could identify to differentiate it from other strata in the earth record. Such a term takes for granted that there will be scientific observers – and thus human beings – to carry out such observations indefinitely into the future. It builds into our conception of the present the notion that it will be subject to analysis by a human scientist in the future. As Srinivas Aravamudan comments, the notion points to a "physical layer of the planetary ter-rain, anticipated from some future standpoint that could very well be a vantage point beyond human existence."[9] But if what marks our era is to become visible in a scene with no human observer, the record will also disappear as an object of observation, erasing this and all other geological eras as objects of thought. Indeed, as Günther Anders argues in a related context, human extinction would destroy the past itself, for after such an event "the past will not even have been the past," for every conceivable reference to it will have been expunged.[10] Under the prospect of the terminus, we live not in the Anthropocene – nor in a series of alternatives to the term proposed in many critiques of its naive evocation of a universal humanity – but in strata visible to no one, composed of nothing, made of oblivion.

A similar objection applies to the phrase "the world without us," popularized by Alan Weisman's book of that title.[11] Weisman depicts what would take place on earth if humanity suddenly vanished, using the best current knowledge to project how that future might unfold. But in doing so, he relies on the perspective of human knowledge and necessarily describes it as it would appear to us – even though on his own premises no human observer would be present in that world. Thus as Eugene Thacker points out, the "world-without-us is a paradoxical concept; the moment we think it and attempt to act on it, it ceases to be the world-in-itself and becomes the world-for-us."[12] Moreover, this scenario resembles that found in the idea of a posthuman future, which as Marija Grech argues, simultaneously invites us "to think of a future devoid of any human presence . . . and anthropomorphises this humanless future into a world that the human can continue to see, reflect and read itself in."[13] It also confirms that broad pattern identified by Claire Colebrook, whereby "the only world is the human world, and the only apocalypse or end that we imagine is one in which we lose ourselves. Extinction and apocalypse become events of the subject."[14]

These concerns even pertain to the notion that humankind may go extinct. Because the notion of extinction arises within the frameworks of modern geology and biology, which demonstrate that species appear and disappear from the fossil record, one must rely on those frameworks to speak of human extinction as well. Once again, then, this term relies on the observational status of the scientist, and thus on a human observer's impossible presence in a world in which humanity is absent. Moreover, the designation of this event as extinction applies a biological notion to a cultural catastrophe, placing it in the framework of the material history of the species rather than of the conditions that forced that history to take place. What we endure is not merely extinction; it is an economic, cultural, and political disaster, one that includes the context for science as well as for what the scientist observes. In short, it describes as extinction an event that transcends a purely material description, classifying as extinction what is actually a form of self-erasure.

This approach to the question of human extinction reframes the concerns of recent speculative realist thought, especially in the work of Ray Brassier, who emphasizes the philosophical import of the eventual extinction of the sun.[15] In his work, however, such questions arise from the prospect of an event that exemplifies the logic of a world whose processes transpire without any reference to humanity whatsoever, and thus a world that exists outside of humanity's perception of it. While speculative realism's attempt to think a world truly exterior to thought remains urgent for anyone reconceiving of humanity's situation today, its emphasis on a distant event – and one not caused by human action – keeps in place an extinction caused by purely astronomical and biological processes.[16] As I have suggested, however, the terminus speaks of something more: insofar as its potential arrival merely a few decades from now arises from the impact of human actions, it belongs also to a cultural and political history through which humanity may bring about its own annihilation, and what is more, an erasure that it hastens to bring about despite ample and vigorous forewarning.

These examples suggest that it is no easy matter to attempt to conceive of the present outside a traditional anthropocentric viewpoint. Because even depictions of a world without human beings assumes the spectral persistence of human observation or thought, our situation requires us to adopt an even more rigorous approach whereby human thought conceives of its own disappearance.[17] A scrupulously nonanthropocentric response to the terminus acknowledges that with the terminus, thought itself disappears and that as a result, no one ever attains that final overview of human history. Neither science nor thought, neither our proleptic figures of finality nor our present surmises of that nonhuman future, will survive, for the terminus will bring about the annihilation of thought itself.

In that case, one who wishes to incorporate the implications of the terminus into one's thought today must perforce bring that future nullity to bear – not on humanity's future extinction, for reasons given above, nor any other *objective* condition, but rather a condition that befalls the *subject*: thought's own disappearance. One can apprehend the significance of this moment only if one thinks through the forthcoming erasure of thought itself. "The idea of human extinction implies the death of all human beings," writes Thacker, "including those who would think this idea and bear witness to its reality."[18] In that case, as he argues elsewhere, "extinction can never be adequately thought, since its very possibility presupposes the absolute negation of all thought."[19]

Thus the impossibility of perceiving human extinction from outside it – of surveying the terminus of human history – instances *another* level of extinction: not only the cancellation of mastery itself, the undoing of the very prospect of an overview, but also the notion that thought can adequately address its own preconditions *even in the present*. To bring that future prospect to bear, one must accept a certain radical nullity of thought even now. If thought cannot offer itself to its own future, if it disappears even as it is articulated, unworked even in its most basic operations, then is it still thought? But if it is not, what is it? What appears even in the midst of that disappearing? How is thought still thought in the midst of its extinction?

Le débris de. – At a culminating moment of deconstructive articulation, Jacques Derrida brings *Glas* to its terminus with the words "le débris de," hinting at a pun with the author's name and thereby placing himself within the heap of signifiers that is this text. Furthermore, these final words in that text's right-hand column – "Today, here, now, the debris of" – echo the opening words in the left-hand column, "what [sic], after all, of the remains(s), today, for us, here, now, of a Hegel?," point to a certain recasting of the recursive structure of Hegel's *Phenomenology*. For Derrida, it seems, Hegel's dialectics can appear "here, now" only in the medium of debris.[20]

In *Glas*, deconstruction haunts the immense trash-heap of articulation, living on where the logic of the signifier has reduced the tradition to a pile of rubble. Perhaps it, too, has already survived a terminal thought. Perhaps the undoing of the cultural legacy has already taken place, quite apart from any crisis in the biosphere; perhaps a certain event, toward which Derrida at times gestures, has already made the transcendental signified no longer credible, no longer capable of centering the architecture of thought.

Yet to arrive at such a stance, deconstruction requires the patient work whereby thought dismantles thought, examining significant articulations to trace how signifiers unravel the texts in which they appear. The very labor of deconstruction that sets it apart, that makes it such a bracing performance, arises because those writings have not yet explicitly and evidently unwoven themselves, because despite all odds, what Derrida considers the tradition of Western metaphysics endures, even after its closure.

In stark contrast, terminal thought considers an event that unworks texts without requiring any such labor of deciphering – an event that erases the very space of thought, the matrix of articulation itself. Rather than patiently demonstrating that the text unweaves its transcendental signified, that no form of essence or center can remain valid, terminal thought delineates the traces of an undoing of thought that sweeps away any activity of deconstruction along with any essence to be deconstructed. For the same reason, it cuts through the mode of rhetorical reading initiated by Paul de Man, no matter how rigorous or demystifying.[21] It does so because the thought of the terminus refers to an event that takes place even if no one ever undertakes the conceptual labor of demonstrating its effect on articulation or on thought; that event transpires not through the medium of careful rhetorical reading but even *against* such a medium, cancelling the preconditions even of deconstruction.

Some might object that such an undoing of the preconditions of thought comes to pass without any such labor, in a materiality that, even if it operates in language, takes place outside human reference. De Man, for example, in keeping with his consistent emphasis on the anti-anthropocentric implications of rhetorical figuration, at one point refers to the "fundamental non-human character of language."[22] In a similar vein, Martin Hägglund argues that a radically nonhuman activity infests the very logic of signification, aligning the Derridean thematic of the trace with certain aspects of speculative realism.[23] Moreover, Monique Allewaert suggests that a radical decentering takes place on the level of "materialist figuration" – in the displacing movements within the field of matter itself.[24] But if figuration operates in its own nonhuman domain, it will endure beyond the activity of rhetorical reading per se; it will outlast the annihilation of humanity. Thus insofar as such arguments identify aspects of an activity that is always already underway, decentering language and materiality *in general*, they cannot anticipate the thought of the terminus, which exemplifies not only what that logic permits but also an imminent and contingent *event*. It is not enough to theorize a figuration that may endure even after the disappearance of humanity; as I suggested above, the thought of the terminus must go further and think the cessation of thought itself – even the cessation of our ability to decipher the nonhuman dimensions of figuration.

Yet this terminus, however alien to thought, does not transpire in a space utterly hostile to it, for thought can register it, contend with it, and make it felt even where it remains inconceivable. Thus thought confronts an erasure that takes place elsewhere while remaining an urgent fact for thought itself, a fact that, it soon discovers, undoes what it is. Insofar as thought in this process confronts its own annihilation in a procedure one might call *terminist* argument, it might seem at times to resemble deconstruction, but in fact it operates otherwise, for it considers how thought is undone by something that militates against conceptualization, articulation, and reading alike. The thought of the trace or of the figure, it turns out, is not yet the thought of the terminus: only the latter names a blankness that overrides our tracing of the trace, that decimates even our apprehension of figuration.

Time unredeemed. – In those theses, Benjamin proposes that the coming revolution will redeem the dead; rather than being condemned to a history irrevocably contained by historical time, past generations will be redeemed from the Antichrist, from the ruling classes who have "never ceased to be victorious."[25] Taking place in the radical, messianic "now-time" that explodes the "continuum of history," the revolution will grasp the past in a flash of recognition, releasing the losers of history from their subjection.[26] In such a moment, humanity's past will become "citable in all its moments," each of which is now an instance of Judgment Day.[27]

But under the pressure of the terminus, thought recognizes that this messianic moment may never take place, for today the sheer momentum of change in the biosphere may override even revolution. The past may well remain unredeemed, unreleased from its exile. Even more, because the carbon dioxide we currently emit will continue to circulate in the atmosphere for over a century, cancelling in advance the potentially positive effects of future political interventions, future generations will be confined to a fate dispensed by the present. Still worse, insofar as the present takes place under the sign of a future that may never redeem it, it too falls into the fate of that past, captured by a history whose continuum it cannot explode: in that case, the present is already consigned to a defeat that it shares with the past and the future.

Thus the terminus cancels the hope embedded in messianic time. The latter makes itself felt through its very absence, through the gap that a missing revolutionary possibility leaves in the continuum of history. The generations of the past, present, and future call out for redemption; the dead, the living, the unborn reach out their hands, seeking release from this catastrophic history. But the terminus condemns us all to our place within the debris, within a defeat from which no new victor will redeem us. In a telling irony, this time even the victors will be defeated as well: the Antichrist will be brought down by his own weapons, progress by its own storm.

Paradox of terminal judgment. – Is terminal thought a lament for the end of the West, a dirge for a dying tradition, an expression of love for something we have lost? Or is it a realization that this tradition brought forth an immense horror, that it embodied and produced an immeasurable disaster? Are we caught within what is passing, feeling the loss of something to which we are attached in innumerable ways, or are we aware that this culture is killing us, devastating the very conditions for our lives? Insofar as this latter judgment must take precedence, cutting through our fidelity to the societies in which we live, it does so against our habits of affiliation with them, violating a loyalty to what they represent. We resist this judgment even as we find it irresistible.

A similar paradox arises in the context of scientific research into the state of the biosphere. Careful research establishes probabilistic scenarios of what will take place under the pressure of various destructive human activities, delineating the most likely changes in the biosphere. But such research also reveals the cost of the entire cultural and material infrastructure that creates the conditions for research itself. The assessment of what our own activities cause elicits a judgment of the mechanisms that made it possible to arrive at that assessment in the first place.

In both cases, the judgment regarding disaster is also a judgment regarding itself: here judgment seems to fall into an aporia. Such an aporia, one might argue, echoes the aporetic features of Kant's critical philosophy, in which judgment also reaches an impasse as it examines itself.[28] But today, the impasse is imposed not by the deficits inherent in the faculties of mind but by a limit that the terminus imposes on thought, a terminus that thought can neither dismiss as alien nor thematize as part of itself. Accordingly it can no longer examine its condition by means of a critique of its own capacities; its procedure must contend with a factor that is at once contingent – what seems to be the merely empirical event of its approaching cessation – and imperious, at once less than and more than an aspect of itself. It is caught by a terminus that mangles the categories by which it has comprehended itself.

Yet even in the wreckage of critique, thought can attempt to register its new condition. When the judgment of disaster becomes a judgment of itself, thought almost seems to cancel itself, to erase its own validity. Yet this judgment is not, for all that, invalid: what it finds still holds. Accordingly, we reach the paradox that in judging itself as disaster, disastrous judgment speaks the truth. Indeed, it is only because it speaks the truth about itself as disaster that it enters this aporia. A similar paradox applies in another feature of this situation. Judging itself, judgment also finds that the conditions that led to its action should never have appeared on the field of history; it decides against its own emergence. Yet it can do so only because of that emergence, because it appeared on the field of history. Thus thought can only judge itself as disaster thanks to its place in a disastrous history – and can only know its untruth because it knows its judgment about itself holds true. Judgment's truth and its aporia emerge together.

Judgment's self-disabling act makes possible a devastating insight into our situation. It ultimately reveals the fundamental untruth that we live so intensely, the untruth of our culture, the untruth even of science itself. Yet in doing so, it liberates us from being entirely bound to this untruth; it cracks open the history that has produced us, enabling us to acknowledge the gap in our history that indexes the revolution that did not take place. It enables us to gain a fidelity to what did not happen, an event that could have intervened into modernity itself. It attaches us, then, to the impossible – to a principle we can invoke even if our history did not allow its realization.

Yet the notion of the impossible event brings with it a further contradiction, a political aporia. Because that event did not occur, our awareness of it returns us to our judgment of the history we actually do occupy, the field of debris in which we find ourselves. The thought of the terminus enables us to reach this judgment, but it also speaks of the liberating event in the idiom of the impossible and thereby binds us to the field that the impossible event would have repudiated, the field of the merely possible. The thought of the impossible at once proposes an alternative history and erases it, bringing forth the prospect of an event that it expunges in the same gesture. It both liberates and confines us, or rather teaches us that when we gain some sense of a lost liberation we become aware that we are truly confined. Caught within and against our own history, judging beyond and against ourselves, we remain at an impasse, lost within the domain whose emergence we condemn. The judgment of disaster is disaster's judgment of itself.

Who, we? Who is this "we" of whom I speak? It cannot be a biological species, for such an entity does not organize itself through a linguistic statement; nor is it a political collective, since no single collective could encompass it; nor is it a universal humanity into which all partialities are subsumed, as if it constitutes something like the *anthropos* invoked in a word such as the Anthropocene, for the prospect of the terminus shatters the notion of human ascendancy and coherence embedded in that term. Nor is it the "we" of Martin Heidegger, which, as Derrida argues in "The Ends of Man," evokes the concept of an underlying human essence.[29] Nor is it the "we" of Jean-Luc Nancy, for whom the "co-implication of existing is the sharing of the world" and the creation of that world, for today we abide not with its creation but the prospect of its erasure.[30] Today, it can only be the "we" of those who share the condition of radical exposure to humanity's possible annulment across the untold array of divergences between us, across the countless alterities that compose our now shattered "being singular plural."[31]

Such a "we" can never become a "they" for any human speaker; to insist on the third person is to disclaim participation in this exposure, to reduce this situation to a problem for distanced regard or objective knowledge. "We" insists on mutual implication, shared suffering, a common and vulnerable condition; it insists that the prospect of the terminus is a crisis for those invoked in a first person pronoun. Yet such an insistence cannot always override immense differences in responsibility; indeed, any honest account written from the midst of the West must use "we" in describing the actions of privileged participants in its history and the emergence of capitalism, as well as attitudes within polities in the developed world. To remove all reference to *this* "we" would erase the fact that assymetries of power have shaped our world. Yet to cling to this narrow "we" when speaking of a collective exposure would deny the humanity of all those who are not primarily responsible in this way. Thus one must ultimately set aside that occasional narrowness and return to the "we" that moves across alterities, that evokes the shattered, impossible collective of those who endure this new condition.

The call from amidst the ruins. – Given the conditions for thought today, it cannot take up the project of philosophy, which attempts to answer fundamental questions in systematic arguments or at least rigorously integrated claims. In attempting to answer these perennial questions, philosophy participates in an ancient tradition of reflection and thus rests on the assumption of a continuity of human experience, invoking in its very name an ethically freighted notion, inherited from another age, of loving wisdom. That continuity has ceased; that inheritance is no longer quite our own. Nor can thought maintain the project of theory, a term often used in the Anglophone world for intellectual developments arising from post-phenomenological Continental philosophy and extending to an array of projects that set out to expose the internal fractures in virtually every discourse and practice of the contemporary West. By perpetually carrying out an internal critique of that kind, theory sets aside a problematic that operates below its threshold of attention, on a level external to those discourses and practices – or perhaps even more internal to them than theory has previously suspected – and that accordingly disrupts them in an even more definitive manner.

In asking new questions, in facing new exigencies, thought survives after philosophy and theory alike. Perhaps its concept of itself today can be drawn only from the terminus that it confronts, a factor that defines it through and through: it is unmistakably a terminal thought. Cut off from the past, pursuing an interrogation that will last only for a moment, denied any future good it may serve, this orphaned thought nevertheless persists, revealing more than ever that thought may pursue its task without alibi, without any purpose outside of the questioning itself. Persisting in its haunted and depleted state, its extinct condition, thought may no longer be capable of marshalling coherent answers to its questions. But it does not, for all that, fall silent: it will call out from amidst the ruins until humanity itself is lost.

2 The dialectic undone

Phenomenology of Anti-Spirit. – In the Hegelian dialectic, substance is subject. According to the Preface to the *Phenomenology of Spirit*, the subject, mediating itself through its othering, negates this simple negativity; the result is a "self-*restoring* sameness," a "reflection in otherness within itself," which alone is "the True. It is the process of its own becoming, the circle that presupposes its end as its goal, having its end also as its beginning; and only by being worked out to its end, is it actual."[32] Moreover, since the "True is the Whole," and the whole consummates itself by undergoing its complete development, arriving at the Absolute only "as a result" of this process – an Absolute that becomes actual as Spirit – the Substance that is also World-Spirit must "take upon itself the enormous labour of world-history," a process that will allow Substance to show itself as "essentially Subject," so that Spirit will have "made its existence identical with its essence," having overcome the separation of object and subject, "knowing and truth."[33] This entire sequence, this unfolding of the dialectic, alone can ground a science of Spirit, for "the True is actual only as system" leading to the "Absolute as *Spirit* – the most sublime Notion and the one which belongs to the modern age."[34]

How does this argument look today, under the sign of the terminus? According to a dialectical account, today's subject mediates itself in the objective logic of climate change, negating this negativity to reflect that otherness in itself, and by doing so allows the dialectic of world history to come to completion in itself; in this process it discovers the actual in the prospect of its own dissolution, making its disappearance "identical with its essence." In effect, then, it reconciles "knowing and truth" by recognizing annihilation as intrinsic to Spirit. Moreover, in this account, insofar as the end of this process is also its beginning, then humanity's self-erasure has been at stake throughout the dialectical process in the Subject's self-mediation through otherness in a development that culminates in humanity's disappearance. Only from our vantage point, after the dialectic follows the course of world history well past Hegel's moment through many further phases, can one see that all along a certain *Anti*-Spirit has moved through the process of its becoming to reach its end. In such an account, then, history constitutes not a positive dialectic but a dialectic of disaster that develops across all these phases of becoming, so that this array of successive sublations leads at last to the realization of an Absolute in human nullity. In the Preface to *Elements of the Philosophy of Right,* Hegel writes, "What is rational is actual; and what is actual is rational." But today one who adheres to a dialectical approach must conclude that what unfolds itself over the course of this history is the quintessence of the *irrational,* of unreason, of Anti-Spirit.[35]

Would rewriting the Hegelian dialectic in these terms sustain it? By insisting on the place of that nullity as the Absolute of this long development, that dialectic might seem to adhere to the notion that the truth is the whole. But by revealing that the whole is humanity's erasure, the culmination of unreason, it would demonstrate that the system ultimately works out the terms of its own shattering. Moreover, because that erasure will interrupt the process of becoming, cancelling the arrival of the Absolute, it will also destroy the "whole" on which the truth of the dialectical procedure rests. By exposing how a retrospective sublation of the entire sequence into a whole becomes impossible once subject returns the substance of human disappearance into itself, it would indicate that there is no truth of the whole, no moment of totality, no arrival at Spirit, but rather a moment when this reflective turn exposes the falsity of the entire enterprise, the imposture of a totality that, in dissolving, leaves in its wake only the scattered waste of its futile process.

Tarrying with the negative. In the same Preface, Hegel famously writes that Spirit "wins its truth" in a life that does not shrink from death but rather one that "endures it and maintains itself in it," a Spirit that "is this power only by looking the negative in the face, and tarrying with it."[36] This is the negativity that, through its place in the self-mediations of Spirit, helps generate its transformations across all its phases of development. But now that this sequence leads to the terminus, can we truly regard that negativity as productive, as a feature of Spirit's self-development?

Here one could follow the lead of Adorno and discern how the unfolding of that dialectic has all along subsumed the individual and the particular into a violent universality, leading not to a realization of Spirit but a much more dire state. "No universal history leads from savagery to humanitarianism," he writes in *Negative Dialectics,* "but there is one leading from the slingshot to the megaton bomb. It ends in the total menace which organized mankind poses to organized men, in the epitome of discontinuity. It is the horror that verifies Hegel and stands him on his head." A realization of the totality in the "self-realizing absolute" would today "be the absolute of suffering."[37] Adorno at once inverts and "verifies" Hegel, arguing that his constrained, narrow, ideological version of the dialectic, which mirrors the development of the modern state, culminates in absolute horror.

In such moments, Adorno exposes the mendacious self-assurance of the West, its belief that thanks to the Hegelian cunning of history, it has in one way or another engendered a suitable final phase. Indeed, in a commonsensical account, the West might exclaim that it has emerged from a very cunning process indeed, that its movement through such developments as the emancipation of slaves, the arrival of mass education, the increase in living standards for all, and the defeat of the Nazis has in the end created what Francis Fukuyama once described as the end of history in the form of liberal democracy.[38] But for Adorno it was already clear that this movement produced anything but an affirmative state, that history, rather than bringing about what we might wish, leads to a horrific result instead.

In reworking the Hegelian argument into a negative dialectics, Adorno wins his way toward exposing Hegel's complicity with a history that has led to such a horror; he makes it possible to trace the ideological violence endemic throughout the system. In this mode one might well trace how the central development of the modern West sublates one level of violence into the next until it reaches a state of annihilation that erases the entire scenario. Such a sequence, like a revision of the Marxist critique of Hegel, would exemplify a material, rather than spiritual, logic: it would unfold across successive phases of the exploitation and immiseration of vast portions of humanity, as well as the biosphere, in a progression that culminates in the terminus itself. This reading of modern history would displace thought's preoccupation with its own forms, foregrounding instead the practices of fossil fuel extraction and consumption that made possible the lifeworld in which thought could proliferate. In that case, modernity might also reveal itself in a sequence from Hegel through Marx to terminal thought, from spirit to the proletariat to anthropogenic climate change: it would hint that this sequence often provided spiritual or revolutionary cover for a much darker scenario, creating a philosophical or political mask for the scarcely noted, hardly mentioned conflagration on which it relied.

But in pursuing such an argument, one would, with Adorno, verify Hegel; one would point to "an absolute of suffering" rather than the erasure of humanity. One would thus remain within the purview of a critique of history rather than entering into an encounter with its disappearance. Today, thought tarries neither with death nor with a productive negativity, but with the extinction of humanity and thus of thought itself.[39] This terminus surpasses even horror, even suffering, for it culminates in the utter disappearance of the dialectic as a whole.

Thus today it is not enough to say, as does Adorno at the beginning of *Negative Dialectics*, "Philosophy, which once seemed obsolete, lives on because the moment to realize it was missed," and that
accordingly, "[h]aving broken its pledge to be as one with reality or at
the point of realization, philosophy is obliged ruthlessly to criticize
itself." By now it is clear that philosophy has not only missed that
point; encountering the moment of its own erasure, it has reached the
point of its *derealization*, its evacuation through and through. When
thought must tarry with the prospect of the *death of thought*, with the
absolute eclipse even of Spirit, it cannot sublate that prospect into a
criticism of itself that endures; the recursive movement collapses, and
as a result, the entire sequence fails to reach its end. There can be
no dialectics of disaster: that disaster undoes the dialectical process
itself. The thought of the terminus is the terminus of thought.

3 Another covenant

Generations on the land. – The Judaic ten commandments first speak of duties to God, then of duties to humankind. One might think that they do not speak about duties to the earth. But the second commandment establishes that one must not worship any "graven image," for this God is "a jealous God, visiting the iniquity of the fathers upon the children to the third and the fourth generation of whose who hate me, but showing steadfast love to thousands of whose who love me and keep my commandments." The fifth commandment, the first on duties to humankind, establishes that one must honor one's parents "that your days may be long in the land which the Lord your God gives you" (Exodus 20:5, 12). These two commandments, along with the initial statement that God "brought you out of the land of Egypt, out of the house of bondage" and the reference in the fourth commandment to how God, after creating the world, rested on the seventh day (20:2, 11), bind together the whole decalogue, grounding it not only in God's creative and redeeming power but more crucially on the underlying demand that his chosen people remain faithful to the covenant whereby he gives the land to his people. Their loyalty to God, then, is bound up with their commitment to abide on God's land over countless generations, to sustain this gift in perpetuity. This demand, it turns out, is *collective*: it requires Israel *as a people* to abide by it, for if it does not, the Lord will impose a punishment on subsequent generations, much as one generation's failure to care for the land would have dire consequences for later ones. The commandments thus take for granted a long-term fidelity to something that the people itself does not and cannot own, to a land that must endure so that the people itself may endure as well.

What does this deeper commandment say to us today? It suggests that in breaking out of that generational continuity, modernity violated the ineradicable gift of the earth, subsuming it into human purposes, transforming it into the means for a vain and rapid conflagration. The results of that endeavor are now clear, even if such consequences are imposed on us not by a supernatural agency but by merely physical processes. Judgment day, it seems, takes place in and as history itself – not at its end, but within its very contours. Disaster brings about a judgment against itself.

Intimate disaster. – A host of contemporary discourses begin by promising to reveal "what they won't tell you" – a secret that hides behind

the appearance of power. Such discourses take for granted that *someone* actually runs the world, that a coherent intention underlies the
divergent powers that be, that an ultimate Secret explains all. How
well this notion of a hidden Truth fascinates its adherents – how spell-
binding are these tales of conspiracy!

Yet if the secret of our time is difficult to see, it is so not because
it is hidden, but because it is *too evident – too close* for us to sense
it. It transpires across every society, every ecosystem, every life –
continuously, incrementally – but in ways we can easily overlook or
neglect; it surrounds us on every side, infiltrating every aspect of our
experience, shaping our unconscious attitudes and the very fibers
of our bodies. It is so close to us that we typically forget that it is
present at all.

This stunning intimacy calls to mind a surprising aspect of the
Christian tradition. In the garden of Gethsemane, on the even of the
crucifixion, Jesus addresses God as "Abba," the informal term for
father, bringing what is apparently the most distant into the most
proximate (Mark 14:36). Such a term may be quite fitting for a son's
address to a father; it is not unexpected for Jesus to use such a term.
But Paul scandalously permits such usage to all believers, who, in
receiving "the spirit of sonship," may make the same cry in their
own right, as if, alongside God's own son, they too may experience
the intimacy of the divine (Romans 8:15-17; Galations 4:6). In such
moments, transcendence becomes the closest presence of all.

Today, in a dark echo of that moment, a supervenient disaster
comes as close to us as ourselves. Whatever we attempt to do, whatever lives we lead, are now shaped without reprieve by this force.
Should we address it by means of a familiar "you," in an intimate or
familial term? But this supreme exigency comes to us not as a person,
not through the familial metaphor, but through an insistently anonymous process, a ubiquitous and invasive intervention that admits of
no appeal. This alien intimacy, this impersonal closeness, erases us
as it comes near. Perhaps we can address it in no other way than with
a gesture before language, outside of speech – a gesture with which
we, like those who have come before us, might greet the approach of
our own deaths, unknowable as they are, but today can also greet the
disappearance of humankind.

Absent judgment. – In his reconstruction of Solon's teaching that we
must "count no man happy until he is dead," Vivasvan Soni argues that
happiness, rather than an affect we experience when we are alive, is
given in a judgment that others reach concerning us after our lives are
over. By drawing on Solon's teaching – and emphasizing happiness

rather than justice – Soni dares to shift from a focus on God's act on the Day of Judgment to a human act after one's death, expanding on a classical alternative to Christian eschatology. Embracing this teaching, Soni suggests that in modernity we have abandoned such judgment only at great cost, for the revision of the judgment of happiness in eighteenth-century British narrative ultimately made "happiness and politics seem incompatible" and led to "a radical impoverishment in the horizon of our political possibilities."[40] Yet he emphasizes as well that the responsibility to render such a judgment is "excessive and difficult," in part because those who would render it have only limited knowledge of the lives of others. To evaluate the judgment of happiness involves "inordinate difficulties," for it forces us to face "the tragic condition of finitude."[41] Nevertheless, he argues, only such a judgment can anchor our experience, giving it the narrative integrity and ethical coherence that we seek.

What happens to such an arrangement today? Can we imagine any such judgment coming to pass on our shared history? To be sure, the shift from individual life to a collective history radically alters the scale of concern. But a judgment of individual happiness is never separable from a judgment of the cultural context in which that individual lived a life, of the historical projects within which individual intention took shape. Indeed, the very process of reaching such a judgement takes for granted a commonality of reference and value, a shared enterprise of action, embedded in a society's own implicit understanding of itself. To judge an individual life, then, requires at least a tacit judgment of its underlying contexts, its place in that broader enterprise, even if the latter greatly exceeds the former in its scope. Today, the Solonian judgment of happiness must dare to expand its scope in precisely this way, attending to the more capacious questions that any individual necessarily faced, even if unconsciously, over the course of a life.

But does such a shift leave intact a key component of Soni's teaching: the contention that happiness is to be found in a posthumous declaration? Can one reach this judgment *before* the death of the collective? One might think that the thought of the terminus makes such an act possible: insofar as we can anticipate the potential erasure of humankind under the pressure of an extravagant, disastrous modernity, perhaps we can already reach a judgment on that history. But because that event calls into question virtually every dimension of our society, virtually every form of value on which we rely, the validity of that judgment would itself be called into question, undercutting the power of any attempt to anticipate that final perspective. Yet without enacting that scandal, without allowing someone alive to commit that act in anticipation, no such judgment would ever take place; the refusal of that act would also be offensive, cancelling the ethical framework that might give integrity to our lives. Thus it seems that the ethical project of humanity – if it exists – may rest on a premature act that is partial, ignorant, and self-interested.

But perhaps no human being need render this judgment; the fate of humanity may be sufficient in itself to do so. Perhaps the objective logic of disaster may be enough: the biosphere itself may carry within it a force that can subsume transcendent and finite ethical determinations alike. Such a judgment would be neither flawed nor belated: it would be definitive, taking place throughout our moment and even after we are gone. Perhaps the last judgment speaks to us at every moment in the voice of the nonhuman world in which we are immersed.

Yet the disaster sweeping over us is not, in fact, a judgment; it is only the consequence of our history. The catastrophe now unfolding merely transpires; it does not speak; it makes no ethical claim. Rather than providing a definitive judgment, it deprives us of one. It withholds from us any final view, any perspective that might survey our history from outside or beyond it, any knowledge of the whole, any genre of commemoration. It leaves us nothing more than the baffled search for a judgment where the perspective on which it relied has disappeared.

Listening to the grass. – In his "Critique of Violence," Walter Benjamin suggested that only a divine violence – or its equivalent in a general strike – could cut through the oppressive, end-based violence of the state. Moving cryptically between the theological and political registers, between the messianic and the revolutionary, he leaves the ultimate referent of his argument unclear, as if to hint, despite all appearances, that these two might belong to the same category of experience, that the divine and the revolutionary collective arise from the same principle.[42]

Under the sign of terminal thought, such a violence imposes itself through the ordinary actions of the biosphere: the altered climate forces changes across the world's ecosystems, producing an uncounted number of effects throughout our experience. The biosphere itself has thus become the agency of a divine violence, the earthly face of a supervenient means without end. Yet it is clear that this version of ruthlessness, far from blending its force with revolution, reveals the consequences of that revolution's absence. It impresses itself through a radically material principle, through an *interstitial* violence, as if (to borrow from a famous passage in George Eliot's *Middlemarch*) it wished to force us at last to hear "the grass grow and the squirrel's heart beat," even if in doing so – in forcing us to abandon the practice whereby "the quickest of us walk about well wadded with stupidity" – it would ensure that "we should die of that roar which lies on the other side of silence."[43] Today, that sound addresses itself to us with even more severity; it cuts through that wadding, forcing us to listen to a vast human and nonhuman suffering, to hear to that infinite roar, long after we had ears to hear and did not. It sweeps over us with a violence that may indeed erase us entirely.

In saecula saeculorum. – In a speech late in 1798, Richard Price, a leading Protestant Dissenter, greeted the French Revolution in the words of the *nunc dimittis*, in which Simeon blessed the infant Jesus: "Now lettest thou thy servant depart in peace" (Luke 2:29).[44] Such an evocation of biblical enthusiasm over the arrival of a new dispensation ramifies across Price's broadly millenarian political theology, which everywhere speaks of his eager embrace of what he sees as a redemptive event. In response to Price, Edmund Burke wrote his *Reflections on the Revolution in France*, repudiating Price's millenarian stance in favor of a starkly contrasting political theology – one in which the sacred dispensation is incarnated in the historical continuity of the church and eventually the state. Where Price seeks a divine event that cleanses and reoriginates history, Burke sees it as having already taken place at the substitution of the church for the apocalypse, ecclesiology for eschatology, making any such apocalyptic expectation not only redundant but pernicious. In effect, he holds that apocalypse must give way to the undying presence of salvation in a historical continuity, the divine event to the institutions which are to endure *in saecula saecularum*, over the age of ages (a phrase that appears in the Vulgate translation of Ephesians 3:21), and accordingly in his view the millennium is not an age to come but is already transpiring in the continuity of the church and its heir, the traditions of the British constitution and its common law. Placing his emphasis on the sanctity of this historical continuity, Burke describes it as "the great mysterious incorporation of the human race," alluding to the idea that the *corpus mysticum*, the sacred body of Christ, is united with the church through the Eucharist, a usage that had long since been applied as well in secular contexts, including to the idea of the body politic.[45] The divergence between Price and Burke points to a constitutive ambivalence in Christian eschatology, which simultaneously cherishes the redemptive actions of Jesus and looks forward to apocalypse, in effect suggesting that history has already been redeemed, even if it is yet to be redeemed. Within that ambivalent tradition, Burke places his emphasis on what is already at work in historical institutions, which for him in their ordinary operation perpetually enact a version of God's redemptive agency. Insofar as Price and Burke are representative, then, the British response to the Revolution arose from competing political theologies, from a broadly millenarian stance characteristic of Protestant Dissent and a Catholic and Anglican stance regarding the relation of divine justice to human history.[46]

Burke's argument highlights a strong continuity between the medieval church and the modern state, extending as well to the processes that take shape under that state's auspices in the form of political, social, economic, and legal history. In one view, at least, the sacred endures in the form of the secular – in the historical traditions that, if not severely interrupted, constitute (in the King James translation of Ephesians 3:21) a "world without end." The secular, in one sense, is what never ends. Whether its sacred import is explicit or implicit may not matter: the secular relies on the notion that history can substitute for apocalypse, that the endless can stand in for the end. From a perspective grounded in this sense of the secular, any polity that does not respect its longstanding traditions is in danger of suffering from perpetual discontinuity; in such a state, writes Burke, "No one generation could link with the other. Men would become little better than flies of a summer."[47] For Burke, the only form of existence worth cultivating is one that endures over many generations; the individual is only a moment within the long continuity of a collective subject.

What happens to this version of the secular under the sign of the terminus? Insofar as it defines history not as the process of working through a constitutive tension between a fallen state and an eventual redemption, its perspective seems to survive the terminus rather well. After all, in its view the telos of history has already been incorporated into enduring historical institutions. Yet in fact this stance is also shattered; the terminus reveals that this highly valorized continuous history is vulnerable to an absolute interruption – a shattering erasure that will reveal how this continuity was not in fact the site of a mysterious incorporation, not a domain permeated by a divine presence, but a contingent construction. Ultimately the terminus proposes that nothing endures *in saecula saeculorum*; just as the continents beneath our feet morph and move over time, just as species emerge and disappear, so also human institutions arise and fade away; all of them are "little better than flies of a summer." Or rather, since this terminus is *caused* by this particular history, the implication is even more dire: perhaps only a culture that applies the language of the sacred to its own contingent institutions, assuring itself of its worldly survival over the ages, and thereby dismisses outright signs of its vulnerability or its violence, could consume the earth to such a degree that it would bring about its own dissolution. Perhaps only a culture that sees itself as eternal brings about its own extinction.

Another covenant. – In *Night,* his unforgettable account of surviving the Shoah, Elie Wiesel recounts how, on seeing the chimneys of the crematoria for the first time, his belief in all divine assurances disappeared. He depicts that moment in a passage so searing, so infinitely bleak, that one cannot help but find in it his version of a negative revelation that destroys the covenant under which he had previously lived: "Never shall I forget those flames which consumed my faith forever," he writes. "Never shall I forget those moments which murdered my God and my soul and turned my dreams to dust. Never shall I forget these things, even if I am condemned to live as long as God himself. Never."[48] In effect, that moment ushers him into another era in salvation history – into a time defined by the erasure of any covenant with the divine, bereft of any hope of redemption. In the wake of passages like this, one might extrapolate that for Wiesel, the time of Judaism would henceforth not be covenantal time, but a time defined by Auschwitz, by the evil *omphalos* of those chimneys.

How does this moment speak to us, now that our experience takes shape under the sign of the terminus? Since the moment Wiesel captures is one of the darkest in human history, an evil hour that nearly erases all memory of the good, how might we respond to a coming moment that will erase all thought of good and evil alike? Since the scene he captures here speaks of a vast evil that human beings perpetrated directly on others, how might we conceive of the evil of an indirect violence against us all? The Shoah already beggars speech, already makes us mute before its annihilating darkness; how could we possibly even begin to utter the darkness of that terminal hour? Would that future event, in causing far more deaths than the Shoah, an annihilation so great that it would leave none to remember in its wake, usher in yet another phase in the history of annihilation? Or would it extend and renew the event to which Wiesel bore witness? Does modernity's legacy of ash, that smoke from countless industrial fires, drown out the smoke from those infamous chimneys, or does it multiply that smoke indefinitely, spreading it across all the planet's spaces, wounding the biosphere itself? Here a beggared speech is lacerated even further; the muteness that befalls us after Auschwitz gives way to an even starker incapacity, to a silence that no longer has any memory of speech.

Hail, Satan! – At one point in the television series *Better Call Saul,* the protagonist, a lawyer, relinquishes an idiosyncratic effort to serve justice and concedes to the superior power of the corporate law firm for which he works, in that moment exclaiming, "Hail, Satan!" In this gesture, he reveals what is at stake in the pragmatism that virtually any social agent in our time must cultivate to survive, an attitude whereby we accept what seems inevitable as we allow the institutions that have power over us to thwart our efforts to do justice.

Such a pragmatism is inherent in the settlement that Christianity reached with secular power from the start: even though it was grounded at least in part on an anti-imperial stance, especially in the epistles of Paul, already in its canonic texts it proposed that one should "[r]ender therefore to Caesar the things that are Caesar's," accepting the sway of imperial power even as it opposed its principles (Matthew 22:21).[49] If, as Paul writes, Christianity battles against "the principalities, against the powers, against the world rulers of this present darkness, against the spiritual hosts of wickedness in the heavenly places" (Ephesians 6:12), then in leaving secular authority in the hands of those rulers it too said, in effect, "Hail, Satan!" Indeed, that concession created the template for principled opposition ever since, for nothing is more familiar in the history of the West than the pragmatic endurance of injustice. Yet this pattern has allowed that secular power so much sway that it has almost entirely forgotten any check against its domain, permitting it to absorb even ideas of divine justice into its own languages and practices. Thus Christianity – and not only Christianity – concedes to the very powers it pretends to chasten, sustaining an indirect fidelity to what it sees as the present darkness.

This pattern has held true as well in recent centuries, even as the environmental cost of an exponential growth in productivity and population has become increasingly clear. As Christophe Bonneuil and Jean-Baptiste Fressoz demonstrate in *The Shock of the Anthropocene*, a critique of capitalism's effect on ecosystems started early in the nineteenth century, coinciding with the rise of capitalism itself, and has persisted in tandem with it all along the way. Modern industrial production has always known that what it brought about was damaging the earth and pushed ahead with its project nevertheless.[50] In doing so, it followed ample precedent, casting aside principled critique and choosing instead to pursue a seemingly unlimited increase of power and wealth.

Under the sign of the terminus, however, the promise embedded in that ancient concession to power falls away, erasing the prospect of redemption, revealing instead that those dark powers now expect us all to make one last concession, to accept the demise of humanity itself as the cost of modernity. Perhaps the West has never actually sought to realize justice: perhaps its true if unstated motto all along has been, "Hail, Satan!"

Sacred rage. – At the core moment of the Exodus from Egypt, the children of Israel elude the grasp of the Egyptian armies as the waters of the Red Sea drown them. Here Israel's emancipation takes place through the divine slaughter of its enemies. Such a scenario reappears at the end of the Christian Scriptures as well, where the redeemed enter into the New Jerusalem only after divine violence annihilates all others. Thus while liberation theology holds the Exodus dear as a fundamental symbol of emancipation, insisting that the biblical tradition is on the side of justice for the enslaved and the poor, one cannot help but notice how often in that tradition redemption is premised on mass killing, sometimes of ethnically defined others – on a violence that from a more recent perspective verges on genocide. A similar pattern persists well after the biblical canon is closed: stories of a saint defeating the dragon, of conquerors decimating indigenous people in the name of settler colonialism, and of the lone gunman cleansing the frontier town all speak for a fundamental assumption that right will prevail through might, that a sanctified mission may justly resort to an annihilating rage. The long history of this pattern shows that the polities of the West have long since incorporated the mythos of God's wrath into their mode of dominance, assuming lethal powers once intrinsic to a cosmic governance, even if religious teaching ostensibly places divine violence outside the depredations of the modern state. This pattern applies as well to the state's attitude toward the ecosystems on which it relies: the nonhuman world must submit to its commands and accept a similarly devastating violence (the draining of wetlands, the removal of forests, the damming of rivers, the irrigation of deserts, and the settling of plains) as it serves the purposes of a humanity that sees itself at the pinnacle of creation.

Thus it seems that the religious traditions of the West do not merely *concede* to dark powers; the language of violence endemic to them helps *establish* the sway of a certain darkness, ultimately leaving the world at the mercy of an endless train of brutal regimes. In that case, the discourses of divine or state violence bear within them a trace of radical evil, a Satanic dimension, precisely so that they can dominate in an apparently hostile world and thereby impose a specific view of cosmic right on a recalcitrant reality.

Yet one must also remember the counter-tradition according to which, as Paul writes, there is strength in weakness (2 Corinthians 12:9), or in what Benjamin, perhaps referring to that passage, calls "a *weak* messianic power."[51] As Giorgio Agamben argues, for Paul

the messianic is found in rendering vocation, power, and law inoper-
able, in hollowing out the things of the world, in treating them "as
not."[52] But this strength does not overcome secular power, for on
the contrary it remains caught within a world still under that power's sway; consigned to "the futility of what is lost and decays," the
whole creation "groans as it awaits redemption."[53] As Percy Bysshe
Shelley's *Prometheus Unbound* suggests, if an apparently nonviolent
power ever dismantles tyranny, it will do so only through miraculous
violence; ironically, Benjamin's weak messianic power will prevail
only through a divine, cleansing annihilation.[54] Weakness relies on
strength; the alternative to power relies on an extreme version of
its own. At first one might think that this impasse is an instance of
what Derrida would call the autoimmune disorder of justice, whereby
"justice as relation to the other" must always take place at the risk of
injustice.[55] But in fact it exemplifies an even sterner logic, where by
the very act of realizing justice may contradict what it hopes to bring
about, may do injustice in doing justice.[56]

Today the thought of the terminus disfigures this problematic. Does
the environmental disaster of our time reveal the nonhuman world's
vulnerability to human dominance, its weak messianism? Or does
it enact the biosphere's version of sacred rage, through which a certain ineradicable might at last cuts through all the claims of secular
domination? Or does it pass beyond both of these scenarios, revealing the radical indifference of forces that need not obey the categories
of our history, that unfold in terms well beyond our own, or in no
terms at all?

Justify whom to whom? – Over the course of the history of Christian
theology, various figures sought to provide a theodicy – that is, in
John Milton's words, to "justify the ways of God to men."[57] This
endeavor implicitly distinguished between justice and divine action:
even if virtually all those who wrote in this genre did so to explain
how evil and misery could exist in a world created and ruled by a
God they regarded as at once just and omnipotent, their very effort
revealed their awareness that such an argument was not immediately
credible, that a sense of God's justice was not obvious. Furthermore,
these arguments took for granted that God's reign was tolerable only
if one could demonstrate that it served the good of his creation.

Thus in taking up such a project, one inevitably embarks on a haz-
ardous enterprise. One opens up the possibility that one might fail,
that one might discover how God may have to repent of his ways
and perhaps even atone for them to those he has wronged. The very
notion of justifying God evokes and inverts the usual emphasis on

God's justification of humanity, so central to Pauline theology. If one takes this inversion seriously, one begins to notice the rather scandalous possibility that the death of Jesus on the cross may atone not for humanity's error but for God's. Yet that prospect has its own redemptive implications: if even God may suffer in this way, then humanity can find in its own suffering an echo of that divine self-sacrifice, that utter submission to powerlessness. Perhaps God is worthy of faith not because he is omnipotent but because he, too, is frail and governs not through force but moral appeal. In that case humanity finds its place within a vulnerable version of what William Blake called the "human form divine," the collective body that divinity and humanity share.

Such might be the cost of justifying God's ways to man. But this entire effort relies as well on the assumption that God should not be more sovereign than goodness, should not be able to cast justice aside in the name of his supremacy. That assumption harks back to a key difference between the thought of Thomas Aquinas and that of the nominalists who succeeded him: for Aquinas, theology could remain coherent only if God was bound by the forms he had made through the assertion of his loving will, for otherwise the principles of creation would be neither stable nor knowable, rooted in neither grace nor the good, and would accordingly become inaccessible to the human intellect.[58] For the nominalists, however, any such argument limited divine sovereignty, making God subject to the forms he made and thus depriving him of his transcendence. Aquinas sought to save God from instantiating an arbitrary transcendence beyond form; the nominalists, from becoming subordinate to form that shared a status like that of his creation.

These explorations of divine justice, however, may be far less daring than the approach outlined long before in the book of Job, one of the most ancient texts to be incorporated into the Hebrew scriptures. Job calls God to account for forcing him to endure untold suffering – in effect, for falling prey to the evil dimension of divine power, represented in this book as God's willingness to allow Lucifer to test the endurance of the faithful (1.6-12). Job and his friends debate the essential questions of theodicy at length but come to no conclusions. At last, God himself speaks from the whirlwind, repudiating any attempt to call him to account, exploding any sense that the universe has a moral order and mocking the sheer vulnerability and finitude of human beings in the face of the monstrousness of his creation. This God is beyond justice; his sovereignty serves no good; rather than curbing the violence and inhumanity of his creation, he celebrates it (38-41). The book concludes as Job, intoxicated by this monstrous God, surrenders to him (42:1-6). As it turns out, it is possible that something other than a moral appeal, something other than divine justice, may sway human beings, for there is an irresistible sublimity to the nonhuman wildness of the creation.[59] Perhaps God becomes truly divine only when he abandons any attempt to proclaim his justice.

Today the whirlwind speaks to us again; we who live after the researches of modern science, aware of the amoral reaches of astronomical, geological, and biological history, are stunned by a universe infinitely vaster and more powerful than ourselves. Now we learn, in our own idiom, that the processes of the universe do not transpire on our behalf, that they greatly exceed any moral demands we place upon them. Like Job, we may discover that we need not seek a theodicy, for we may be moved to awe by forces far beyond the reach of our interrogations. Perhaps only what retains the power to violate us without reserve can strike us as truly other to ourselves, as truly enacting a principle beyond our concepts.[60]

Yet even Job's theology is disfigured in our time. The whirlwind that devastates us today reminds us of the effects of our own actions on the biosphere; because we have pushed it into patterns even more dangerous to humanity than before, it now speaks of *our* amorality, *our* refusal to accept limits on our actions. In this respect, we do not share our position with Job: this whirlwind implicitly accuses us of a collective misdeed, a provocation that intensifies the destructive power of the nonhuman world. In its disastrous intrusions, it shows us the face of a *de facto* judgment so stark that it admits of no justification we could ever provide, no atonement we could offer. We have become the agents of a destruction so fierce that it unworks the idea of creation on which this entire tradition relies. A humanity capable of erasing itself is no longer subject to a creator, however conceived, nor can it any longer demand a just universe. Nor can it in any simple way be swayed by awe at the natural world's monstrosity, for today that monstrosity is ourselves. We are the whirlwind that will destroy ourselves.

Triumph of an insidious evil. – For most of Western history, theologians held to a privative notion of evil: rather than having a weight and force contrary to the good, evil was the failure to serve the good. In this way they avoided falling into a dualism that pitted God against Satan, that created an interminable dispute between the Almighty and an equally powerful counterpart, for doing so would have given Satan a much greater status than he actually possessed as one of God's creations. Only with the coming of modernity did the West begin to argue that one could assert evil *positively* over against the good, to *choose* evil with all deliberate intent.

Today, however, this concession seems partial and incomplete. Only a more robust version of evil may convince us today: a form of evil capable of damaging the telos, the moral good toward which the universe ostensibly moves. The terminus tells us that evil can positively intrude upon, and even defeat, the very architecture of the good. Far from being in a dualist struggle, one that would presumably endure in perpetuity, we find ourselves in a battle where evil wins; the victory of evil in this case is so great that it even cancels the overarching narrative space in which we may organize ethical action.

Yet this account may provide too assertive a notion of evil to convince us. The evil that triumphs today scarcely rises to the threshold of consciousness: it operates in such an apparently peripheral domain, in such easily overlooked aspects of daily life, that it hardly seems to correspond to our sense of deliberate action at all. Its consequences are similarly elusive: it is as if evil undercuts our shared world in the way that rust, mildew, or mold can destroy – in a molecular or chemical process of which we might easily remain unaware. For us today, evil is not only a disorder of the will; it is a malady in the preconditions of human flourishing, a disease that infests goodness like an unknown virus, the antibody to which goodness does not possess.

Devil's dismay. – Hearing of the terminus of human existence, Lucifer falls into renewed despair. How can his wickedness, his power over human affairs, succeed so well that with humanity's disappearance, no new recruits will ever arrive in Hell? Whom can he tempt now? What evil might he do? He still has so much work to do, so many projects of human wretchedness to complete! In utter anguish, he contemplates his denuded future: how can his victory be so great that it *exceeds* his designs, that it imposes an utter triumph *prematurely*? Suddenly his dark eminence realizes that in such a triumph comes his defeat: to eradicate humanity is to erase his own purpose. Now without a future, Satan regrets his past. He wishes he might leap into the deepest abyss and annihilate himself. But Apollyon, the Angel of the Bottomless Pit, holds the key to those depths and blocks his passage. He is caught in his own prison: he must now suffer his empty fate forever.

The mortal soul. – The received belief within Christianity that the soul is immortal is hardly credible today, when we confront the prospect that humanity as a whole – and many aspects of the biosphere that have so amply enabled human life to flourish – are doomed. Such a belief was already suspect when astronomers determined that the universe itself would eventually fade away and when evolutionary biologists conceded that humankind would ultimately become extinct. For a century or two, the notion that the individual soul exceeds the universe or the species in its temporal scope has not been compelling, and that notion is even more doubtful today as the terminus approaches.

The notion of immortality scarcely does any better when modern philosophers attempt to salvage it. Kant argues that only over the course of an infinite future, only thanks to the immortality of the soul, could a finite subject eventually comport with the moral law.[61] Yet as Lewis White Beck points out, this notion of how the individual might gradually approach ethical perfection takes for granted a temporal process – and thus places the soul once again within the realm of time.[62] What Kant really seeks, as Alenka Zupančič argues, is the immortality of the *body* – that is, of mortal time itself.[63] Indeed, any philosophy that inherits the insights of that system, which insists on the limits of human cognition and embodiment, faces similar difficulties with the concept of the soul's immortality. The twentieth-century tradition of phenomenology, for example, demonstrates that fundamental aspects of human consciousness and cognition are bound with a thousand ties to the basic orientations of the body, making it virtually impossible to imagine a truly cognizant soul that lacks such orientations. Furthermore, the recent critique of the solitary subject at the center of Enlightenment thought suggests that the focus on the individual mind neglects the more pivotal question of relationship.[64] These shifts toward embodiment and relationship overleap aspects of Christian thought and return us to the Judaic sense of redemption, which emphasizes an embodied, mortal person's participation in a shared covenant and its historical unfolding.

These developments hint that the insistence on individual immortality is complicit with an individualist triumphalism, a subordination of human and nonhuman others to an imperious assertion. Indeed, certain versions of the ideology of freedom hint that what that triumphalist individual seeks is freedom's capacity to surmount materiality and circumstance altogether – to overcome any constraints on its autonomous sway. Yet one does not improve much on this stance to insist on the dominance of humankind as a whole; extracting ourselves from our corporeal relatedness to the widespread networks of life or imagining that we can outlive our material conditions condemns humanity to a useless, imperious solitude. Analogues of that belief in the political and economic domains are largely responsible for getting us into our present dilemma; accordingly, today humankind may be learning that we cannot be sovereign over creation without condemning ourselves to annihilation. The claim to immortality, it seems, brings with it an even more severe cessation. Our only real prospect for cultivating human flourishing has been to accept a modest place in the web of existence we share with all mortal beings – a prospect that may ironically become visible to us just as we glimpse the possibility of our own disappearance.

Above us only sky. – In one of the most moving secular hymns ever sung, John Lennon invited his listeners to imagine a world with no heaven above us, only sky. Rather than to the God who once occupied that heaven, he paid homage to a humanity that, giving up thoughts of transcendental justifications for sacrifice, could join together in peace and live for today. That open sky, in effect, symbolized the absence of something that people had often invoked as they committed violence against themselves and each other. Yet by invoking that sky, Lennon in effect relied on its power to remain *only* sky, to remain the domain of that absence.

But the sky is no longer simply that space; our actions have altered its composition and behavior, transforming it into an active and intrusive agent, a space that absorbs emissions of many kinds – and one that in consequence is the scene of forces that undercut human flourishing. It is no longer *only* sky: this sky that opens up after the disappearance of transcendence also endures after secular modernity falters, after the purely human future dissolves. If we once lived in a secular state that followed upon the history of the Christian West, as Gil Anidjar argues, in an ironic, further development of that religious tradition we now live in a phase after that state, when even the secular world gives way to a more dire condition, when even the sky has ceased to be what it was.[65]

Vanity beyond vanity. – The preacher of *Ecclesiastes*, surveying the state of humankind, noting that "there is nothing new under the sun," that everything that happens occurs again and again, concludes that "vanity of vanities! All is vanity" (1:9, 2). The endless circling of history, the perpetual vacuity of human achievements in the face of time, makes merely finite, immanent life futile: only submission to God has any weight.

What might this preacher say today, when there *is* something new under the sun, when environmental catastrophe brings with it a condition unprecedented in the memory of humankind? Whereas the winds once circled to the south and the north, returning on their circuits, and the streams flowed to the sea, only to flow again (1:6-7), now the winds and streams depart from their ancient paths, becoming volatile, unpredictable. Having broken out of the ancient patterns of shared life, humankind now finds itself *beyond* vanity, in an even *less* rewarding condition, as the terminus reveals that the endless round can cease, that vanity may pass away. Moreover, insofar as the terminus undoes

our confidence that we can rely on an enduring transcendence to ori-
ent our lives, it leaves us exposed to nullity without recourse. If there
is a time to be born and a time to die – a time to weep and a time
to laugh – in what time do we live now? Perhaps the preacher might
conclude with renewed emphasis, "Better is the end of a thing than
its beginning" (7:8), or – voicing a strikingly antinatalist sentiment –
declare once again that the "dead are more fortunate than the living
who are still alive; but better than both is he who has not yet been, and
has not seen the evil deeds that are done under the sun" (4:2-3).[66]

Renouncing renunciation. – In the Tantric variant of South Asian
renouncer traditions, ascetics who turn away from ordinary life take
up habitation in the domain of the dead, in the taboo zone of the cremation ground.[67] Settling into that space, they embark on spiritual
practices of many kinds to attain distinctive forms of spiritual power
or achievement.

Do we who share Job's condition in the face of the whirlwind,
repenting in dust and ashes (42.6), or who abide in a state even more
empty than that of the preacher in *Ecclesiastes*, participate in a similar
mode of renunciation? We too know that human endeavor is vain, that
we breathe in a legacy of ash. But in that case, our state is not volun-
tary but forced; the earth itself has become our cremation ground, its
condition already detaching us from the lives we once thought were
ours. Even further, our situation does not speak of a departure from
the everyday but of our dwelling in it; the renouncer is no longer distinct from the householder, no longer an ascetic who gives up ordinary life to seek a spiritual path, but one who lives alongside others
in the world we all share. Today the seeker turns not away from the
world but toward it, drawing even closer to the barest truths and sim-
plest facts of ordinary time. In our moment, the renouncer is invited
to accept a place in the rubble of this culture, the charnel house
of humankind.

This turn damages the spiritual legacies of renunciation. In one of
the greatest traditions of renunciation, Buddhism, the bodhisattva not
only seeks enlightenment for herself but also vows to liberate all sentient beings. At first it might seem that one can fulfill this vow today:
one might, for example, seek to liberate all sentient beings from the
illusion that this reality has substance, that it constitutes the only
framework in which we might live; one might suggest that the terminus reveals the emptiness of what we have so long taken for granted.
But the thought of the terminus forecloses the prospect of fostering
liberation for all. The disappearance of humanity erases the preconditions even of this vow.

Thus in turning toward the charnel heap today, renouncing one's attachments to ordinary concerns, one also renounces renunciation itself. Even when one takes this vow and serves the enlightenment of all, one does so under no illusion that this universal liberation will ever come to pass. Perhaps one is left only with a more radical stance, a renunciation that abandons even the project of redemption, that accepts the emptiness even of one's most sacred vow. Perhaps only a stance that accepts the emptiness of all conceivable purposes can endure today.

4 Shadows of the flame

Already past. – As the prospect of the terminus approaches, as the idea of a historical process leading to a legible future for humankind dissolves, the tension that drives history, its living energy, subsides as well. Social, political, and economic developments of every type now lack the prospect of enduring realization. Even as such developments continue, this fate falls irredeemably on the entire sweep of historical change extending from the past through our present into the period to come, so that all of it is now consigned to a past without purchase on any credible future. Although this past now includes even the present, it does not simply weigh down the living, for it too has become hollow, evanescent, ghostly. Yet since it is impossible to dislodge, too powerful to undo, it also constrains our actions in every conceivable way. Thus it is at once infinitely heavy and impossibly light, an immense burden somehow lacking any force, a paradoxical object at once freighted with significance and utterly useless, a bank of toxic fog one must breathe but cannot seize.

An archive for the sun. – For those who study the past, the archive is indispensable; how greatly they must rely on papers recording births, marriages, deaths, decrees, laws, taxes, harvests, contracts, property transactions, financial accounts, legal rulings, legislative debates, articles of indenture or apprenticeship, and manumission, not to mention books, manuscripts, correspondence, diaries, logbooks, notebooks, newspapers, maps, reports, flyers, posters, advertisements, postcards, and photographs. Fortunately for researchers, the enormous archive of the past is now moving even more from private to public hands even as it is also becoming digitized; in principle it will eventually become available to people around the world in formats more searchable than ever, making possible more comprehensive and accurate depictions of the human heritage.

Yet what is the status of the archive for researchers into the course of human history? From one angle, the archive seems more neutral than the museum, through which a society erects a secular shrine to itself, or the monument, which absorbs the commemoration of heroism – or of loss – into an affirmation of its history. The archive, which is less visible and less ostentatious than these, may seek to preserve the past without placing it in an ideological frame. Nevertheless, its import changes as a new relation to the past shapes our response to all these remainders. Now that we in the United States see the removal of monuments dedicated to slaveowners or exemplars of racist prejudice and the emergence of museums focusing precisely on the injustice endemic in our history, we also see that the archive is becoming a resource for those who wish to disinter the underside of this nation's history and expose it to view. A similar effort is underway in relation to other nations: as Thomas Richards and others demonstrate, British imperial governance operated precisely through bureaucratic discourse, through ordinary administrative acts executed on pieces of paper eventually gathered in the archive.[68] Read in these ways, the archive is becoming a resource for those who, with Benjamin, read history against the grain: it now shows how the documents of civilization have indeed been documents of barbarism, how the shrines to state history preserve the evidence of a long defeat for most of humanity.

Under the sign of the terminus, such a turn must expose as well how the violence of the West, imposed not only on most of humankind, extends to the entire biosphere and indeed to the preconditions of human life itself. Examined with an eye toward this long imposition, will the archive become a record of a vast, incremental erasure, a patient, quotidian annihilation of humankind? Will it bear witness to the patient unfolding over centuries of a catastrophe still taking place before our eyes? Will we learn that every document of civilization is a document of disaster as well?

Under the pressure of such questions, other markers of the past take on new significance. Memorials to the war dead, for example, sit oddly within the context of the endless wars of our time – and take on an even more dubious status within the framework of our participation in the ongoing violence against all of humankind. Such markers of respect for the dead look increasingly spurious, for in offering occasions for us to remember the dead of our own nations, they set aside the violence we have done to others, or indeed our awareness of the broad legacy of violence across human history. Moreover, in marking losses that one can interpret as safely contained in the past, they hide from view our general unwillingness to recognize the catastrophic losses befalling the earth's ecosystems and humankind itself today and into the future. They may thus distract us from our actual situation, reassuring us that we live in a stable and coherent society that has survived and overcome those events. In response to such pitfalls, however, we might learn to view these monuments in a new way, to see them as memorializing those already dead and those still to die from the devastation now being visited on humankind, even potentially the death of humanity itself; we might read them as markers of specific moments within a broader history and thus as occasions for a much vaster commemoration.

But the material remainders of the past not only mark the legacy of a long history of violence, for they are also becoming targets of forces that would destroy them, and along with them, a certain memory of the past as well. This aggression toward the past takes many forms: the bombing of museums and archives, as well as archaic sites, during military incursions, for example, or the demolition of historic quarters during the modernization of major cities. These instances indicate that the physical remnants of the past are often in danger today.

This violence against memory, in turn, reminds us that the approach of the terminus exposes the entire archive of human history to the whims of a turbulent, increasingly destructive biosphere. Whatever portion of the archive has been made available online will eventually fall prey to the disappearance of the internet and of every digital interface, leaving only its offline form to remain. This material archive, vulnerable to fire, flood, and the neglect that may befall research in societies under duress, will gradually sink and decay, a victim of dark times. Where Derrida once surmised that there could be "no archive desire . . . without the possibility of a forgetfulness," without a "death drive" that would sweep away "the spatio-temporal conditions of conservation," the terminus now implements this destruction through an external, material process, so that we now abide in an archive fever made physically manifest, a drive operating even beyond the psyche, a forgetfulness befalling humanity's entire history.[69]

Yet the fever of which Derrida speaks will infest not only the archive but also those who haunt its domain. When the terminus comes, who will survive to read it in in its frayed, molding, and charred state? For whom will it be a resource? It is now offered up to a nonhuman ignorance, an implacable indifference. Perhaps only the monuments will endure, commemorating nothing, remembering when we will not. As humankind disappears, the archive will speak to no one, to the blank face of the wind, to the empty sky, to the blazing eye of the sun.

The history of the West as the history of disaster. – In the wake of the French Revolution, the modern West began to assume that history had before it an open, unknown future. At the same time, by other accounts, a certain historicism emerged across the disciplines, in the dialectical outworking of spirit, in histories of the modern nations, and in a developmental logic one could find in such disciplines as linguistics, biology, and political economy (as Michael Foucault argues in *The Order of Things*).[70] The opening of the future, suspending a knowable or secure framework for human action, effectively located history's site of significance not in its ultimate telos but in the developmental process itself. Such a logic often conceived modernity's internalization of its telos positively as an inner resource whereby history could perpetually reinterpret its own stakes, learning from its development to posit ever further new outlines of its coming-to-be. Out of the very erasure of a destination, then, modern history could continue to imagine itself within an ongoing narrative, suspending any specific definition of its future in order to safeguard the process whereby it could endlessly generate more refined conceptions of its destination.

Yet this notion of history's perpetual renegotiation of its stakes masks the mark of negation at its heart, the sign of the erasure of any positive definition of its trajectory. One might well borrow from the work of Joan Copjec, who in an argument inspired by the teachings of Jacques Lacan proposes that "if history has no outside . . . if history is without limit, then it must accommodate or be invaded by the infinite, the never-ending, by undying repetition, or the undead." The cancellation of creation or apocalypse, the divine origin or end of history, now appears *negatively* within history, for "if one wants to prevent the formation of an outside," then one must "inscribe in the interior a negation that says 'no' precisely to the possibility of an outside," thereby installing "the real as internal limit of the symbolic," as an "obstacle that scotches the possibility of rising out of or above the symbolic."[71] Thanks to this move, one no longer locates power within any positive entity, such as a king, for within modern constitutional democracies, various presidents come and go, occupying only for an interval what Claude Lefort calls "power's empty place."[72] In much the same way, Ernesto Laclau shows that the political antagonisms perpetually at work within those same democracies do not lead to any positive instantiation of collective will but rather seize on a hegemonic signifier, fashioning an ideological *point de capiton* that quilts the political order together without creating any positive, substantial signified.[73] One might find still another counterpart in a rather different domain: the cancellation of divine origin or end for the creation takes place in part by rendering human societies subject to the intrusion of natural disasters, which, as obliterated versions of divine transcendence, can bring the "undead" force of amoral catastrophe into human time at any moment. Modern history, then, does not revolve around its perpetual growth and maturation, but its internal limit, the mark of the cancellation of a transcendence or external limit, one that disarranges it on every level.[74]

Elsewhere I have analyzed at length certain effects of this transformation for conceptions of history, aesthetics, politics, and ethics
around 1800, effects that have continued to play out across Western
culture ever since.[75] Modern societies have cultivated versions of
what I have called disastrous subjectivities throughout this period,
exploring an aesthetics of the sublime, for example, alongside a sense
of modern society's emergence within the strikingly contingent processes that shape the history of the earth.

But this formation of the internal limit alters once again under the
pressure of this history's approaching dissolution. Now it is clear that
modern societies relied on geological knowledge not only to fashion
new subjectivities but also to exploit that history for material purposes, creating the modern fossil fuel industry – and especially the
oil industry – that has enabled the growth of their economies ever
since, thereby altering the conditions for human life itself. In effect,
the West produced a disastrous *objectivity*, a transformation in the
physical contours of the biosphere, as it incorporated aspects of the
nonhuman world into its own logic.[76] To borrow a term from Lacan,
one might say that the world is now extimate to modern society, that
is, at once external and intimate to it, an element that, even if material
in its operation, belongs well within the central dynamic of the West.
In that case, the history of annihilation is the counterside of the history of progress, the back side of modernity's infernal Möbius strip.
The creation of a material catastrophe is that history's most defining
feature; that external history *is* its internal history, the most telling
instance of its characteristic logic. The history of the West is the history of disaster.

Planned obsolescence. – In his essay on Kant's "What Is
Enlightenment," Foucault suggests that Kant points to an aspect
emerging with Enlightenment thought, its investment in the specific
opening taking place in the present. In effect, Kant asks, "What difference does today introduce with respect to yesterday?"[77] Such a
question, Foucault proposes, contains a "critical ontology of ourselves" that "has to be conceived as an attitude, an ethos, a philosophical life in which the critique of what we are is at one and the
same time the historical analysis of the limits that are imposed on
us and an experiment with the possibility of going beyond them."[78]
This attitude, however, takes for granted the necessity of surmount-
ing the previous moment in a logic that, if implemented in perpetuity,
would invite those in the future to regard one's moment as woefully
superseded, if not entirely benighted. Thus if one can argue that each
new phase somehow develops out of the previous one, foregrounding

possibilities evident only in that new moment, one can also maintain that the new devalues what came before, setting it aside as inadequate for critical thought. The equivalent of this process in the commodity world is to determine that yesterday's artifacts are kitch, that the past is not merely past but out of fashion, discredited, devalued.

A related logic is at play in the dialectic. Where Hegel held that *Aufhebung* cancels and preserves previous stages in the unfolding of spirit, in fact each new stage does not entirely preserve what it has overcome – for if it did so it could not overcome it – but leaves in the past what it does not retain. Thus sublation abandons a host of superseded aspects of spirit, an archive of what has been jettisoned, a museum of the outmoded. Progress is a version of planned obsolescence. The trash-heap that is our history is no accident; it is the result of a deliberate practice, modernity's longing ceaselessly to overcome itself.

Clamor of the silent histories. – For Benjamin, the fact that only the victors write history makes the entire narrative of progress false, for it selects only those elements from the past through which the ruling classes attempt to justify their dominion.[79] His critique suggests that if one reads history against the grain, another possibility appears. Whenever history takes one path – whenever one social force defeats another and can therefore impose its notion of progress – it abandons another; as a result, each event is a swerve from the possibility of others. A narrative that selects only what happens thus suffers from an immense confirmation bias, an enormous preference for actuality over possibility and for the narrative of what took place over what did not. In this perspective, then, the revolution will finally bring to pass what was possible but never realized, opening up a direction for history that it once repudiated.

Benjamin's conception shares much with that of Jorge Luis Borges, who in "The Garden of Forking Paths" similarly imagines a history taking place over a vast web of diverging scenarios.[80] But where Borges surmises that history is still taking place along all those paths, as if transpiring within the same overall reality, Benjamin suggests that only one history has actually taken place. Yet he would also contest the idea that one scenario alone is real; disputing the claim of Leopold von Ranke – that the historian must capture history "the way it really was" – Benjamin would include unactualized histories within reality, placing the actual and virtual side by side within a space no longer defined only by empirical events. In Benjamin's view, the totality of history includes the immense range of events that did not occur as well as those that did.[81] A fidelity to actual events betrays the true shape of history, which in its range vastly exceeds the mere positivity of appearances; once its submerged direction surfaces in the messianic event, it will defeat the forces that depended on that apparently positive history.

Today, as the prospect of a messianic event recedes and the dominant history rushes us toward a shared annihilation, the invisible, submerged, alternative possibilities do not, for all that, disappear; even in their silence, they clamor to be heard. Under the prospect of the terminus, the dominant history, despite its annihilating power, still bears the imprint of what it is not; sweeping away all human possibilities, it defeats even itself, revealing that the story told by victors was fraudulent all along, that they never did truly achieve what they sought, that the revolutionary critique of its sway holds true. Though the forgotten of the earth may not triumph, they may nevertheless know that the terminus liberates humankind from a belief in the legitimacy of that history, from accepting the justice of that disaster.

Emancipation from life. – Popular conceptions often imagine the history of the West, especially in the last 150 years, as a series of emancipatory developments extending over generations, each new phase enfolding and surpassing the previous ones, in a kind of collective *Bildung*, a course of gradual awakening, a process whereby humanity becomes progressively mature. But under closer scrutiny, this story of historical progress takes on a different look. Where modernity tends to read its past selectively as a series of emancipations, a long train of events releasing humankind from its confines, from another angle it is simultaneously a series of much darker acts, whereby it enslaved people, subordinated them to the logic of capital, colonized most regions of the world, decimated indigenous populations, and eradicated or devastated countless ecosystems. Progress is also antiprogress, enlightenment also endarkenment. Modernity does not necessarily move forward, for when it emancipates people from previous confines, it simultaneously creates unprecedented forms of immiseration, new styles of destruction. As the West emancipates itself with ever greater daring, it also violates the world in acts of ever more devastating force.

One may see this pattern repeatedly in the history of the United States. The founding fathers, for example, overcame a potentially fatal impasse at the Constitutional Convention only after southern states were in effect guaranteed the capacity to expand slavery into what would become new states south of the Ohio River, inscribing a perpetually enlarging domain of racial oppression into the ostensibly progressive future of the republic.[82] In the late nineteenth and

early twentieth centuries, the democratization of the American polity
– and expansions in workers' rights – took place in part because of the
radical activism of coal miners, and thus in tandem with the exploitation of coal reserves, tying an emancipatory politics to a vast increase
in the burning of fossil fuels.[83] Moreover, the direct enslavement of
captured Africans and their descendents gave way to less overt but
still legally sanctioned forms of slavery, while coal democracy was
superseded by the far less worker-friendly context of oil exploitation,
suggesting that history may unfold not as a series of gentle reforms
but through the adoption of more strategic forms of exploitation, more
euphemistic types of oppression, more subtle devastations.[84]

Thus even as the history of the West over the past two centuries or
more led to a stunning, unprecedented release of human productivity, population, and knowledge – an explosive transformation in every
arena – at the same time it subjugated humanity to its sway, spread
a layer of nuclear radiation across the surfaces of the globe and into
the living bones of its people, and is now producing the sixth great
mass extinction in the planet's history. Taken all together, this history exemplifies an analogue of the Nietzschean transvaluation of all
values, for it has erased virtually all moral limits on action, all illusions of the subject, transgressing a thousand norms in the name of no
specified purpose. Indeed, wherever the modern state has managed to
consolidate itself with increasing rigor, to coordinate its citizens more
powerfully, or to organize its information with improved sophistication, it has made possible greater crimes, more daring violations of the
limitations placed on finitude. What we may see, in short, is not a tale
of progress but of extravagant transgression, the emergence of a will
to commit more lethal crimes, to leap into the abyss with ever greater
daring. What we inhabit is the history of humanity's emancipation
from life itself.

The inevitable revolution. – In their analysis of modern political relations in *The Communist Manifesto*, Karl Marx and Friedrich Engels
posited that capitalism's exploitation of the proletariat would eventually immiserate it to such a degree it would rise up in a great revolution, overthrow its oppressors, and institute a classless society.[85]
Today we might imagine a counterpart of that argument, according to
which capitalism, exploiting the nonhuman world beyond its capacity
to endure, would similarly incite it to respond with a countervailing
violence, decimating capitalism and the societies that rely on it. But
even in such a scenario, what might follow such an event? Would such
a revolt necessarily lead to a transformation in power? If thousands of
species go extinct, if ever more powerful hurricanes decimate major

cities, if changed weather patterns force millions of people to migrate and possibly take up arms as they enter new territory, if warmer weather inhibits the production of grain and decreases the food supply, if that weather creates the conditions for wildfires to proliferate and send smoke over large tracts of land, and if countless other such disturbances profoundly alter the prospects for human flourishing across the globe, *even then* states do not respond with sufficient boldness to ward off further devastating events. Nothing whatsoever ties immiseration – whether of the proletariat or the biosphere – to a particular outcome. Even the awareness of further disaster does not necessarily lead to transformation.

These histories suggest that rather than leading to liberating action, a catastrophic history more typically brings about radical indifference. Marx and Engels were still under the spell of the idea that a vast cause would have a great effect, that the logic of history is coherent. But the opposite may be the case. Perhaps a cause as large and severe as irreversible climate change may have little effect at all. In that case, the state is not the scene of revolutionary transformation, the site where history works out its inner logic; instead it may be where the coherence of history runs aground, where its worklessness comes to the fore. Perhaps the state is obtuse, indifferent, a force for historical inertia so vast that it can override even the greatest urgencies without difficulty. Perhaps the most surprising talent harbored by the modern state is its capacity to persist well into an era when its legitimacy and rationale have long since disappeared – when it can no longer pretend to care for its people or even ensure its own survival. It may be that the endurance of capitalism well past the moment when its extraordinary violence against the proletariat became clear is only a harbinger of an even more dire fate, for now capitalism persists even after its cost for humankind is manifest to all.

Shadows of the flame. – As we have seen, Koselleck argues that around the last decade of the eighteenth century, interpretations of Western history broke out of the assumption that the history of the state "remains trapped within a temporal structure that can be understood as static mobility." A new notion of progress intervened, "open[ing] up a future that transcended the hitherto predictable, natural space of time and experience and thence – propelled by its own dynamic – provoked new, transnatural, long-term prognoses," a future "characterized by . . . the increasing speed with which it approaches us" and "its unknown quality."[86] But Koselleck goes further; he shows that in the wake of this development, histories in the plural gave way to a singular History, which could be "conceived as a system that made possible an epic unity that disclosed and established internal coherence."[87] Thus the very unpredictability of the future made it possible for the "Final Judgment" to be "rendered temporal"; as Friedrich Schiller wrote, "World history is the world's tribunal."[88] The telos that vanished from the historical future reappeared within history's underlying unity, allowing it to retain aspects of traditional ideas in a new form.

Yet the very notion that history has an internal order falsifies its radically unpredictable future, the open temporality within which it now moves: as I suggested above, what is incorporated into history is not that telos, but its cancellation, its internal limit. That mark reveals history's exposure to revolution, natural disaster, and the eruption of previously unknown forces; modern history is vulnerable to developments that may violate every expectation, disasters that may interrupt at any time. Accordingly, the notion of a systematic, unitary history constitutes an attempt to deny the danger in that opening, to close the gap introduced by an unknowable future. In effect, historicism seeks to protect society from its own modernity. A discourse that sought to capture modernity's actual condition would set out instead to map what could never be systematized in that way, never rendered whole; it would trace the shape of what disfigures narrative, noting those features of history in which this mark of a radical ungrounding, of a severely antinarrative principle, appeared.

Today the attempt to reduce our multiple histories to a central, unified narrative is especially suspect, if only because the terminus makes it even more evident than before that this history has no destination it can defend, no logic that actually coheres. If historical narrative is still available to us today, it would perforce adopt a mode of writing never previously attempted, an articulation of how historical trajectories are inhabited by a useless negativity, a worklessness that erases them even as they appear. It would outline the shape that annihilation takes through the very medium of progress, as if to trace the patterns cast by a flame that consumes the world. But in that case, we have outlived the era of historical narrative; we live in a world whose tale vanishes as it is told.

5 Liberty as annihilation

The hollow public sphere. – The current state of debate concerning how to ward off a catastrophe in the biosphere amply demonstrates that the notion of the public sphere, if it were ever valid, no longer obtains. Where one might have expected a summary of scientific findings regarding the effects of climate change on the biosphere and on the planet's ecosystems to have forced a substantive public debate on how to address those effects, in fact for several decades most citizens and politicians in the United States – and in many other countries – have been reluctant to press for political, economic, and social change on the necessary scale. Rather than a domain for an active debate between informed and rational participants, the public sphere is a space for the collective to assert its indifference, its inertia, and even its contempt for specialized knowledge, especially where that knowledge points to the absolute necessity of changes in daily life for all.[89] As it turns out, the fairly strict conventions of public debate tend to exclude any discourse that challenges habitual assumptions or makes an imperious demand for wholesale change. By dismissing what it considers "alarmist" predictions or "extremist" conclusions, that debate reveals its investment in the status quo, its fidelity to sociodicy – to a society's underlying justification of itself – and thus to a broadly Burkean sense that a society should never question its premises. As a result, rather than actually constituting a domain for rational discussion, the public sphere is a means for a society to reiterate its received ideas, often under the guise of adopting incremental reforms, in effect substituting mild alterations, if any, for the far more ambitious transformations that truly rational debate would demand.

A key factor in maintaining this arrangement is the continued influence of arguments that militated against reforms several generations ago – ideas that, opposed to enlightenment, are in effect calling for endarkenment, for regression to more abusive public norms. While the latter tendency is not always dominant, incapable of perpetually limiting the restless search for social transformation, it nevertheless constitutes a nearly permanent bar against more daring change. Ideas opposed to the extension of civil rights to previously disenfranchised groups, for example, even today effectively shut out many attempts to bring about social justice. The pattern whereby certain societies resist taking concerted action in response to climate change is not an exception but instead exemplifies the longstanding state of such polities. The tendency of some modern democratic societies may thus be to countenance their own demise, to hold to their previous assumptions so long that they will *insist* on creating the conditions for their own disappearance. Rather than a matrix for gentle improvement, the public sphere may be among the strongest forces for the annihilation of humankind.

The will to falsehood. – Scientists who speak out about the dire consequences of climate change have so far not succeeded in persuading their various publics to take sufficient action not because of any contingent flaws in their research, in their ways of articulating knowledge, or their modes of engagement with the public but because the public sphere receives whatever they say within the long-sanctioned and narrow conventions of political disputes. This reception of climate science is not unique: modern societies give an even less welcoming reception to those who, like philosophers, theorists, social scientists, cultural critics, musicologists, art historians, literary critics, or scholars of religion, among others, also set out to articulate knowledge. Despite the lip service that the public gives to the enterprise of knowledge, in fact it regards it as relatively marginal, useful primarily for instrumental or ideological purposes. Societies accept it only on the condition that it is contained within the university, or better yet, within the space of specific disciplines, placed in a zone outside of what the public must acknowledge, confront, or absorb.

Contained in this way, the quest for knowledge cannot overcome the cultural authority of indifference. While no doubt disciplinary forms of knowledge rely upon and exercise certain forms of social power, as Foucault argued, their containment suggests that they fall under the greater sway of what Eve Kosofsky Sedgwick designated as the privilege of ignorance.[90] Such ignorance has at its disposal varieties of skepticism, the inertia of public opinion, and the enervating effect of a hyperabundance of information, all of which the "merchants of doubt," as Naomi Oreskes and Erik M. Conway have called them, have exploited as they set out to muddy public perceptions of climate research.[91] Yet these accounts do not yet go far enough: the fact that the public so often *prefers* its ignorance to what would dispute it, that it is bent on *defending* the indefensible and crediting the discredited, shows that it submits to a will-to-falsehood, a craving for illusion. It yearns for pretexts that will allow it to abide by its previous attitudes, that will permit it to rest within a familiar ignorance rather than accept a new and unwelcome reality.

Despite this overall context, scientists continue to rely on the assumption that the public truly seeks to know and to learn, that it is still shaped by a will-to-truth; accordingly, they have remained committed to the paradigm of education, hoping to find strategies of engagement that will bring about a sea-change in the public mind. With this end in view, researchers have often leaned heavily on their colleagues in the social sciences to discover what precise strategies would best enable them to reach the public. There are now countless findings about how best to frame, exemplify, or elucidate climate science so that it may avoid coming across as too technical, too alarmist, or too distant from ordinary concerns. But such advice often comes down to the insistence that scientists speak within the terms that are already acceptable to the public and thus avoid contesting widespread assumptions about the viability of our ways of life. Faced with such advice, any scientist who attempts to convey her findings is asked to decide whether to violate those assumptions, thereby presumably failing to reach her audience, or accept them, conveying a false impression of our current state. Because scientists retain a broadly Enlightenment conception of the public, they typically remain committed to sharing their findings in this way, attempting to overcome public resistance through a labor of endless patience.

Such an approach, while it has much to commend it, nevertheless fails to come to terms with the situation in which scientists and many others find themselves today. Their situation reveals that the promise of the Enlightenment – that modern societies could be arranged in such a way that the search for knowledge might become available to the public and to those in power, making it possible for those societies to become ever more just – is not, and perhaps has never been, credible, for on the contrary such societies regard such disciplined endeavors (except for those in some disciplines, such as economics, history, or sociology) as separate from the pragmatics of governance or the realities of daily life. Where Kant once argued that rational agents excluded from power would be able to criticize public policies and institutions freely for the benefit of all, today we see that practitioners of knowledge are excluded from power so that whatever they say may be treated as trivial.[92] As a result, the public sphere sets aside a rational critique of contemporary institutions and merely rehearses already recognized debates, allowing full sway only to established antagonisms. In this context, the demand for action on the global environmental crisis is reduced to legislation that environmentalists promote and free-market ideologists oppose, becoming another weary iteration of familiar disputes.

One must conclude that what modernity accepts least of all are insights that pierce accepted conventions and reveal their fraudulence through and through; it is founded instead on the hatred of truth, an enmity with reason. But as I have suggested, when faced with such resistance, knowledge too readily accepts its diminished role, accepting its place within the framework outlined by social norms, comporting with a certain style of bureaucratic rationality rather than attempting to challenge it. In this respect, thought should attend to Jacques Lacan's differentiation between knowledge and truth: insofar as what knowledge has to convey ultimately challenges a conventional framework, it should attempt to transcend its diminished state, moving beyond the outline of a disciplinary object to adopt a discourse of truth. It should enact a mode of statement that addresses the core resistance of the subject, that moves beyond conveying content to challenge the defenses that protect public indifference.[93] In shifting from knowledge to truth, thought would take up the task of speaking the latter without reserve, precisely where it seems to be outrageous, scandalous, unassimilable. Only such a forthright speech would refuse to compromise with the stupor of our times, with the violence of an infinite indifference, for it would foreground what is least acceptable in truth, its rebuke of the comforts on which the public depends. In our time, only an openly revolutionary discourse that starkly repudiates ideology and indeed all the dominant assumptions of social life is legitimate.

Such a discourse would never promise itself that it will achieve success; it would never authorize itself through pragmatic calculations about its ability to persuade. Its purpose is wholesale transformation, not gentle reform. Accordingly, it is quite likely that its truth will be realized only in the eventuality of which it speaks, for the hatred of truth is already leading to the erasure of modern society, as well as humankind as a whole, in a terminus that may in its own way cut through the illusion of our times.

Unenlightened self-interest. – Over the course of early modern thought, various thinkers proposed that the collective could be organized through the enlightened self-interest of individuals. As Albert O. Hirschman argues, they conceived of interest as a protection against the passions, which were too destructive and unpredictable. In a range of arguments proposed by such thinkers as John Locke, Baron de Montesquieu, Adam Ferguson, and Sir James Steuart, there emerged the idea that those acting in their own economic interests behaved in a much calmer, sweeter, and more predictable fashion than those acting on their passions, and as a result a society organized to serve such interests could become the basis for a democratic polity, whose governance could abandon arbitrary measures and become much less intrusive.[94]

If one can rely on this account as a credible reading of the emergence of the modern political order, which does indeed tend to rely on the notion of a self-interested, predictable economic agent and citizen, one can immediately see several problems with the world it inaugurates. For one thing, individual interest necessarily has in view the consequences of action within the lifespan of the economic or political agent; the individual will seek a general good that is consistent with his or her own eventual flourishing. Such a stance does not easily take into account the long-term effects of present economic action. Moreover, since the good of the whole is taken to be that which best protects the interests of each, one is never asked to sacrifice self-interest to safeguard the whole. Thus a society grounded on self-interest can scarcely imagine how it might enter new arrangements *against* established economic practices in order to ensure its own longevity, especially if it places threats to its flourishing some distance into the future. The adoption of an *ethical* core to the shared polity, which would subordinate interests to other ends, would force a reconception of economic and political action alike, requiring a revision of collective life so severe that it would constitute nothing less than a revolution, an overturning of the existing order, and accordingly would meet with vast and prolonged resistance.

One is thus forced to conclude that far from constituting a form of "enlightened self-interest," the pursuit of one's own interests militates *against* a truly rational conception of collective life. But it never promised to do so. As Hirschman reminds us, the notion of interest arose largely in order to protect the polity against the danger of the passions; it was broadly defensive in intent, designating the lessening of disorder rather than the adoption of a fully rational basis for a new order. Moreover, a theory that emphasized how a social order founded in interest may flourish necessarily had in view a relatively limited temporal scope; it never did lay claim to the long-term consequences of such a model. The rationality of this conception, in short, lay only in how interests were relatively more rational than the passions, not in society's capacity to evaluate the whole according to a rational estimate of this model's eventual effects.

Today, under the sign of the terminus, we can now see that the entire model rests on what is ultimately *irrational* self-interest, on a theory that protects self-interested citizens from confronting the eventual consequences of their actions. The notion that the mutual interplay of self-interest may establish a relatively secure polity is nothing more than a fiction, a once-useful postulate, whose value fades quickly under the pressure of global environmental disaster. A similar corrective applies to the paradigms of economic theory; the postulate that one can buy everything essential in a market whose mechanisms are self-correcting loses credibility when so-called "externalities," that is, phenomena the market generates that it does not take into account, interrupt its sway. These externalities, such as a fairly dramatic change in the condition of the biosphere, make the irrationality of the overall system unmistakably clear.

As it turns out, then, models based on interest could never provide more than a partial account of the collective; by placing a broader concept of reason in abeyance, they helped make modern societies forever vulnerable to what interest alone did not wish to envisage. Indeed, by suspending the political passions, they placed out of view motivations that could exceed pragmatic considerations, that could invoke or address supremely important concerns. This choice for the partial, however, was precisely the point, for only such a determination could save the social order from being torn apart by passionate, mutual recriminations. After all, it once seemed legitimate to contain actions that justified themselves through appeals to transcendental principles, that is, through appeals that others might not recognize as rational or binding. Neither the passions nor the interests, then, can enable a society to grasp its condition. Yet reason alone can scarcely find purchase in human affairs without mediating itself through such lesser appeals. Thus it is highly unlikely that reason ever could have much sway within the lived situation of any social order. The notion of an enlightened society is itself a myth.

Liberty as annihilation. – In his canonic essay "On Liberty," John Stuart Mill argues, "The only freedom that deserves the name, is that of pursuing our own good in our own way, so long as we do not attempt to deprive others of theirs, or impede their efforts to obtain it."[95] Although this principle has been modified by contemporary societies in many ways, it still underlies attitudes regarding civil liberties, whereby government steps back from regulating the many activities of private life. Needless to say, the constitutional protections extended to civil liberties of this kind establish the basic principles of modern liberalism, a characteristic mode found across virtually all developed democracies today.

These basic principles of liberty, however, obligate one to accept the opinions and actions of others, even if in one's view the latter may eventually counteract the principles of liberty. In many polities around the world today, people find themselves in the position of tolerating the opinions of those who support an authoritarian politics and thus pursue a version of ideology that undermines liberty itself. In such instances, as in Derrida's initial analysis of the suppression of elections in Algeria in 1992, democracy suffers from an autoimmune disorder, providing the means to undo democracy even for the purpose of protecting itself.[96] Arguably, the recent drift toward the taste for an autocratic politics within modern democracies began with the general tolerance for climate denial, for political positions that repudiated the findings of science without apology and without an undue loss of public support, creating the template for a further range of openly mendacious and abusive positions. Thus it is no surprise that it goes hand in hand with another persistent demand of our time, that citizens accept versions of climate denial in their peers. Yet in imposing this demand, liberalism perforce allows a stunningly violent set of opinions to have full force within political debate and in the ordinary interchanges of social life; one is now compelled to remain civil to those who collaborate with forces that may ultimately annihilate humankind.

But liberty is not merely caught in its own autoimmune disorder, in what indirectly undermines it, for today it also does *direct* harm to others. Almost any act within our current infrastructure damages the environment in some way, whether it generates fossil fuel emissions, consumes natural resources, contributes to the waste stream, or disrupts the survival of many species – and through these means harms vast numbers of other people as well. Today it is virtually impossible to act in such a way as not to harm others. This impossible situation befalls liberty in part because our very births already violated this principle, for our presence as living beings in these large numbers and in these economies forces us to participate in systems that damage the wellbeing of others and of ourselves. In effect, we inhabit a disorder not merely of democracy but also of embodied action itself; merely to subsist today is to take action in ways that directly undermine that subsistence. The assertion of life brings about death.

This situation, however, reminds us that even in earlier eras, liberty did direct harm, for it depended upon political arrangements that positively required the subordination of the disprivileged. The citizens of ancient Athens or Rome, as well as those empowered to vote in early modern England, received their status in part through the enslavement or subjection of others; the political sphere itself took for granted a logic of exploitation that by definition fell outside of political concern. Moreover, in the context of the United States, as Kathryn Yusoff argues, "freedom and its conceptual apparatus were built on" the subjection of slaves, so greatly that "escape from captivity is only possible within the indices of that grammar of captivity and its interstitial moments, never as idealized outside of it."[97] Thus Afropessimist thought rightly teaches us that such histories reify the social position of privileged masculine political agents of European descent into a false concept of the human; indeed, one must perforce extend that argument to suggest that it did so by consigning all others – especially Black others – to a position outside of humanity, outside any status worthy of survival, thereby treating them as worthy of annihilation and thus subject already to the logic of a culturally imposed extinction. The enlightenment subject, it seems, is founded on human extinction. Liberty in its various forms, in its multiple legacies, intrinsically depends not only on structural violence but also on the annihilation of the human.

Today, with virtually universal suffrage, we may imagine we have overcome this benighted history. On its own face, such a claim is dubious at best. But even further, as Andrew Nikiforuk argues, the fact that modern nations such as the United States replaced slaves with fossil fuels – with coal and oil – demonstrates that it now relies on the exploitation of the earth's resources, in effect keeping a version of enslavement in place.[98] The logic that produced a notoriously persistent structural violence against Black bodies has also generated an annihilating structural violence against the biosphere as well.

Yet this is not a mode of oppression we can overcome through still another emancipation, through an extension of the logic that brought us to this moment. Only a radical and thoroughgoing refusal of this entire sequence can release us. As Chris Washington argues, only the extinction of an anthropocentric framework makes hope possible today; only by entering a "posthuman history" can one "establish communities for living with human and nonhuman others."[99] The shattering of that false concept of the human finally makes possible the emergence of a justice that Western political history has so long denied. But such a breakthrough, if it happens today, comes too late, for it may well be followed by an all-too-literal extinction of human embodiment. We are bound by the consequences of our enslavement of the earth; we are already abandoned to the terminus. Today, the legacy of liberty imposes annihilation on us all.

Ambivalent modernities. – After World War II, as colonized nations gradually achieved independence from European powers and entered the postcolonial and decolonial phases of their histories, they pushed back against imperialism in a new way, contesting the exclusions embedded in colonialist versions of personhood, politics, language, history, economy, religion, society, culture, and much more, thereby contributing to a multiplicitous and wide-ranging critique of European modernity itself – a mode of engagement analogous to, but distinct from, other postwar forms of political and cultural resistance.

Yet to articulate the exclusions embedded within that modernity, these regimes borrowed on its terms, relying on modern notions such as the state and nation, for example, or on the discursive possibilities afforded by that quintessentially modern genre, the novel. In effect, then, even as they mobilized distinctively non-European cultural traditions, practices, and norms, they placed them within a framework inherited from the colonizers. As Homi K. bhabha writes, they thus brought into play "a process of hybridity, incorporating new 'people' in relation to the body politic, generating other sites of meaning and, inevitably, in the political process, producing unmanned sites of political antagonism and unpredictable forces for political representation."[100] In doing so, they entered into fractured versions of modern temporality, deploying reinterpreted versions of the historical break from the premodern past so dear to modernizing ideology while displacing many of its characteristic accents and doing so across a wide range of traditions, creating what one might well describe as "multiple modernities."[101]

In recent years, a further version of this ambivalence has emerged in the relation these new nations sustain to the dominant global system. While many of the world's states have invoked the project of decolonization over the past several decades, they have also pursued policies to claim a greater share of the world's wealth, often doing severe environmental harm in the process. One might think of such well-known instances as Nigeria's exploitation of oil resources, the inundation of vast regions through the construction of large dams in India and China, and the decimation of portions of the Amazonian rainforest in Brazil.[102] These instances exemplify a new kind of ambivalence: a strategy of replicating models of Western development precisely to address the problem of immiseration brought about by colonial domination. Such devastated landscapes are complex cultural texts in their own right: they speak of a longing to overcome the legacy of poverty while also echoing the logic of violence imposed by colonizing regimes. They are thus instances of a hybrid discourse, sites of political antagonism of a new kind.

As the climate crisis accelerates, these nations find themselves again in a liminal zone, at once primarily victims of the long-term consequences of Western development and yet also aspirants to join in the wealth that such development can provide. Caught between a productivist ideology and an acute awareness of its costs, they take into a new phase the ambivalence that has informed their formation from the start. Today this pattern has devolved into a stark blend of aspiration and horror: building new states within depleted landscapes, they endure in a blend of indigenous, colonial, and postcolonial temporalities under the sign of the terminus, caught by the most brutal hybridity of all.

Modernity as inertia. – Although modernity defines itself as a departure from the premodern world and its premises, and thus in part through the notion of a historical break from the past, building discontinuity and disruption into its notion of itself, in fact it too becomes habituated to its institutions and practices, resisting fundamental change at every turn. A society shaped by a written constitution, for example, tends to establish practices that are consistent with that document over time, and as a result legislative action cannot really hope to bring about more than incremental reform; military bureaucracies often insist on organizing preparedness in response to the last war; and social and economic institutions put immense effort into maintaining themselves over time. Furthermore, events that interrupt long-term continuity end up shaping expectations for generations thereafter, establishing a new continuity. The experience of surviving World War I inspired a huge array of political and military scenarios across many nations in the 1920s and 30s, much as the terrorist attack on 9/11 has informed the development of foreign policies and military interventions ever since. Eventually modern societies become aware that surprising events are bound to happen, and accordingly they create institutions whose task is to prepare for them and maintain the existing material and cultural infrastructures as much as possible. Despite its claims, then, modernity too develops enormous inertia, holding to its practices with a truly impressive fervor.

How is this pattern consistent with modernity's evident fascination with the new? It is so insofar as modernity expects and even requires novelty – often in the form of the emergence of new cultural and social trends, the appearance of new kinds of commodities, and the creation of new technologies. Without such developments, many aspects of modern society would scarcely function; capitalism relies on the endless renewal of commodities, just as the arts forever demand original interventions. But perhaps the most characteristic attitude within modernity is the expectation that one should not merely be prepared for new developments but should also see their arrival as inevitable and accordingly embrace them without objection or reserve. In effect, modernity treats the new as normative. But since this expectation is built into existing relations, since the entire ideological infrastructure of our societies circles around it, it promotes a stunning refusal of an actual change in those political, social, and economic relations themselves: modernity has made perpetual transformation into a form of stasis.

Yet because that transformation relies on the limitless expansion of international capitalism, along with its immensely destructive effects on the planet's ecosystems, the inertia of this system drives it toward ever further destruction, making the whole into a mindless momentum toward the eventual decimation of humankind. Modernity's inertia does not keep it still; it demands a continuous movement onward, continuous growth, continuous absorption of all things into its productivist regime, and thus a continuous violation of what human beings, and the earth itself, can bear. In the end, its most definitive innovation will the abyss itself.

The impasse of the disciplines. – Over the eighteenth and nineteenth centuries, practitioners of knowledge invented the modern disciplines, abstracting distinct objects of knowledge from the vast panoply of interrelated phenomena and differentiating each from the others. In this way, they constructed fictions of self-consistent, demarcated, stable entities capable of sustaining prolonged and systematic examination, fictions that were eventually received as objects existing in the real world and functioning independently of knowledge itself. Western societies eventually came to believe, for example, that one could extract something called "literature" from the realm of written texts in many arenas and analyze it as a distinctive practice, that one could find a consistent arena called "religion" within various religious practices around the world, that one could differentiate between the analysis of politics, political economy, and society, and that an entity such as "culture" – the object of anthropological knowledge – was to be found in traditional, not modern, societies. Incorporated into these fictions was also the sense that each object, organizing ineradicable properties of human collectives, was by its very nature enduring over time, consistent with itself, and accessible to rational analysis. Taken together, the disciplines created the groundwork for maintaining that the constitutive domains that underlie modernity's institutions are at once rational, stable, and enduring, and thus that the infrastructure of modernity itself is effectively legitimate.

Yet the reception of climate science in recent years indicates that the social order, far from being attentive to how scientific research points to the absolute necessity of massive change, is more inclined to maintain its fidelity to existing arrangements instead. This attitude seems consistent with the legitimating function of those disciplines, as if taking that function more seriously than the particular findings that they reach. The divergence between knowledge's legitimating tendency and its capacity to reveal the need for transformation, however, points to a split within modern society between a belief in its fundamental rationality and its assent to reason's analysis of its limitations.

In an optimistic reading, this divergence should inspire modern societies to reform themselves, to bring their ordinary activities ever closer to what reason demands. But the resistance to what knowledge teaches indicates otherwise: it suggests that these societies fundamentally dispute the orientation of knowledge itself, refusing to accept what it teaches. One could draw on a psychoanalytic discourse here and suggest that the collective, like the subject, is riven with unconscious drives, most especially the death drive, through which it perpetually violates its own best interests.

In that case, the disciplines find themselves confronted not with stable objects of knowledge but with self-subverting domains. If anything, each disconfirms reason's belief in its consistency, exposing instead its tendency toward a condition other than its ostensible purposes. In response, knowledge could find itself analyzing that slippage, tracing the collective's yearning to become other. But it could not do so without becoming another kind of discourse, without transforming into a theory of alterity. This shift in discourse, however, would threaten the fiction of modernity, undercutting its claim to possess a stable architecture and revealing instead that it is subject to an alterity in conflict with that claim. One would no longer be able to differentiate it from the irrational, inconsistent condition it believes it has surpassed. As a result, one would perforce place it in a strong continuity with previous formations, considering it as an indirect and sophisticated means for traditional society to adhere to its archaic premises. While modernity has its own distinctive claims about itself, most specifically in its claim to *be* modern – and must therefore be taken seriously as a formation in its own right – in the end such an approach would demonstrate that it is strongly embedded in what preceded it, so that despite itself it sustains what it pretends to have overcome and must find its place in a long *non*modern continuity.[103]

As it turns out, then, when one examines modern society's indifference toward its own slide into oblivion, one can come to see that it is not modern at all – and that the disciplines devoted to its interpretation must entirely reconceive of themselves. But what might an anti-discipline teach us now? For what purpose would it speak? Or would its own teaching reveal that it is no longer needed – and never was?

6 Living in the void

Living in the void. – In his pivotal work *Myth of the Eternal Return*, Mircea Eliade demonstrates that in their annual rituals, archaic cultures enacted the end and the regeneration of time.[104] The act of creation was not marooned forever in the past, a single origin for a perpetually expanding history, nor was the apocalypse only an event to be anticipated; these cosmic events took place in ritual time, *in illo tempore*, during which the gods, in tandem with the collective, repeated the originary act of creation. Each year, such cultures cancelled and renewed time by reenacting the primordial event, and in that way relieved the collective of the burden of history. Altering this pattern, Judaism split apart origin and end, installing a linear history between them, creating a cycle that took place not annually but over the entirety of earthly time.[105] Retaining some hint of the archaic in Yom Kippur, in which participants repented of the faults committed over the past year, it still placed such events within a positive conception of history, which now became the domain for the unfolding of God's redemptive action across a vastly expanded version of ritual time. This concept of history eventually became the foundation for the Christian understanding of time, and in its wake, for modern historicism, which retained a sharply revised sense of salvation history in its own sense of progressive liberation and enlightenment. Underpinning even a progressive sense of history, then, lay that fundamental substrate, that evocation of a cosmic cycle, whereby history's culmination in apocalypse erases the errors of the past and brings about the reorigination of the world.

What remains of this cosmic cycle under the sign of history's terminus? The dissolution of a redemptive notion of apocalypse implies the disappearance of creation, and indeed any sense that history is rooted in cosmic events; it points on the contrary to the radical contingency of human existence, to the happenstance of human emergence within the evolutionary history of lifeforms and the inevitable disappearance of the species at some future date. Furthermore, it points to how human action, generating this disappearance well before any evolutionary, geological, or astronomical process would bring it about, reveals a contingent dimension of the human well beyond its biological finitude. But for Eliade, such concerns would not capture the full stakes of this new scene. In the absence of any version of the ritual event, history would remain unpurged, its errors unredeemed; the

vast assortment of profane events would accumulate beyond all limits, so that the wreckage of time, in Benjaminian parlance, would pile
up to the sky. It would expose us without recourse to what Eliade calls
"the terror of history," that aspect of time that ancient ritual sought to
abolish.[106] Moreover, without an origin or end, the anchor points that
give coherence to time, what seems to be history would transpire in a
temporality without shape or direction. Finally, with the disappearance even of distant derivatives of that archaic ritual, no language or
practice would remain that could confer symbolic status on the whole,
that could inaugurate the reality of time; through its brutal erasure of
any such capacity, the terminus would cause the derealization of time
and its world, leaving it weightless, suspended in the void. For where
ritual cannot exclude chaos and institute order, cannot overcome radical contingency and institute a divinely ordained necessity, the world
collapses, returning the cosmos to a state without boundary or name.
A time marked by the terminus is the terminus of time.

When rituals are forgotten. – Certain elders within indigenous peoples today maintain that if "people abandon and eventually forget
the ancient rituals," then "the end of the world" will be inevitable.
As the ethnologist Stefan Parmento writes, one elder in the Q'eqchi'
people, which lives in parts of today's Guatemala and Belize, stated
that "[w]hen all rituals are forgotten . . . humanity will experience
difficult times: the harvests will yield nothing, the animals will die,
and people will starve."[107] Such a statement captures the archaic sense
that only ritual action enables the natural world to thrive, to pass from
season to season, and to respond to human endeavor with its provi-
sions of abundance.

How might one interpret today's world from such a perspective?
Now that many indigenous societies have lost the opportunity to
maintain their archaic traditions, in what sense do they live on? Here
one might be tempted to build on the analysis of Jonathan Lear, who
examines the moment when Plenty Coups, a member of the Crow
nation, speaking long after the demise of that nation's traditional
ways, declares, "[W]hen the buffalo went away the hearts of my people fell to the ground, and they could not lift them up again. After this
nothing happened."[108] For Lear, that statement indicates that with the
end of a "vibrant tribal life," so also the "mental states that are salient
and important" to Plenty Coups come to an end, so that "[a]ll that's
left is a ghostlike existence that stands witness to the death of the
subject."[109] But Lear goes on to argue that "[t]here is reason to think
Plenty Coups told his story to preserve it; and he did so in the hope
of a future in which things – Crow things – might start to happen

again."[110] From this suggestion, Lear turns to the question of how any one of us might develop a similar courage to conceive of the devastation of our culture and discover an ethical response to that possibility: how might one best conduct one's life in the face of such an event?

It is unquestionably crucial to ponder an ethical response to such a dire situation, as I will do below. But here it is more pressing to consider the implications of Plenty Coup's declaration: he speaks quite simply of the end of the world.[111] This statement is uncanny, for Plenty Coups makes that remark after having lived on for several decades after everything ceased to make sense, after the archaic practices he knew had lost their value. One could speak, then, of the possibility of surviving after the world's end, after indigenous reality gives way to the devastated, senseless, modern world. In that case, one could also say that indigenous peoples have already endured, and continue to endure, the end of the world, the ends of many worlds, and that in consequence they have learned how to live after that end. As Rebecca Roanhorse, a fantasy novelist of Ohkay Owingeh Pueblo descent, remarks, "We've already survived an apocalypse."[112]

But the perspective voiced by the Q'eqchi' elder suggests another possibility: with the loss of archaic ways, the world is indeed coming to an end. Such an insight would suggest that the modern world, having lost its archaic rituals, is also fated to collapse: without any spiritual significance to the life it makes possible, that life cannot persist. That perspective is borne out by the events of our time: with the cancellation of a spiritual respect for the lifeforms in which they thrive, modern economies have created the very scenario that may well lead to the terminus. Jettisoning ritual practices of symbolic exchange between human beings and nonhuman others, modern society chose to regard the nonhuman world as a mere resource for its own activities, so that nothing forbade it from decimating the earth. As I have argued elsewhere, such a turn against archaic practice also included the abrogation of symbolic exchange between social elites and commoners – a process that required an immense and ruinous effort in the era that formed the political framework that made modern capitalism possible.[113]

It is not only indigenous people, then, who live on after the end: that is the very situation of *all* of us who live in the modern world. It follows that we, like Plenty Coups, inherit the legacy of a dire event and endure in a merely literal, "ghostlike" existence. While one might in consequence attempt to absorb indigenous peoples into a modern temporality, Mark Rifkin shows that doing so would subject them to the time of the colonizer.[114] Our fate today reveals the necessity of proposing the reverse, the reinterpretation of modernity from the vantage of an indigenous sense of time. The extinction of humanity, if it transpires in the coming decades, will take place as the consequence of an event that has already taken place: the collapse of the symbolic practices that make the world possible.

Putting extinction back at stake. – In *Symbolic Exchange and Death*, Jean Baudrillard draws on premodern premises to illuminate the logic of capitalism. He points out that in a traditional logic, a victor could choose not to kill a prisoner of war but save his life and thus make him a slave; in a modern twist on this reprieve, the capitalist emancipates the slave to employ him in a wage economy. In doing so, the capitalist removes the worker from the exchange of death for death, subordinating him to the threat of a deferred death. "This is the violence the master does to the slave," writes Baudrillard, "condemning him to labor power." By deferring that death, by removing the defeated from a symbolic interplay, the master subjects the slave to a position outside of relationship. It follows that "[n]o revolutionary strategy can begin without the slave putting his own death back at stake." Thus the act of subordinating the worker calls forth its counterpart, whereby the worker repudiates this deferral and puts himself at risk in open combat against his oppressor.[115]

One can trace the contours of a similar argument in analyses not of slavery's imprint on capitalism but on the status of Black subjects in the United States. In *Slavery and Social Death*, Orlando Patterson argues that "the slave's powerlessness always originated (or was conceived of as having originated) as a substitute for death, usually violent death." As a result, the slave became "a socially dead person" who "ceased to belong in his own right to any legitimate social order" and lost all claim on his ancestors and descendants. He became subject to social death – to a status outside social relations *tout court*.[116] Building on this analysis, Frank B. Wilderson III argues that to this day Black people in the United States continue to live in the mode of social death, outside of a human status, time and space, and the resources of narrative, suffering an ontologically distinct condition.[117] Since for Wilderson this exclusion of Black people from humanity founds the very possibility of ontology, of a world, their liberation would require nothing less than the "end of the world."[118] A similar perspective informs Christina Sharpe's evocative rendition of what it means to live "in the wake" of the slave ship, to endure in a social context still defined by its legacy, so that those living in Blackness are subject to "the ejection, the abjection, by, on, through, which the system reimagines and reconstitutes itself."[119] And Fred Moten riffs further on these themes, arguing that "[m]odernity is sutured" by the "hold" of the slave ship and that it retains "at its heart, in its own hold, this movement of things, this interdicted, outlawed social life of nothing."[120]

Yet it does not follow that those who inherit the legacy of slavery are placed in an ontological status outside humanity. Moten emphasizes Black fugitivity, the capacity to steal away, to elude state power, and to undermine the many features of state-thought.[121] Jared Sexton, pursuing this argument, argues that the attempt to police this fugitivity "is aimed . . . at its irreducible precedence," the precedence of social life.[122] If the police can maintain their power only through a perpetual violence against those who perpetually steal away, it follows that social death is never secured, permanent, or ontological; it is inherently *relational*, insecure, open to a possible intervention – embedded, that is, within a relation of symbolic exchange. Rather than simply being imposed on slaves in a manner that forever defines them, it arises from within a dynamic they can deploy in reverse. Thus as Achille Mbembe demonstrates, Frantz Fanon envisioned a process whereby colonized subjects would rise up and claim a place within humanity, giving meaning not to their lives but to their deaths.[123] Indeed, for Fanon this reversal of colonial violence would bring about what Wilderson refers to as the "end of the world," the destruction of the colonizing regime.[124] In Baudrillard's terms, the colonized would in this way put their deaths back at stake, undoing the deferral of death by risking their lives in defiance of their ostensible masters.

This repudiation of deferred death, this seizure of one's own death to put it at stake, would constitute a moment of liberation of all those who inherit the legacies of slavery, whether in the form of racism, capitalism, or indeed of racial capitalism. It would ramify into a range of other domains as well: it would cancel the illusions of state-thought, the belief that settler colonialism constitutes a truly settled order, that whiteness is intrinsically ascendant, or that *any* social order ever gains an ontological status. Moreover, it would usher in an era after capitalism and its state, after the familiar regimes of governance that grounded themselves on the exclusion and immiseration of virtually all actually existing human beings. It would do so in part because it would revive the archaic understanding of symbolic exchange, of the ludic stakes of violence and contest, and thus renew a logic akin to that of ritual – a logic that makes possible a relationality within and to the world.

Today this logic takes on still further resonances as capitalism claims the right to impose a death on humankind as a whole. For most of its history, it has dismissed and attempted to cancel the logic of symbolic exchange not only in relation to its subordinates but also to nonhuman nature. Yet in the end it cannot, even on these terms, over-come that logic: as it contributed to environmental harm, it created a form of symbolic exchange that, however debased and literalized, endured in the exchange between violence against the environment and the biosphere's response. Moreover, by producing a false abun-dance out of the postponement of disaster, it has attempted once again to create the scenario of deferred death. All of us today, whatever our races may be, now live in the wake, and in the hold, of that deferred death, that enslavement. But that disaster will no longer be deferred; the potential disappearance of humanity approaches rapidly, reveal-ing that even a strategy of literal deferral is reversible, that the post-poned event can impose itself in turn. The reversibility of symbolic exchange now appears in domain of the biosphere as physical forces battle with capitalism for the stakes of life and death.

Needless to say, if that terminus arrives, it will erase the possibility of defiance and liberation. Nevertheless, the overall logic of symbolic exchange reveals that humanity could seize this moment to put its death back at stake in open revolt against the forces of terminal gov-ernance; all of us, facing the prospect of imminent extinction, could cancel the deferral of our deaths, put ourselves at stake, and bring about a revolution.[125] In taking such a step, we could declare a revolt in the name of all those suffering the legacy of slavery, whether in the form of race or of capitalism, and of all creatures and forms of life in the enslaved nonhuman world. In an act that repudiates the coloniza-tion of our histories, our subjectivities, and the biosphere itself, we could at last repudiate an existence granted to us on a specious basis, however divergent our place within these impositions may be. In that way, we would put the terminus into play in a new form, as a truly encompassing end of the regimes that have long been destroying us – and enter a mode beyond life and death as we have known them.

Tradition and disappearance. – In his essay "Tradition and the Individual Talent," T. S. Eliot argues that the new literary statement does not merely take its place in a succession after previous ones, but that "what happens when a new work of art is created is something that happens simultaneously to all the works of art that preceded it. The existing monuments form an ideal order among themselves, which is modified by the introduction of the new (the really new) work of art among them."[126] One might add that the same applies in a rather different but still valid way for each new material development, each generation's new sensibility, each historical era's departure from what came before; with each such emergence, the entire past is altered, appearing in a new light, characterized by previously unsuspected imperatives and intentions.

The thought of the terminus alters the past as well; it forces us to reconceive of humanity's history, to reinterpret the West, to ponder every aspect of culture anew. Yet it does so not merely by altering that past; it forces the entire tradition to incorporate a shocking new awareness of its radical contingency, the possibility of its cessation. This new moment has an overweening power over the past; its capacity to intervene, to force a new estimation of everything we inherit, is so sharp that it threatens the ideas of tradition and of historical temporality alike. Yet while it shatters the past, it still abides by the logic Eliot outlined, entering its place within the overall order to which it belongs.

What results, then, is a shattered order that still endures, a tradition that is scarcely recognizable in previous terms. Suddenly the works of the tradition, which evoke such a range of apparently secure contexts, now appear fragile, undone. Their confidence in the endurance of serious assertion has been rendered hollow; while their place within a long cultural history once seemed to assure them a place within a permanent legacy, now it is clear that the history to which they belong may well bring about their utter erasure.

Now that their premises are lost, their claims to significance in ruins, something else in them speaks to us: their capacity to survive as texts even after the world to which they belong has vanished, to manifest a mode of articulation that endures even in the midst of oblivion.

Without posterity. – Those writing ambitious literary works have long since assumed that the audience for those works would gradually form over several generations and that their writing would receive its proper estimation in posterity. Milton draws on this assumption in his hope that *Paradise Lost* will "fit audience find, though few."[127] In such a confidence, writers took for granted that their attempts to enter the canon, if successful, would give them a place within an enduring ensemble of respected works, that they would become a permanent part of their literary cultures. Shakespeare, taking his own immortality for granted, reassured the addressee of his sonnets that he was giving him an "eternal summer," for "So long as men can breathe or eyes can see / So long lives this and this gives life to thee."[128] In this astonishingly immodest claim, the poet contends that the canon, and every referent within it, will last as long as human beings live.

Even if such assertions are no longer typical today, serious writing still takes for granted the key role that posterity must play in determining the value of literary works. Writers of every kind are aware that books beloved in their own time might be forgotten soon thereafter and conversely that literature scarcely heard of in its own moment might be given pride of place by a later generation. In recent decades critics have accelerated this process, at last attending seriously to writing by women and those not privileged by the color of their skin, bringing new attention to dozens, and perhaps hundreds, of authors whose work is now pivotal to our sense of literary history. Accordingly, for many generations authors have written works with an eye toward the future as much as the present, even attempting at times to fashion a sensibility that might eventually triumph over present taste and thus to give their own work a special status.

Such attitudes permeate many other fields. Those who participate in or comment on public affairs often invoke the idea that certain deeds "will go down in history" or comment that "history will judge" what happened. These attitudes alongside those in the literary sphere point to a sense that the present depends for its significance on the future, perhaps even on several phases of the future; by implication, without such a judgment from another moment the present loses much of its value. In many ways this temporality reflects a certain secularization of culture, whereby people look not to the judgment of God but of human beings, though this shift toward an immanent framework is tempered by the belief that only mortals blessed with a sufficiently distant perspective can truly grasp the import of a given text or deed. Such beliefs suggest that we now understand our lives as participating in a shared history extending over many generations; for us, the present is a moment whose audience includes not only our own generation but also those toward whom we gesture in that appropriately distant future.

Under the sign of the terminus, however, as posterity disappears, as that useful distance dissolves, the import of the present alters. Whatever we do and say may not have an audience living even a few decades from now. In that moment, we ourselves will not be remembered, nor any of our deeds or words, nor any context for what we have done. Much as immortality has dissolved, so also does an immanent framework or a mortal judgment; as a result, the present is stranded on the verge of a great absence where there will be none to hear its voice. In the absence of this future, the present ceases to be itself; denuded of its contexts, lacking its addressee, it sustains a merely apparent existence, persisting within an oblivion that has already swept it away.

What is the grass? – In one of the most defining moments of American literature, in section six of Walt Whitman's *Song of Myself,* a child approaches the poet and asks, "What is the grass?" Before long the poet suggests that the grass grows "among black folks as among white," among "Kanuck, Tuckahoe, Congressman, Cuff" and "give[s] them the same [and] receive[s] them the same."[129] Growing everywhere, for one and all, it is a metaphor for radical democracy, even racial democracy, erasing hierarchies of difference in the new American polity.

A century from now, however, if the grass grows in a world denuded of human beings, it will no longer speak of any political condition, nor indeed of any human condition whatsoever; it will cease to be a metaphor for human concerns. Yet on further consideration, one can see that it has never spoken of our concerns; no one but human beings ever considered it to be a metaphor for features of our condition. The grass is not about us. But is it possible for human beings to live without natural metaphors, without investing the nonhuman domain with human significance? Can we see spring and fall, sunrise and sunset, in a truly neutral manner? Even if we could, what would it be like for us to live in a world we would no longer interpret in this way – in the solitude of the merely human, bereft of a world through which to speak of our concerns? Would a nonviolent humanity cultivate the ability to see the nonhuman without such metaphors, without even figural appropriations?

On one level, we might hope that a humanity capable of such a practice would not be solitary after all, for it would instead become a part of the nonhuman world at last, one of its endless profusions, living side by side with the grass in an even more radical version of democracy. Much as Levi Bryant writes of a "democracy of objects," outlining a politics for an object-oriented ontology, one might conceive of a democracy that forms of life could share, a mode of relation without imposition.[130] But to conceive of humanity's relation to other living forms in the terms of democracy would be to place those forms within a human framework. Here again, the attempt to place ourselves in a world without us sustains an anthropocentric focus despite its intention.

Thus to recognize that the grass is not a metaphor for our concerns requires us to see it as bearing no human significance whatsoever; it remains thoroughly other, living in a mode and in a domain radically apart from our narratives, projections, and metaphors. If as it so happens human beings disappear entirely, the grass will grow on, supremely unaware that any event occurred, flourishing as now in a mode of life we cannot know or speak. Or rather, since the grass is not even "unaware" of us, since its mode of life is not even "unknowable" in our terms, one must acknowledge that it lives outside of these negations, in a domain where even these erasures are erased, where even the forgetting of humanity is itself forgotten, where human thought falters and vanishes away.[131]

Yet in an almost paradoxical way, even as the grass lives on in this domain, without reference to humanity, it remains beautiful. Perhaps what we might recognize in the beautiful today would be this radical indifference to us, this extravagant performance for no one and nothing. If we adopt such a perspective, the coming of the terminus can make no difference for the beautiful, for it arrived eons before and will persist eons after any human spectator. For us, natural beauty may exceed any reference to the aesthetic as a category for the human subject – but for that very reason is beautiful. The grass dreams not of beauty and speaks not to us – and thus to us it is most beautiful.

After tragedy. – At one point, Lacan remarks that the sin of Oedipus does not take place years before the main action of *Oedipus Rex*, not when he slays his father and has intercourse with his mother, but rather when he insists on following through on his demand to know. In his account, when Oedipus demands to hear the truth at all costs, pushing past everything that might halt his quest, he ultimately stumbles into a knowledge on the basis of which he condemns himself and tears out his eyes.[132] One might conclude that Oedipus's insistence on knowledge is a tragic flaw, a hubris that comes at his own expense, as if he would have done better not to pursue such knowledge. But such a reading would overlook the exigency that befalls him as king of Thebes: the most relevant context is not the one provided by an analysis of the tragic hero (as Aristotle's discussion of tragic form would suggest) but rather by that figure's place within the crisis of the

city, the collective demand voiced in the play's initial scene that the
king end the pestilence and blight afflicting it. The tragedy arises in a
conflict Oedipus cannot evade – that between the demand that he save
the city and the cost for himself of doing so. This conflict is evident in
the paradoxical status of his fate, and indeed of his person, as the play
comes to an end: here the logic of the *pharmakon* applies, since the
remedy for the city is poison for him, as well as that of the *pharmakos*,
because, as René Girard argues, Oedipus becomes the scapegoat for
the crisis, a sacrificial victim whose exile at last restores the city.[133]

How might the import of this play bear on our own situation? By
pursuing a thorough knowledge of the condition of the biosphere and
of the earth's ecosystems, are we embarking on an enterprise like that
of Oedipus? Such a quest may force us once again into a version of
that tragic conflict, that clash between the necessity of seeking and the
devastation of gaining a certain knowledge. We too may learn that our
previous actions were unconscionable; we may condemn ourselves for
participating in a great crime. After receiving this knowledge, we too
may wish to blind ourselves. But such acts of self-condemnation will
not dispel what we have come to know, nor will it bring the pestilence
to an end. Today, tragic knowledge leads to no catharsis, no resolution;
no symbolic act on the part of the one who knows can bring the crisis
to an end, no exile call it to a halt. The logic of neither the *pharmakon*
nor the *pharmakos* works today. We now live in a world after tragedy
itself is defeated, after the symbolic gestures on which it relies have
lost their efficacy. Today we are exiled in a city where the pestilence
itself will rule – and eventually sweep us away.

Transgression without limit. – In a classic Restoration comedy, such
as William Wycherley's *The Country Wife*, the characters who have
pursued illicit pleasure throughout the play gather in a final scene,
prevaricate about their previous actions, and arrive at understandings
that bring back a rather fragile, if still recognizable, social order. Over
the course of such a comedy, the playwright exposes the hypocrisy
of social norms, the pleasure various characters take in transgressing
them and deceiving each other – as the leading women violate their
marriage vows, for example, and indulge in intercourse with Horner,
the principle rake – inciting our laughter and our enjoyment all the
while, only to bring such indulgence to an end at the last moment,
gently let it pass, and reinstate the appearance of good behavior. In
this play, the resolution itself produces a further comic effect, as
everyone collaborates in reassuring Mr. Pinchwife, the most jealous
husband, that Horner is indeed impotent, although Pinchwife's own
spouse, Margery Pinchwife, the titular country wife, unaware of the

turn events must take, attempts to contradict them and testify that "to [her] certain knowledge" Horner can indeed cuckold such husbands as he.[134] She is too naive to play along when it is time to hide the truth. In response, of course, her more quick-witted peers, women who like her secretly enjoyed Horner's company, leap in to interrupt her and bring about the final, necessary deceptions.

This comic form in some measure echoes the overall shape of inversion rituals, present in virtually every traditional society as well as early modern European carnivals, during which everyone in the collective is invited to participate in abrogating familiar norms and hierarchies, mocking the rules that apply in ordinary life, and then expelling this wholesale disorder and reinstating those norms as the ritual comes to an end.[135] Comedy thus bears within it a strikingly complex, if implicit, commentary on collective life: it exposes the fictional status of norms and yet treats them as necessary to the basic functioning of social relations, in effect unmasking the artificiality of collective codes while insisting on their ultimate value. *The Country Wife* evokes the subtlety of that stance in its own way, insisting on the return of social fictions even as it hints at their basis in hypocrisy; it puts a specifically Restoration twist in a traditional pattern.

Today, however, it is clear that the West has long since abandoned traditional norms without ever returning to them. The erasure of limitations to economic expansion in capitalist and socialist economies alike over the past two centuries or so has allowed for a mode of transgression so perpetual that it has become the very definition of the ordinary, creating an expectation so fundamental that a government failing to meet it loses much of its legitimacy. Replacing the symbolic excess of the carnival feast with literal abundance and the sense of playful inversion with a non-ludic regularity, the limitless economic expansion modernity seems to require ceases to evoke a giddy sense of misbehavior or inspire laughter; instead, it takes form as a routinized excess, creating the norms of a society that expects to live with a perpetually rising standard of living and thus of a system that expands its ecological footprint *ad infinitum*. By now the laughter intrinsic to traditional comedy has given way to the enchantments of perpetual growth – or, in societies acutely aware of income inequality, to the demand that abundance be shared with all. While versions of transgression or inversion may endure in other contexts, in the economic domain they have now dissipated, their scandal long since dissolved; today in some measure we live in a world after transgression, after comedy, indeed after any memory of the limits that once applied to collective life.

Yet modernity has not in fact overcome the logic visible in ritual inversion; its pursuit of a literal abundance abrogates a biological limit, the carrying capacity of the earth, as is now evident in the literal response of the biosphere. The subtlety of comedy, in short, has succumbed to the interplay between human imposition and environmental catastrophe, into a sharply nonsymbolic exchange between material forces. Playful provocation has given way to a brutal scenario, whereby an insistence on pleasure that never curbs itself confronts a material rejoinder beyond all appeal. In seeking to live in a mode after transgression, after comedy, we have succeeded only in living beyond the limits of the earth.

This unreal world. – In a bracing critique, Amitav Ghosh argues that the realist novel takes for granted that the world it depicts in all its quotidian glory is highly predictable, a reliable domain in which the protagonist may negotiate the challenges of a stable social world.[136] Over its history, one might add, the novel has been flexible enough to incorporate into its fictional space certain cultural disasters, including the devastations of war, which thanks to their strong continuity with quotidian histories still belonged within that world. But in an era when lives are more and more often interrupted by natural disasters unprecedented in their timing, size, ferocity, or effects, one can readily see that these conventions have always been arbitrary, for in excluding an array of happenings from its definition of realism, the novel constructs a highly constrained, even artificial notion of reality itself.

The novel's claim to realism today is even more suspect in part because its reliance on those conventions enables it to protect a manifestly fictional construction from the onslaughts of actuality, enabling people to regard catastrophic events as bizarre, exotic, even in some sense unreal, simply because they depart from the expectation that we live in a predictable world. People often respond to those events as if they erupted from disaster movies into the real world – as if they belong to outlandish subgenres of fiction – hinting that the respect people accord to the realist novel permits them to dismiss entire categories of contemporary experience. The hierarchy of genres, it seems, is replicated in a hierarchy of credibility people impose on the events in their lives.[137] Indeed, a restrictive notion of reality may help explain why so many people cannot quite see climate change as real: it departs too much from a bedrock belief in the stability of the world.

The novel's reliance on predictability should remind us of the idea, arising when the novel itself emerged, that the collective should ground itself not on the passions but the interests, in part because

when people act on their interests, their behavior is more predictable. A polity of interests, then, makes for a much more stable collective. But as we have seen, a society defined by interest does not
even attempt to take into account the consequences of its operations;
it creates externalities without attending to them. In much the same
way, the "ordinary" world constructed by the novel produces the very
catastrophes that interrupt it, yet the fiction of that world bars the
novel from treating them as real.

Might one therefore argue that science fiction is the exemplary
genre of our time, that only its scenarios can do justice to what we
face? But Ghosh's argument already demonstrates that people treat
certain events as taking place in a science-fiction world in order to
give them *less* credence, in order to place them slightly *outside* reality. What science fiction captures, then, is not yet regarded as reality:
it is too anchored in a future, in speculation, in fantasy, for it to be
regarded as a window on the actual present world.

One cannot help but conclude that what Ghosh ultimately describes
is an ideology of reality itself, a conviction that holds so tightly to
the known and predictable it cannot fully grasp what is taking place
today. But it would be a mistake to see this conviction as a contingent error one might easily correct, a mere byproduct of the history
of genre. In fact, this sense of reality is embedded in the foundational
assumptions of historical narrative, scientific inquiry, legal precedent,
the social and political unconscious, popular psychology, and many
more institutions and practices: it is the bedrock faith of the modern world. The actuality that undermines the credibility of the novel
cracks open the ideology of reality itself. Under the sign of the terminus, our reality becomes unreal. That unreality, that impossibly surprising and incomprehensible state, is our reality today.

The horror of the human. – With the coming of "black metal theory,"
as well as of Thacker's exemplary discussion of the "horror of philosophy" in our time, we might well turn to the mode of horror fiction pioneered by H. P. Lovecraft as a genre fitting this moment.[138] In
the classic stories at the inception of that mode, human protagonists
encounter forms of life utterly outside ordinary experience, confronting the possibility that species unknown to us might potentially dominate on this planet and even decimate us.[139] Such a mode, of course,
takes into account the radically anti-anthropocentric stance implicit
in the modern sciences, which must make way for an awareness of
our relatively contingent place within astronomical, geological, and
biological history – within a universe that contains forms of life well
beyond what we might control or master.

Yet even that already bracing mode cannot do justice to our condition today. In Lovecraft's stories, the horror comes from an encounter with something outside human knowledge, outside any previous dimension of our experience. But today our condition eclipses even horror with a more quotidian, and yet more brutal, possibility: *we ourselves* are destroying the conditions for our continued existence; *we* are the exotic species that threatens to exterminate us. We live in a world more horrifying than even horror tales can capture.

The anti-sublime. – If classic and modern genres alike crack apart, if the fundamental frameworks on which they have relied no longer hold together, what about the distinctive aesthetic possibilities that emerged with modernity? Consider Kant's analytic of the sublime, that linchpin of his critical philosophy and of modern aesthetic theory. According to Kant, the sublime requires a magnitude that is "absolutely great," great beyond comparison, so great that it suspends other faculties of mind preoccupied with the tasks of understanding or reason, such as considering the purpose of such greatness or comprehending it as an object of knowledge. Although for Kant such a magnitude cannot exist in the empirical world but only in the mind, he nevertheless argues that the mind must find a trigger outside itself – some vast or overwhelming natural object – to encounter its ability to conceive of the infinite.[140] One might find a useful counterpart to this Kantian analysis in Percy Bysshe Shelley's poem "Mont Blanc," where the glaciers, emanating from the peak of that mountain – a symbol for the poet of what lies beyond any human comprehension – enter the human world in a "flood of ruin," with a stunning, amoral "scorn of mortal power," as they breach "The limits of the dead and living world," the domain where mortals live.[141]

Today, however, the glaciers of the Alps are melting away, disappearing rapidly in the warmer conditions imposed by climate change. Those who view their remnants – or indeed the empty valleys where they once flowed – now know that there are forces greater than they, interpreting them within the terms of scientific knowledge, thereby reducing their absolute to a relative magnitude. The same fate has befallen other natural objects; the increasing force of vast storms reminds us that the alterations in the biosphere now make such phenomena more intense than in the past, so that when we encounter them with this knowledge in mind, we can no longer experience them in purely aesthetic terms as instances of the sublime. Climate change melts not only the glaciers, but the Kantian sublime as well, removing virtually every trigger of the idea of absolute magnitude from our experience. In Kantian terms, at least, we now inhabit a planet denuded of the sublime.

Indeed, today we are the force that scorns the power of glaciers, overwhelming them with our amoral violence; we have reversed an ancient dynamic, imposing ourselves on the physical processes of the biosphere itself. But such a shift does not give the sublime a new home in ourselves; on the contrary, it reveals the cumulative impact of small, quotidian actions, below the threshold of the senses, which together irreversibly displace the significances of the nonhuman world. We now experience a radically altered aesthetic; we now live in a world shaped by the anti-sublime.

Waste Land. – This scene of rubble: haven't we been here before? Don't we visit it whenever we read *The Waste Land*, that pastiche of citations from the tradition?[142] Isn't that space also inundated with the voices of the dead, polluted by the trash of history, haunted by the absence of renewal? Perhaps the overall stance of the poem accords well with much of what I have outlined here: insofar as it relies on its rendition of archaic myth, organizing its passages around the recurrence of archetypes and marshalling them within a narrative pattern from Arthurian legend, it too suggests that the world of its moment has fallen into disarray as a result of departing from archaic patterns.

But in describing its present moment as a counterpart of the "waste land" over which the impotent fisher king presides, it ultimately places itself within the arc of that older narrative, suggesting that it will be possible to renew those old forms and rescue modernity from its condition. In some future moment, the fisher king will undergo a spiritual breakthrough and once again become generative; such a change may coincide with the arrival of the rain, some hint of which gusts across the poem in its late lines. In the poem's fantasy of anthropocentric, reproductive futurism, once the king becomes potent again, the waste land will burst forth and call a dead tradition to life, completing the pattern inscribed in this particular thread of Arthurian quest-romance. Rather than consisting of debris, then, the poem shores its fragments against the ruins, evoking a redemptive conclusion it does not directly depict, placing itself within a framework defined by a resolution to come.

The thought of the terminus thus takes us well beyond the aesthetics of this poem: our present condition belongs to no ancient tale, our actions replicating no archetypal failure. Indeed, today we can see that the anthropocentric framework of the poem's narrative arc can produce the very waste land we now inhabit: an insistence on the idea that a human vitality will lead to the flourishing of the world may well be the curse under which we suffer. Writing in the wake of World War I, Eliot seeks a pattern that might call forth a potential recovery from the experience of devastation. Thinking under the sign of the terminus today, faced with a prospect that makes war itself subordinate to a vaster crisis, we can no longer hope to evoke such a recovery. No narrative resolution awaits us; no archetypal pattern can depict our fate. We are past all myth, confronted with the dissolution of any *arche* that might still pretend to define us. The archaic gives way to the terminus; the type to its disfiguration; the notion of the human to its own nullity. The poem of fragments now finds itself in a pile of debris.

Terminus of an endless end. – Over the course of the last century and a half, the task of bringing about the end of philosophy has generated successive waves of speculative innovation that have ironically sustained philosophy and given it greater conceptual range and subtlety. Writers such as Nietzsche, Heidegger, Wittgenstein, Derrida, Rorty, and Laruelle have challenged the premises of philosophy in styles of thinking that, while bracing and novel, nevertheless are still recognizably within the institutions and speculative traditions of philosophy, so that precisely by setting out to end it they enlarge upon it, redefine it, and give it a range of new possibilities. Over roughly the same period, literary writers have carried out a similar project in relation to literature; as Roland Barthes argues, in such figures as Flaubert, Mallarmé, Proust, the surrealist writers, and Robbe-Grillet, "literature appears to destroy itself as a language object without destroying itself as a metalanguage," creating "a dangerous game with its own death."[143] One could easily extend this argument to the plastic and visual arts, where over the extensive history of the avant-garde, modernist and postmodern investigations have used the resources of those arts to expose their previously tacit premises. In such efforts, the practices of high culture paradoxically persist by means of apparently destroying themselves, as if to create a strangely endless end over the course of an entire lineage of self-erasure.

Today, however, this endless end is now exposed not to an end but a terminus, not to a conceptual scouring of certain inherited premises but an erasure that overwhelms them from outside. As a result, the material preconditions for these cultural practices become surprisingly visible, cutting across these familiar styles of self-critique with a threat they cannot metabolize. Here the affect of avant-garde practice – its yearning for a scandalous break from tradition, from inherited assumptions and gestures – dissolves under the force of a development infinitely more scandalous than any mere scandal, the erasure of humanity as a whole, which takes place non-intentionally, non-conceptually, without any provocative gesture, outside any staging of an event and any reference to the new. The terminus hollows out tradition and the avant-garde alike, aligning itself with no cultural category of any kind. While the practices that it promises to erase may be able to attend in some way to what this threat brings, such responses will not contribute to a further elaboration of a meta-language but will reveal the fragility, indeed mortality, of those practices themselves. The mode of internal critique now gives way to an externally imposed erasure, taking us from the thought of the end to a terminal thought, one that, in thinking the undoing of each practice, must perforce think its own extinction as well.

8 The fading of the virtual

Ideology today. – In *The Sublime Object of Ideology*, Slavoj Žižek, drawing on Lacan's reading of the dream of the burning child from Freud's *Interpretation of Dreams* as well as Marx's theory of ideology, demonstrates that ideology does not enable us to avoid our reality but provides the terms through which that reality gains its consistency, through which it holds together. What we see as reality is itself our ideology. Our direct experience is a lie: this ordinary day, this familiar scene, obscures an unbearable truth – the Real – from which we hide ourselves at all costs. Protecting ourselves in this way, we create the framework for carrying on with what seems like our ordinary lives.[144] As Žižek points out, whatever we may believe about our world, whatever we may say about it, whatever politics we may advocate, our ideological investments are ultimately far more visible in these everyday acts, in the underpinnings of the most banal practices in which we participate.[145] Ideology is most visible where we notice it the least.

If all this is the case, then how might a leftist politics opposed to ideology conduct itself today? On the basis of its fundamental principles, it would expose how nearly everything in our apparent reality is derived from the domination of capitalism and dare to shatter that reality with a revolution that is at once a version of the psychoanalytic Act and a politics of the Real. Today, however, capitalism's reality is eroding in the face of the terminus, a literal version of the Real. The biosphere is bringing about what might seem to be the fiercest critique of ideology imaginable, exposing the costs of imposing capitalism on humanity and the nonhuman world alike. In doing so, it might seem to have a revolutionary force of its own, as if it retains some reference to an alternative, to a collective flourishing. Yet in fact, it threatens to cut through any political response to ideology with its inhuman intervention, to sweep away all possible ethical responses under the force of its biophysical reply. Today, the critique of ideology goes so far that, in becoming literal, it imperils itself, potentially engulfing every Act we might carry out with a supreme intervention of its own.

The fading of the virtual. – In recent decades it has become more commonplace for social agents to form identities by appealing to mediated images. With the gradual inclusion of gay, lesbian, and trans people on television shows, for example, and with the emergence of shows including more people of color, many viewers in the United States have felt that this society might actually affirm them: the representation of people with a certain identity has made it more possible to claim marginal identities in socially recognized and effective ways. This pattern reveals that the same has been true all along for those with more privileged identities; indeed, it demonstrates that for a vast number of people living in a postmodern world, the formation of identity takes shape in part through an engagement with visual narratives. In effect, the media serves as the central space for the presentation of authorized identities. More recently, this practice has also operated through representations people make of themselves on social media; the more people can consume images from others like those they might create for themselves, and the more coherently they can represent themselves through this medium, the more they can claim a socially viable identity.

This architecture for identity suggests that rather than mediating a reality that lies outside itself, the media has become primary; it is now the privileged domain for framing that reality, enabling it to come into existence. Like previous versions of such framing in myth, religious teaching, literary narratives, or psychoanalytic scenarios, these visual stagings are prior to what they capture, sites for the origination of a shared world. Although people are aware that the images they construct of themselves on social media are in part fictional, distortions of a certain reality, they do not for all that regard those images as secondary or derivative; these mediations retain the ancient privilege of the symbol, the power of a convincing artifice.

The same follows for the construction of our shared "reality" as well: as long as the media represents a phenomenon as real, then it is so; as long as it depicts an event visually, then it clearly took place. In fact, today nothing happens unless it takes a visual or mediated form; if it is not available in those ways, it is not received as real and does not merit public attention. The mediated is now the space for the construction of a shared reality. We inhabit what Baudrillard designates as the "hyperreal," that is, a mediated reality more real than real.[146] The more privileged the virtual becomes, the more empirical reality — including the biosphere — fades away.

The emergence of this mediated reality, however, does not depart entirely from the past. At no point in human history have people apprehended reality directly; they have always read it within interpretive frameworks, excluding or denying certain aspects of experience in doing so. Lacan captures this pattern in his argument that the Real is unassimilable in the symbolic; impossible to name, never fully captured, the Real eludes representation, emerging if at all in the deadlocks of the symbolic, its logical and constitutive impasses.[147] The domain of the symbolic has shifted its domain in part to the regime of visual narrative or social media representations, taking up new abodes to carry out its familiar tasks. In some respects, then, the hyperreal is the most recent strategy for making possible the emergence of identities through an evasion of the Real.

Yet today the costs of such an evasion become ever more evident. Whereas in the past, societies could postpone a reckoning with the Real almost indefinitely, deferring an encounter with its constitutive exclusions and impasses generation after generation, today that confrontation approaches rapidly, exposing the fissures in our systems of mediation with unusual force. It may at times do so through singular events or stunning interruptions, but it also does so perpetually through developments below the thresholds of perception, in sounds too low to hear, changes too subtle to notice, and in processes that our everyday narrative and visual systems cannot apprehend. Where the term "the Real" implies the existence of an entity, a Thing, it arrives today as well through nothing to which one can point, nothing graspable in itself, in the miniscule but perpetual modifications to that vast array of phenomena that we typically regard as the mere background for the drama of our lives.

Nevertheless, we now know without a doubt that this devastating change is taking place, that it flows ceaselessly beneath the surfaces of representation, that it is bearing down implacably on the regimes in which we live. Ironically, through the very disputes over whether it is taking place, indeed through the internecine warfare regarding what actually counts as "truth" in our time, our society becomes ever more attuned to the potential fraudulence of its representations, so that we inhabit not the hyperreal as such but rather an endless antagonism about how to interpret its mediations. As a result, we have become aware that we are immersed in a network of mediations that have lost credibility, that pretend to a definitive status they no longer have.

Despite this awareness, however, our societies still cling in part to the validity of the visible, refusing to relinquish a regime that they suspect. They do so primarily because of an irony in the apprehension of the Real. They still believe that they can apprehend reality through representation, if only a more intrusive, aggressive version than before. If only one could penetrate into the hidden core of reality, into the inner secret of events! If only one could ensure that all would be revealed! Yet like the pornographer who wishes to capture the truth of sex only to discover that the mere filming of the act cannot do so, one attempts to represent the secret of our world only to learn that the Real cannot be solicited in that way. In attempting to go beyond the regime of mere representation, our societies replicate it, exposing its fraudulence while also submitting to its lure. We are still spellbound by a nostalgia for a real that we can grasp; we cannot quite accept that it is unassimilable within any regime of representation. The teaching of Lacan has not yet hit home.

The desperation with which our societies attempt to overleap the limits of representation, however, perpetually reveals their awareness that its regime is beginning to falter. We live more and more within a symbolic order whose validity has begun to decay. Even in its apparently uncontested sway, the virtual loses its capacity to define our shared reality. While we can never live in the Real, we have begun to sense its capacity to interrupt and undermine the symbolic, to expose the countless gaps in what once seemed to be a seamless web, and to become strangely palpable in its bare, unmediated, uncanny state. Today the virtual regime is beginning to fade away.

From technics to kleptics. – Over the course of many books, Bernard Stiegler demonstrates that in its hyperindustrial form, capitalism immiserates people through the processes not only of production but also of consumption. Previously, he argues, a certain form of libidinal economy took shape as a collective desire that motivated action across time, shaping modes of attention, knowledge, belief, acceptance of constraint and authority, ethical engagement, and more, whereas the current form of capitalism, seeking to mobilize and energize this libidinal flow, ultimately destroys it, leading to an eclipse of that collective desire and all the projects to which it once led and producing a new form of misery – a mode without a project, a past or future, or indeed spirit of any kind.[148] This phase also marks out an important departure within the history of what he calls *technics*. In his account, from the very beginning human societies relied on prostheses, on technologies constituted by gestures and actions surrounding external objects, to shape their practices and make possible the retention of knowledges and skills; the evolution of technics, then, is intrinsic to the evolution of humanity itself.[149] This fundamental feature, typically neglected or excluded by philosophy, led from the shaping of flint in prehistory through the invention of writing and eventually to the construction of the industrial apparatus in early phases of capitalism. But in the present phase technics ceases to be a feature within the passionate engagements of desire and instead, especially in its digital forms, imposes itself on desire, exploiting consciousness for the purposes of the market, producing nothing less than a vast cultural crisis and indeed the potential erasure of any future. In response to these developments, Stiegler proposes a range of remedies, such as the recovery of a transindividual desire capable of subordinating digital technologies to collective ends.[150]

While this analysis of our current collective state cuts deep, the prospect of the terminus reveals that the immiseration of the collective takes place on still more fundamental levels. That prospect suggests that the crucial turn on which Stiegler's intervention relies – the insistence that all instances of collective endeavor depend on the deployment of technical prostheses and retentions, and that as a result one must rethink every aspect of the human as shaped by technics, challenging virtually every philosophy in doing so – does not yet go far enough. To make it possible to take the terminus into account, one must recognize that the formation of technologies depends, in turn, on the cooptation of material aspects of the environment to produce these technical innovations for collective ends – of stone to make shaped flint, of paper to create texts, or of silicon to produce digital technologies. That unthought feature of collective life, technics, depends on something even less thought, what one could call a *kleptics* (from the Greek *kleptein*, to steal), whereby culture perpetually appropriates the affordances of the material world and relies on its supposed capacity to tolerate such theft indefinitely. This kleptics is also a constitutive feature of the collective, and indeed of subjectivity, providing the preconditions of technics as well as of the very consciousness that can begin to analyze its condition in this way.

A philosophy capable of thinking kleptics would thus radicalize every feature of Stiegler's argument: it would show that the market immiserates not only agents of production and consumption, colonizing work and desire alike, as he argues, but also ecosystems as well as atmospheric and oceanic systems, attempting to reduce even the biosphere to a proletarian status.[151] In doing so, it interrupts not only the affective investment in the future – including the capacity to care about the future of the climate and thus of humanity itself – but also the material conditions that permit the biological survival of the human species. If, as Stiegler insists, the dominance of the market is rapidly creating a mass of disaffected individuals, it is at the same time producing what we could regard as an immiserated biosphere. For Stiegler, the market subverts the purpose of technical retentions – their capacity to serve as an external form of memory for collective ends – by imposing a form of digital retention that cancels any such orientation to the future. But in an even more dire development, the legacy of several centuries of kleptics takes the form of carbon dioxide that, retaining the memory of human emissions in the atmosphere and oceans for as much as a century, undermines even hypothetical future action to address the climate crisis and severely curtails the mere prospect of a future for the species. The more that the market attempts to subordinate the environment to its purposes, the more the biosphere repudiates it, making ever more visible the cost of allowing technics and kleptics to hold sway without limit. Our addiction to the affordances of digital technics is thus only a small symptom of an even more consequential development, the erasure of a future not only for collective desire but for the collective itself.

In the midst of this detonation. – It is a commonplace of literary history to demonstrate how the enormous transformations in Western culture following the first waves of colonization, the beginnings of industrial capitalism, and the emergence of urbanization all led to the formation of a wide range of new forms of discourse in the nineteenth century and still further innovations in the twentieth. Among the chief exhibits in this respect are novels of urban life – especially of London and Paris – and Hollywood movies. Both modes turned a potentially overwhelming urban modernity into resources for new forms of emotional complexity, new levels of sophistication and taste, and indeed new possibilities for narrative statement. In making those waves of experience into materials for art, however, they sustained the fiction that people could survive and enjoy radical changes in ordinary experience and thereby enabled their audiences to normalize the slow-moving detonation of the West and of the biosphere alike. Given what we know today about the effects of burning coal and oil to sustain the economies producing all these changes, we can now recognize that these strategies of normalization in effect redescribed that underlying conflagration as a dazzling mode of experience, enabling a transformation in what it might mean to be human. The discourses of modern life, in short, processed a stunning increase in carbon dioxide emissions into a marvelous array of human possibilities, producing a cultural explosion as intense and expansive as its material counterpart.

In doing so, however, these cultural practices created a detonation in the coherence of the West as well: the sheer multiplication of discourses, the very pace of transformation, the impossibility of assimilating or grasping the acceleration of historical change, produced such a cacophany, such an impossible excess, that throughout the fossil fuel era the West has been unable to absorb the import of its own productions. In recent decades, with the even greater pace of historical change, this maelstrom has only intensified, this cacophany becoming even more deafening. What we can hear least of all is the fact of the slow-moving detonation itself, the underlying phenomenon whose signal is buried under an infinity of its effects; having long since become accustomed to these effects, finding our way through them with a truly hypermodern ease, we now find it virtually impossible to discern that they are only features of a slow-moving explosion that is already destroying us through and through.

Fear of experience. – Nietzsche once commented that with the French Revolution, "the text finally disappeared under the interpretation."[152] Something similar happens today in a hundred domains. A single comment by a celebrity may receive hundreds of responses on social media; a single episode of a television show may inspire a thousand comments on blogs and postings; a single piece of legislation making its way through Congress may generate a host of petitions, demands, and comments online, not to mention hours of coverage on nonstop television news channels; and an actual sporting contest may endure through endless replays, analyses, and comparisons, along with discussions of its place in the compilation of statistics. The noise of culture, in effect, drowns out the paltriness of mere events.

A similar pattern obtains elsewhere. Almost every event is photographed, filmed, discussed, analyzed, commented on, in a thousand forums, nearly disappearing into the vast nimbus of its interpretation. As a result, the singularity of the event is effaced, the uniqueness of a specific moment incorporated into the categories of interpretation. In an analogous development, literary and cultural criticism, retreating into an ever more capacious historicism, often drowns texts in a thousand contexts, refusing what in those texts remains irreducible. Moreover, individual people, however singular their lives or unique their contributions, are now merely instances of demographic categories, interpretable first of all as embodiments of abstract populations; indeed, in the United States, it is becoming more and more imperative to present oneself through one's "identity," in order to safeguard the very viability of one's cultural assertion. The singularity of the subject has well-nigh disappeared. Such a pattern is confirmed by the ease with which shooters and terrorists, reducing the significance of people in a similar way, can destroy them as mere stand-ins for a hated high school or despised workplace or as cyphers for entire nations.

This resistance to the specificity of experience is found as well in other trends. By now we – or rather, the more privileged among us – can override aspects of our experience we dislike: we can face off against a warming world with air conditioning, enjoy the taste of fat or salt with artificial substitutes, alter our images using digital photo manipulation, change the very shape and appearance of our bodies with cosmetic surgery, and find sexual partners with any number of apps; we can change the flow of rivers, transform deserts into fertile agricultural regions through irrigation, redesign the landscapes of entire cities, perhaps even produce artificial lakes or islands. More and more, we can reshape reality itself to accord with our demands.

This pattern is confirmed in the increasing refusal to accept that anything is beyond reach, inaccessible, or lost. One can find a vast archive of popular and classical music on Spotify and old movies and videos on YouTube, catch up with nearly every movie on a streaming service, buy virtually any book on Amazon.com, see the entire documentary record of an untold number of institutions online, look up the personal information of billions of people, and indeed roam the world on Google Earth. Thanks to Facebook, one can ostensibly keep in contact with nearly all of one's "friends," never losing track of people one once knew well. Even more, for every devastating loss, one can demand compensation; those whose loved ones were destroyed in the assault on 9/11 have now been reimbursed for the lifelong income of those killed on that day. One is no longer even allowed to feel the anxiety endemic to this era; it, too, must disappear thanks to the emergence of new medications.

No wonder our societies cannot even imagine the possibility of a genuine revolution that would overturn the sway of international corporate capitalism. Such an event is not only beyond imagining, outside a system that now passes for reality itself, but also terrifying in its capacity to put everything one values at risk. Our societies are clearly in the grip of a passion to retain what we know and to sustain what we already have; our singular focus is to keep intact a world already familiar, already interpreted, and in some sense already experienced *tout court*.

In these and other ways, our culture betrays a fear of experience, a horror of the unmediated encounter, a hatred of loss, a refusal of the event. But if nothing is truly lost, nothing is ever vitally present; if no event can occur, then nothing happens. If each person must disappear into a category, no one actually exists. The world thus verges on becoming a mere replica of itself, a mirage. Yet this possibility is unacceptable. Even Baudrillard, the high priest of the hyperreal, endlessly signals its scandal through his very description of it *as* hyperreal, *as* a mode that erases reality; such an account perpetually brings reality along in its wake, exposing what the hyperreal attempts to override without being able to do so. His response signals that the erasure of reality is necessarily incomplete, that the world of pure appearances is forever haunted by what it lacks. Such an awareness can provoke a far less joyous response; indeed, throughout postmodern culture, the dread that the world of mere representations might vanish – or worse, that it is unreal – motivates a defense of reality against its disappearance. Beneath the fear of experience lies a deeper fear, a horror that the world is slipping away. A specter is haunting contemporary culture: the prospect of its dissolution.

Yet in a parody of Lacan's teaching that what is excluded from the symbolic reappears in the Real, creating the conditions for psychosis, today the alterity we deny returns to haunt us in a reality even more alien and threatening than before.[153] The carbon dioxide we emit as we reshape the world to our liking remains in the atmosphere for a century or more, creating a biosphere whose actions will persist beyond all appeal, as if all the denied modes of experience return in an even harsher form. This pattern teaches us that our very refusal of what we fear brings it to pass all the more. The noise of culture, promising to drown out all else, is now faced with the prospect that a great silence will engulf it. Our defense against disappearance is bringing it about; our hatred of loss is taking this world away.

Absence of negation. – In his magisterial book, *Aesthetic Theory*, Adorno explored the intricate dialectic according to which modern art, participating in aspects of contemporary culture, also negates it, revealing its ideological constraints and hinting at revolutionary possibilities that it forecloses. Even as that culture perpetually attempts to fold artistic works into its ordinary processes, they resist that attempt, standing over against its apparently irresistible flow.[154]

At its most powerful, art can expose the ideological underpinnings of our view of an apparently objective reality. As Žižek argues, Kazimir Malevich's painting *Black Square* designates the framework for the artwork, the empty site in which it is placed, and thus serves as the exact counterpart of Marcel Duchamp's urinal, the readymade object that becomes an artwork only when it is placed within that empty place. Where the black square reduces art to its minimal site, the readymade reduces it to an object – any object – contained in that site; in each case, the modernist work cuts through all content, all appeals to art's relation to an apparent reality, and presents a version of the Real, the invisible, nonphenomenal dimension that enables art to emerge as such.[155] These severe negations register a refusal of ideology, providing a viewpoint from which to cut through the commonsensical view of reality, thereby evoking a sense of the Real that can underlie a revolutionary attempt to create a new world.

Yet today, modernist refusal gives way to the postmodern insistence on the mere constructedness of every social reality, as if to absorb the negation of ideology into an awareness (and acceptance) of its fictional status; at the same time, the possibility of revolution dissolves in the face of the belief that there is no alternative to international corporate capitalism, however regrettable the latter may be. On both counts, the negativity of which Adorno speaks falls away. Even where aesthetic statement dares to expose ideology, evoking an alternative possibility, its intervention is absorbed into what is by now a familiar history of the avant-garde, as if it merely elaborates further on the radical gestures of an earlier era. The modernist intervention has become its own orthodoxy; it no longer cuts through the assumptions that underlie a seemingly immovable political complacency. One can trace the effects of this pattern in the overall reception of art. Although exhibits of modernist classics have become strikingly popular with the general public, they no longer have power to shake bedrock assumptions about our common life but have become even more canonic than the works of the Old Masters, even more visibly instances of what Adorno called "the culture industry."[156] Even artworks intended to showcase the dubious assumptions of our era now thematize concerns already articulated in other ways and are thus readily assimilated into familiar political debates. Thus today art seldom escapes the fate of feeding the art market and of reifying still another dimension of the current representational regime.

The eclipse of art's negation, however, makes that regime more fragile. Without the pressure of the negative, culture's positive statements can no longer signal an unstated element that exceeds their manifest content; as a result, they risk becoming pure surfaces, merely virtual. Reacting against that fate, they may attempt to secure some relation to the Real, yet because no revolutionary discourse remains, no prospect of an Act that could disturb the universe, the Real itself seems to vanish, leaving in its wake a society that, unable to evoke its own negativity, loses a sense of its positivity as well.

The victory of the positive over itself, however, has taken place during the same decades as its victory over the biosphere. This pairing reveals that as the negative disappears from a range of cultural domains, it reappears in another, in the material preconditions for culture itself. The only revolution today – and the only avant-garde – is to be found in a radically exterior domain, in climate change. A society that has lost access to its own negation may now find it in a new domain, in a form no longer negative, but catastrophic through and through.

Museum of annihilation. – In lieu of the museums commemorating past eras, today we live in a museum of humanity's future disappearance. This museum may be found in certain objects surrounding us in everyday life – objects that already body forth the practices bringing about the environmental changes that will destroy us. Consider, for example, the signature views of urban centers, with their distinctive skyscrapers, signs of immense concentrations of population, energy, and capital; the industrial plants and warehouses whose efficient operations have perpetually demanded forms of energy harvested from fossil fuels; the freeways that, cutting across any landscapes organized according to a human scale, speak of travel at long distances; the container ships that make the flows of global trade possible; the airports from which people can travel to destinations far away, consuming in a single trip the carbon allowance of an entire year; the overly large and powerful vehicles that people use to commute to work, each signs of a history of ordinary personal travel that has done such harm to the biosphere; the chain saws that, in their quotidian efficiency, make possible the clear-cutting of forests; and the fishing vessels whose equipment permits workers in search of one species of fish to harvest all non-microscopic forms of life within a large swath of the sea. All these scenes and objects, functioning at their greatest intensity within the recent past or actual present, speak of the disaster through which we live, the extravagant devastation we have enacted and still perpetually carry out. Yet we inhabit their domain in a mode of a superb inattention, as if we are bent on enjoying our roles as functions of the objects that surround us.

For those attentive to what will come, all these scenes and objects constitute leading signs of the processes leading to humanity's disappearance. The Real of our era already finds a home in these scenes; today we live surrounded by the machines that are reducing us to ash. Perhaps this is the distinctive anti-aesthetic of our time, this unnoticed display of our own fate, this museum of our will to nullity.

9   Humanity, that antispecies

Homeless at home. – In his discussion of Heidegger's notion of *Heimatlosigkeit,* or loss of homeland, Peter Sloterdijk remarks that it now suggests a profound "denaturalization" as reflected not only in the actual move into "climate-controlled spaces" but also in the recognition that "[a]fter psychoanalysis, not even the unconscious is useable as a home, nor is 'tradition' after modern art, nor by any means 'life' after modern biology."[157] He goes on to emphasize how developments in atmospheric military weapons have taken this pattern further, arguing that since the early twentieth century, roughly since World War I, humanity has become homeless at home, unable to assume that the atmosphere is breathable, and thus fundamentally unsettled in the very place in which it seems to dwell.[158]

Today we cannot avoid radicalizing these points: thanks to severe climate change, even the earth and its biosphere are no longer at home to themselves. The human interference in biophysical processes forces them to depart from their own prior states, to counteract their previous patterns; what military planners only dream of is now being realized on a planetary scale, as the entire earth system disarranges all its elements.

In such an overall context, what happens to the imperative that one cherish and sustain one's local ecosystem? Can one dwell responsibly and respectfully within it? Now that its seasons are changing, its species dying or moving elsewhere, the water flows and landforms altering, the interconnections between essential species being disturbed or lost, how might one sustain what remains? The same questions apply on a broader scale: is dwelling on the planet today a matter of living alongside its disfiguration, its drift into another mode, its discovery of novel and unprecedented forms of biological collaboration? Are we to find a home in this homelessness, to discern in the collapse of all familiar modes the very medium for other arrangements of life? Is sustainability today a matter of learning how to live in the midst of what can no longer be sustained?

Such a mode undoubtedly presses itself on us today. But it is temporary: under the sign of the terminus, we are forced to recognize that even this strategy ultimately commits us to dwelling within a process leading to our own disappearance. What unsettles us from home may eventually make the biosphere entirely uninhabitable for us. In dwelling alongside these transformations, then, we live with the arrival of our own erasure. What we are learning today is how to find a home not merely in our homelessness, but in that imminent extinction itself.

Humanity, that antispecies. – Those who wish to minimize their horror at what humanity is enacting today often resort to the notion that it merely reveals aspects of what is inherent in us, a sharply destructive characteristic intrinsic to us that we cannot overcome. Ironically, such a response often occurs to those who attempt to explain most features of humanity according to evolutionary biology, an impulse that could be interpreted as a way of respecting our place within the earth's systems of life. Yet in fact it does the opposite, for it relieves humanity of any ethical or political responsibility and moreover ignores how we commit our actions *against* those living systems. The fact that we are bringing about the planet's sixth great extinction – and potentially our own disappearance – suggests that even if we are obviously a species, an organism that evolved within the planet's webs of life, we are not *only* that, for the ease with which we disturb the planet's ecosystems places us in a unique category.[159] Furthermore, the difficulty we face in attempting to account for our actions shows that, to riff on Heidegger's thematic of Dasein, humanity is that mode of being for which humanity itself is a question.[160] Whoever resorts to a biological explanation is attempting to answer this impossible question with a merely descriptive answer, to account for our ungrounded situatedness with an appeal to the fact that we are a species. Such an answer, in short, falsifies our situation on several levels, making abundantly clear that our actions have never had biological alibis.

But establishing this perspective is not enough. One who does so must still ask what follows from the fact that evolution could produce a species for whom its very position in the world is a question, who can never simply be *at home* on the earth, never in tune with its preconditions. Such a species, or rather antispecies, cannot be read as necessarily sustaining any specific response to its situation: it might create cultural practices that respect local ecosystems – or it might adopt practices that destroy them.

In effect, then, the earth suffers from an autoimmune disorder proper to a *hospitality to humanity*: such a stance is inherently open to all possible scenarios, including the most affirmative and the most disastrous.[161] To consider this as a mode of hospitality, however, implies that to the Earth humanity is an instance of alterity, a designation that captures well how humanity has no home in nature and can never naturalize its institutions or practices. Indeed, because its position in relation to being and the world takes shape as a question, it may indeed reply to this question in a range of answers none of which the earth's hospitality can exclude. Such a mode of hospitality, in turn, is intrinsic to evolutionary biology itself, which could not forestall the emergence of such an antispecies. To provide the preconditions for life is to be vulnerable to the possibility of such an emergence. In effect, humanity's ungroundedness, its anxious and indeterminate relation to its preconditions, sets it apart as the instance that best exemplifies the autoimmune disorder intrinsic to the planet's affordances of life.

One last voyage. – At the end of Mark Twain's *Huckleberry Finn*, Huck, dismayed by the prospect that Aunt Sally will still attempt to "sivilize" him, famously declares, "I reckon I got to light out for the Territory."[162] Here Huck enacts that characteristic American gesture of heading out to the West to escape some feature of "civilization" that one dislikes. That moment indicates that people entered the frontier not only to find open spaces and claim new territories, but also to evade aspects of their lives or avoid unsolved problems by means of direct physical departure. In that case, the frontier – and indeed much of the initial colonial settlement along the Eastern seaboard – arose from an impulse to abandon historical and political realities and find an alternative space beyond history, outside complication, to launch oneself into a region free of difficulty. America may be the land, at least in part, of evasion.

That pattern holds well after the closing of the frontier; the strong American preference for always looking ahead indicates that the nation experiences time itself in a similar way, as a perpetual departure from a history that it wishes to ignore. This preference appears as well in the space age, when science fiction tales of travel in interstellar space sometimes coincided with the wish to escape the problems of earthly history or to abandon a planet whose environment was in ruins. The Octavia Butler series on living with climate change, for example, which consists of *Parable of the Sower* and *Parable of the Talents*, delves into a wide range of questions with strongly multiracial and feminist insights, pondering such possibilities as whether under the pressure of climate change slavery – especially sexual slavery – will return. Butler's work stands out as among the most culturally and politically savvy writing in American science fiction and indeed in American fiction overall. It is thus quite striking that Lauren Olamina, the initial protagonist of this series, who leads a small group of people she has named Earthseed in their migration from Los Angeles northward, eventually includes this belief in the religion she has initiated: "'The Destiny of Earthseed, / Is to take root / Among the stars."[163] Even in this classic Afrofuturist series, even in a truly insightful exploration of the effects climate change may have on American culture, the fundamental template still applies: the wish to depart from a planet and to settle somewhere among the stars.

A fantasy this embedded in national – and now international – culture has countless effects across many domains. One such effect is the tendency of capitalism to subordinate national perspectives to a global flow, thereby abandoning specific histories to the past as it seeks ever more expansive avenues for growth. Like America, international capitalism wishes to evade the constraints of geographically limited traditions and temporalities and move as freely as possible across global space and time. In this respect, it revives the mentality of settler colonialism in a new mode and on a new scale, attempting to colonize the entire globe – and the biosphere – for its purposes. In effect, the fantasy of space travel reflects this enterprise of seeking an unfettered mobility across the earth and of attempting to bring the entire global market into a domain no longer shaped by previous forms of life, indigenous traditions, or the demands or norms of the past.

As capitalism now embarks on a race for what is left of the planet's energy resources, attempting to push further a mode of endlessly expanding prosperity that more and more obviously violates the limits to growth, and as the consequences to capitalism's endless reifications of its resources become increasingly clear, the fantasy on which it has operated dissolves, bringing into view what lay beneath it all along, a planetary environmental disaster. Those seeking to escape the past now have little choice but to face the ruins that already surround us, the destroyed planet from which there is no escape. The only exotic trip on which we can embark today will be sponsored by climate change itself, which will take us into forms of experience we have not imagined and may not wish to contemplate. We have one last voyage before us: the excursion into our own disappearance.

We who are about to vanish salute you. – Faced with the alterations in the biosphere and in the ecosystems we know, we may well take refuge in the thought that at least the stars endure, unchanged by our actions, and thus along with the sun exemplify a dimension of the nonhuman world beyond all harm. Indeed, we may well wish to join Kant in the reflection with which he concludes his second critique: "Two things fill the mind with ever new and increasing wonder and awe, the oftener and the more steadily we reflect on them: the starry heavens above and the moral law within me."[164] In their capacity to evoke a sense of the infinite, the stars may still trigger a sense of the sublime; moreover, in affiliating them with the moral law, Kant hints at dimensions of his critique of teleological reason provided in a late section of his third critique, already gesturing toward the way these two experiences evoke the possibility (though not the certainty) of a telos for the universe.[165]

No doubt the night sky will always remain a metaphor of a non-human vastness into which all human concerns disappear, in whose spaces even our questions about existence itself – and its origin and end – ultimately confront the unknowable. The sky may speak to us in these ways for as long as we are here to see it. But is it entirely unchanged by our condition?

With the advent not only of modern astronomy but also of evolutionary biology, we have become aware that forms of life not unlike ourselves may have emerged on planets scattered throughout the universe. Accordingly, many people have become curious about whether it would be possible to pick up electronic signals from our counterparts elsewhere, and in recent decades this curiosity has led to the establishment of ongoing efforts to discern such life, primarily through the Search for Extraterrestrial Intelligence (SETI). However, despite the best efforts of various groups, researchers have not yet detected any sure signal from outer space.

What might follow from the absence of such a signal? Researchers have designed a stronger, more capacious system for receiving transmissions; where once they surveyed only a small area at any given moment, now they will be able "to monitor the entire night sky."[166] It is always possible that in its redesigned mode, SETI will be able to pick up a communication. But the absence so far may indicate that any form of life advanced enough to send a message suffers from the same difficulties that afflict us: to create a society capable of that activity may require harvesting a planet's fossil fuel energy in a sustained effort and thus triggering a version of the climate change we are experiencing, thereby causing that society's disappearance. It may be, then, that those living on another planet would be able to send a signal of that kind for only a short period, greatly shrinking the temporal window for potential reception and thus decreasing the probability that anyone elsewhere would detect it. Those who can communicate in this way, in short, may rely on technologies that quickly destroy the preconditions for their own existence.

This is only one possible explanation. Nevertheless, the material context that leads to such considerations indicates that our view of the night sky has changed. The starry sky above us can now remind us of how fragile any technological civilization must be and accordingly how small is the chance that intelligent species will ever be able to communicate with each other. The silence of the night sky now tells us of the possibility that every such species may endure a cosmic solitude, *even if* there are many others like it, for merely to conceive of overleaping the narrow bounds of a planetary existence implies that one is on the verge of disappearing. Every such signal to the universe thus sends this message: "We who are about to vanish salute you."

The experience of the humanless. – In his fiercely insightful "Reflections on the H Bomb," published at the height of the nuclear arms race in 1956, Günther Anders argues that since "modern man [sic]" now possesses a negative form of omnipotence, the power to destroy creation, "we are no longer what until today men have called 'men.' Although we are unchanged anatomically, our completely changed relation to the cosmos and to ourselves has transformed us into a new species . . . . In fact, during the short period of our supremacy the gulf separating us Titans from the men of yesterday has become so wide that the latter are beginning to seem alien to us." Now that we "are the infinite," we are no longer tormented, like Faust, "by his inability to transcend his finitude"; his longing "has become so completely a thing of the past that it is difficult for us to visualize it." Indeed, what the previous generation "regarded as the most important thing is meaningless to us, their sons, the first Titans; the very concepts by which they articulated their history have become obsolete."[167]

Here Anders broaches themes that directly anticipate the concerns of this book: in the arrival of the ability to annihilate humankind, he discerned an event that radically undermined every concept that humanity had inherited. Theorists of our time have tended to capture humanity's new condition through the notion of the Anthropocene, which emphasizes humanity's Titanic power to become a geological force, to imprint itself on the earth's strata. That term implies that in becoming such a force, humanity indeed remains *anthropos*. But Anders rightly insists that with nuclear power, it ceases to be what it was and enters another state, one for which we are not ready and whose challenges we are entirely incompetent to face. Whereas those involved in the extermination at Auschwitz were still "directly involved," physically close to those they were killing, perpetrators in the nuclear era are at a great distance from those being destroyed, so that in this moment "inhuman deeds are deeds without people," taking place in ruthless anonymity.[168] Even in the act of killing, we have taken a step beyond *anthropos*, beyond the one who sees the face of the victim. Yet by the same token, because "we are the first Titans, we are also the first dwarfs or pygmies"; just as we are granted a kind of spurious, destructive omnipotence, we also live with the new truth that "[m]ankind as a whole is exterminable." "This change," he writes, "inaugurates a new historical epoch, if the term 'epoch' may be applied to the short intervals in question."[169] In effect, Anders proleptically shows that with that event, we enter something other than the Anthropocene – an epoch in which humanity goes beyond itself, loses itself in both infinity and nullity, and thus suffers from a radical *subtraction* of humanity from the species, becoming an entity without form or definition. In this sense as well, we are no longer a species but an *anti*species, not only because of our effect on the biosphere and other forms of life, but also because of the capacity to cancel our prior mode of finitude, our own form of existence.

Do we then enter not a geological but a historical era? As Anders suggests, these changes are so profound that we are cut off even from the recent past; the sense that we share finitude, imagination, or desire with previous generations is undone. The prospect of an infinitely shattering power cuts us off from a historical continuity, from any notion of a "human" history.

How might we receive such reflections today? Certainly there is a strong similarity between the prospect of nuclear annihilation and of humanity's disappearance from severe climate change; both instances awaken the thought of our radical nullity. But the possibility of nuclear war emerged from the competition between states for global power; only sovereigns were capable of imposing that fate, even if their power to do so rested on a pervasive ideology and infrastructure of what Edward Thompson called "exterminism."[170] Today, virtually every citizen in the developed world participates in the activities that may bring about humanity's disappearance; our Titanic powers for destruction are now indistinguishable from the most quotidian practices of everyday life. Moreover, the annihilation of humanity may now take place not in a flash but over the course of decades, unfolding even as life seems to go on: life and annihilation take place together in precisely the same experiences, erasing the distinction between finitude and the infinite, between an inherited notion of the human and a new condition.

The historical break, then, is not only a matter of a single event we can locate at Hiroshima; it is also a breach within the temporality of ordinary life. For us, Hiroshima takes place every day. We are simultaneously historical and outside of history; we live a breach that is perpetual, built into the very structure of the quotidian. If we remain in some sense human, we have also lost access to that experience; we are at once present and absent in that finitude. We have become humanless.

10 The time of nontime

The time of nontime. – Should theorists today deconstruct the meta-physics of presence once again? Should they extend Derrida's treat-ment of temporality's exposure to the logic of the trace, perhaps by elaborating further on Martin Hägglund's rigorous articulation of that exposure?[171] To do so would imply that time is still time, that its logic still obtains in a manner consistent with its former operations. But today the present undoes itself in a way not anticipated in deconstruc-tion: this present belongs to a time that in its ordinary course erases any human temporality and as a result constitutes a *nontime*. This nontime is the counterside to time, even to a Derridean time; it insists not in the movement of the trace or of spacing but in their vanishing, creating a movement whereby time bears within itself the dissolution of itself *as* time. This is not the time in which everything dissolves; it is rather a time that dissolves time itself and thus dissolves what we once knew as dissolution – a nontime that erodes the very logic of temporality per se. This nontime destroys not only the metaphysics of presence, but any account that would deconstruct that metaphysics; it erases time and any thought of time alike.

This undoing of time extends to space as well. As Derrida's analy-sis demonstrates, the two are necessarily interwoven, the trace and spacing arising from within the same problematic of *différance*. The cancellation of humanity's future, however, undoes even this think-ing. Thus the pile of debris cannot constitute a place where certain odds and ends are heaped up: in this nonpresent, the debris is a non-place, not even a site for thought. If one takes seriously the prospect of thought's disappearance, then one must also say that the world in which thought takes place today is simultaneously a nonworld, a domain in which thought can find no direction and no markers for orientation.

Although in some sense we now live in a unique time, in an experi-ence singularly of our time, can we indeed speak at all of "our time," if the latter registers the terminus of the historical framework in which such a phrase would have any meaning? Or is our time not our time at all, not even a time in which we now experience the undoing of time? Perhaps we who experience "our time" in fact do not experience it, for nontime is intrinsically beyond experience, beyond what can tran-spire within thought or affect, beyond what can take shape in time. Perhaps we cannot be present for the nonpresent of our time. Perhaps, as Jacques Khalip writes, extinction may be "the improper name for a kind of *counter-life* that is not reducible to the circumstances and practical knowledge of the lived present," a "contretemps" that takes shape as "what is precisely unlived" even within life.[172]

If all this is the case, then one who is aware of the prospect of the terminus steps outside the time still reified by this culture. Is it thus an instance of what Agamben calls the "contemporary," according to which it gazes on its "own time so as to perceive not its light, but rather its darkness"? Does this thought "grasp [its] time in the form of a 'too soon' that is also a 'too late'; of an 'already' that is also a 'not yet'"?[173] But the thought of extinction cannot even be untimely in this sense; it can never be behind or ahead of its time, for it apprehends a time without time, a time of the nontime. This thought cuts through the very notion of the contemporary, locating within time that feature that already brings about the vanishing of thought itself.

Those of us living in this way, experiencing what is unlived within this life, may thus share the status of Lacan's God, who is dead but doesn't know it yet. Perhaps we, too, are already dead. Aaron Schuster, in a Lacanian vein, suggests that such is indeed the case for the human subject, which endures in a mode defined by the death drive. But today this drive insists as well in a radically external form in the operations of the biosphere, instantiating in that domain not only a certain subversion of the subject but also its erasure, rendering it posthumous in still another way. In this account, we cannot be present for the nontime of our time because in some sense we are already dead; we who endure in this moment have in some sense already vanished from it.[174]

Yet despite our having vanished, we nevertheless remain; despite the absence of a space or time in which to live, we persist. What may baffle thought the most, then, is this simultaneity of time and nontime, space and nonspace, experience and nonexperience, this condition of living on within a domain that has already disappeared. This moment is the time of nontime; it is the medium in which we who have vanished nevertheless live on.

The senescence of the West. – If terminal thought exceeds previous modes of thought, does it bring with it a new intellectual wave, a new cultural trend, an aesthetic or philosophical avant-garde, or any other version of conceptualized or commodified novelty? Is it the Next Big Thing? Does it formulate the *ultimate* cutting-edge intervention, the *final* term in overthrowing old shibboleths? Does it, for example, overleap deconstruction, Lacanian psychoanalytic thought, queer theory, decolonial studies, cultural studies, postmodernism, theories of the posthuman, the ethical turn, the religious turn, the affective turn, animal studies, and trauma studies? For many theorists, terminal thought may indeed do all the above and much more. Its intervention may well strike more directly at a host of cherished assumptions, dismantling inherited premises even more starkly, radicalizing all worthy predecessors in its even more stunning provocation. The thought of the terminus may be *the* most avant-garde event of all, taking humanity well into the domain of a "post-" condition without reserve, into a condition that truly and definitively eclipses all that we have received from the past.

But this prospect collapses immediately. To think human extinction is not to participate yet again in the fashioning of novelty: such a thought does not move ahead of the pack, as does the avant-garde, nor does it propose a further conceptual innovation, another round of speculation that would revive thought through its originality. Such a stance perpetually renews the ideology of modernity, attempting to experience again a version of the revolutionary break, the cut against what came before, the intoxication of entering an unanticipated future. Accordingly, the terminus is not a "post-," not an event that, coming either chronologically or logically after prior stages of culture or of thought, might be compared to them; it does not participate in modernity's (and modernism's and postmodernism's) transgressions of what came before, nor does it contribute to a new phase of liberation, construction, or experimentation. On the contrary, it reveals the eclipse of all such breaks by a terminal practice on which they relied but which they never noticed or resisted. Indeed, it shows how the commitment to novelty relied on fraudulent premises; the very attempt perpetually to exceed any limit has been literalized in the arrival not of a break, but of a truly annihilating event.

The thought of the terminus thus has no dazzling slogan, no new command to incite adherents. Where advocates of modernism once cried out, "Make it new!" imposing the demand for a daring reconceptualization of the world, this thought brings a contrary announcement, "It has been made old," registering the impact of a brutal blow, a sudden onset of cultural dementia, an attack on the foundations of aesthetic and intellectual enterprise, indeed of everything familiar to humanity.

To be sure, thought does more than simply feel that impact: it must now labor to interpret its new condition, to examine how this blow has laid waste to its means of understanding. It must absorb the news of its senescence, come to grips with its sudden incapacity. In doing so, however, it does not renew itself but traces how it has already endured past its expiration date, how it can only articulate its own absence.

What, then, is the status of any attempt to think a terminal thought? Since it in some sense still belongs to history, still finds its place within a cultural scene whose cancellation it attempts to grasp, despite itself it too will be received as a new wave of thought. It can reply to this reception only by noting that all such waves of novelty are already condemned to participate in a futile operation, that their significance has been erased in advance. In this way, it can at least acknowledge that it contributes to an "enlightenment" that will be eclipsed in darkness, that its actions and gestures are fated only to be unread, forgotten. It knows that it can be no more than the debris of an extinct thought.

Minutes after midnight. – In May, 2014, two teams of scientists published distinct reports that the West Antarctica Ice Sheet, having melted enough that it now rests on a layer of water at its base, has begun the slow but irreversible process of sliding into the sea – and no outcropping of rock, no geological formation, is in place to halt that slide. That enormous body of ice will eventually enter the ocean and melt away, causing the sea level of the world's oceans to rise by ten feet or more.[175] If these reports are true, this process will transpire over the next century or two and will not cease until it is complete.

Such a process, however long and tedious, can never become dated; it is never in or out of fashion, nor is it ever of its time. Whatever cultural waves transpire in those decades, whatever political movements come and go, whatever new phases of critique may appear, it will simply continue to slide, indifferent and implacable.

We who live at this moment have not yet confronted the worst that climate change will bring; we still typically adhere to the habits of the past, still believe in the logic of a certain history. Yet we now live after having triggered geophysical processes over which we have no control. One might think, then, of the Doomsday Clock by which atomic scientists designate their sense of our proximity to the outbreak of nuclear war; on occasion they have declared that we live just a few minutes before midnight. Such a metaphor has often reminded us that nuclear annihilation is not inevitable but negotiable, an event we can forestall with sufficient will. It has implied that we might turn the clock *back*, that we could distance ourselves from the arrival of that midnight. The sliding of the West Antarctica ice sheet, however, teaches us on the contrary that we now live several minutes *after* midnight, *after* having set off certain slow events, even if we live before their culmination. The same temporality will apply in other domains once we move past certain climatological "tipping points," once climate change alters planetary regions and systems so much that they will begin to contribute directly to further warming on a scale that dwarfs the current human impact.[176] In effect, we occupy a parentheses in time between the end of a familiar mode of history and the terminus; we live in an era when history has been suspended but still transpires, when time goes on even as it ends.

Someday. – Even today, activists and protesters sing the civil rights anthem, "We Shall Overcome," calling on deep reserves of memory, anguish, persistence, resilience, and hope, sharing in the almost unbearable affect of longing for the arrival of justice. Whenever a group of protesters sing it, they partake in a collective that stretches back through time, in a mode of political emotion that, inheriting the prophetic and even millenarian hopes of the downtrodden, carries the weight of the sacred. In the face of the seemingly endless waves of injustice toward African-Americans in the United States, confronted with ever-renewed forms of inequality, violence, abuse, and disenfranchisement, this long movement of resistance invokes a fundamental faith in what is to come. At the culminating moments of this anthem, the temporal structure of this faith comes to the fore, soaring into lyrical heights when it reaches the word *someday.* The moment of justice is still to come, still outstanding. It is out of reach, yet the hands of faith can still grasp it, still consider it to be real.

This is the faith that arises from what the political order has always excluded. Through their moral force, the civil rights movement and its heirs reveal the constitutive injustice of the state, the unauthorized violence on which the law depends. Both speak for those whom history has defeated and thus, as Benjamin suggests, for the past generations that the revolution will redeem. In that anthem, then, one may hear the voice of messianic expectation, the demand for a justice that will overturn a system entrenched by centuries of victory; one hears the voice of both the living and the dead, one that resonates through all of human history.

Yet even Benjamin, by making it virtually impossible to conceive of any ongoing historical causes for the revolution of which he speaks, places it in the category of a truly messianic event, outside the zone of what may ever be realized. Accordingly, one might well take the implications of his stance another step and propose that we abandon the lure of this messianic expectation. Pursuing this approach, Calvin Warren, in a strikingly Afropessimistic argument, suggests that the politics of hope keeps in place a structure that perpetually denies its fulfillment, reproducing "the very metaphysical structures of violence that pulverize black being." In that case, he suggests, "the only 'ethical' response to black suffering" is a refusal to hope for any such realization, to commit the *"political apostasy"* of refusing the faith in what will occur someday.[177]

Such an apostasy falls upon us today with fierce exigency. The movement of resistance continues; the protesters still sing these words; the invocation of that day of justice remains in place. Yet under the sign of the terminus, the *someday* floats free of any possible future realization; it retreats into the domain of the impossible, relinquishing its claim on the future. One who seeks justice may well repudiate its false promise. But one would do so not to abandon the demand for justice, but to voice that demand with even greater clarity. Thus one must reframe the entire question of this faith: today one invokes the *someday* not to signal confidence in the future event but rather a refusal of the progressive modernity that has perpetually excluded that arrival – and thus to suggest that this very history, even if it ends in the terminus, has harbored despite itself a revolutionary possibility that exceeds what will actually have come to pass.[178] To invoke the *someday* would thus mark precisely the prospect of a political Real that this history has perpetually denied. But in that case, this mark hints that apostasy and faith go hand in hand as divergent names for a shared evocation of what lies beyond our historical experience.

A new solitude. – The thought of the terminus does not come to us from a lineage given to us. Nor is it a legacy one can transmit, nor a truth into which one might initiate a new generation. Those who endure this thought thus persist in a moment that is stranded within human and planetary history, cut off from compatriots in any other generation, affiliated only with each other. Accordingly, in some sense we cannot inherit the past, regarding those who came before us as our forebears, nor can we rear new generations of those who will inherit a viable tradition from us and move on into a new phase of history. We are orphans, childless, exiled, lost.

This condition thus makes this moment infinitely fragile; whatever we might declare about our time can only speak of what takes place "for now." Living within this suspended moment, neither within history nor at the terminus, we know that however we live today is only for a moment, provisional, temporary, evanescent. Whatever patterns of settlement, arrangements of power, styles of discourse, or modes of subsistence we can discern today apply only for now. All that is solid has melted into air; all that seemed permanent – even capitalism, even science – becomes temporary; even this thought of evanescence will vanish away.

Salvage anthropology. – For decades, anthropologists studied traditional societies that, thanks in part to this very contact with the West, were fated to abandon their traditional ways. Ethnographers focused on securing a knowledge of those ways practiced a salvage anthropology, recording the old ways before they dissolved. Such a practice captures how modernity often sought to inherit what it destroyed, how it indulged in what Renato Rosaldo called an "imperialist nostalgia," a longing to participate indirectly in practices that it consigned to oblivion.[179]

But today, modernity is dissolving as well; now the discourse that would capture a vanishing culture faces the prospect of vanishing itself. It would be fruitless to attempt to salvage that culture, not only because there will be none to inherit such a knowledge, but also because the very mode of knowledge is passing away. Accordingly, whatever cultural practices one sees today signify no further than their own moment, gesturing neither toward inheritors nor to an enduring knowledge, invoking only the oblivion into which they will shortly pass. Today ethnography survives, if at all, only in the practice of the disappearing encounter, the exchange of those who may be fated to disappear.

Toward a good faith immediatism. – Confronted with the thought of the terminus, one might well reply, "I don't live for the future; I take things one day at a time." But examined closely, such a person most likely has taken out a car loan, pays health insurance, has either a rental agreement or a mortgage, and expects no interruptions to his conditions of employment. Such a person might actually be raising a child as well. That declaration, then, is not uttered in good faith, for it denies what is evident to all – that each of us is, perhaps despite ourselves, immersed in an ongoing temporality that extends well into the future.

Yet a genuine immediatism is indeed possible. It would accept the undoing of all these expectations; it would endure without surprise the vanishing of residence, job, income, health, and more. It would incorporate an acute sense of vulnerability into its ordinary sense of time. Such an immediacy, however, would no longer resemble a self-affirmative sense of the present; it would on the contrary accept the evanescence of the present, its disappearance even from itself. It would live neither in the future nor the present, but in a time that has already vanished.

11 Too deep for tears

The silent bird. – Inscribed above our pathway today are the words that Dante saw above the entrance to Hell; those words tell us that we who encounter the thought of the terminus enter another version of the inferno, a state of desolation without reprieve. That region, supposedly for punishing the damned after their deaths, is now a domain for the living, and even worse, for the unborn; once we enter it, we embark on an exploration that will lead to no purgatory and no paradise. We enter a dark region from which there is no escape.

But insofar as we enter this domain because of the thought of the terminus, rather than a moral failure, one might indeed ask whether we find ourselves beyond hope. In an orthodox account, when one submits to despair, one commits the sin of refusing to hope. But such a teaching assumes that there is a ground for hope, that it is available in some way to the living. Under the sign of the terminus, there is no such ground; the future of humanity is foreclosed. Accordingly, today one can neither hope nor despair, for the entire framework for such morally freighted emotions has dissolved. If we abandon hope today, we do so not because we enter a state of despair but rather because that framework falls away, leaving us in a condition without a future.

In such a case, how might we respond to Emily Dickinson's contention that hope's song "never stops – at all"?[180] Is it possible that it endures even after it is gone – or that it can be found even in the midst of hopelessness? Paul already suggests as much when he writes that Abraham "[i]n hope believed against hope, that he should become the father of many nations" (Romans 4:18), indicating that he considers a hopeless hope to be the very core of Abrahamic faith.[181] Near the end of *Prometheus Unbound*, Shelley voices an associated view as Demogorgon speaks of a "Hope" that "creates / From its own wreck the thing it contemplates."[182] These contentions no doubt endure in Benjamin's messianism – in the bedrock expectation shared by believers and revolutionaries alike.

Yet even in the poem that seems to ratify the perpetual insistence of hope, Dickinson does not entirely endorse it. Although the poem contends that hope's song is "sweetest – in the Gale" and that "sore must be the storm – / That could abash the little Bird / That kept so many warm," her phrasing suggests that someday there may indeed come a storm that *could* abash hope, that *could* silence its song. In this minimal gesture, she anticipates what we now endure: a gale so strong that it silences that bird. But the poem still insists that hope's song "never stops." Does it follow that we can still hear the hope we have lost even in its silence? Is some revenant of hope left to us even now? On the contrary, the terminus tells us that what once seemed endless will indeed end, that the silence is indeed silence. Today we have lost the orientation even to a hopelessness that carries hope within it, even a nihilism that bears the imprint of a transcendental destination it denies; in the thought of the terminus expires hope and hopelessness alike, leaving us with something beyond the scope of such emotions, outside of the time in which even despair could thrive.

The loss of loss. – In our ordinary lives, loss reveals to us our attachments to what we lose; when we confront and accept loss, we affirm the complexity of the web of emotions that bind us to the world. Loss is thus part of the phenomenology of finitude and mortality; our various modes of hope and grief, our relationships of friendship, fidelity, attachment, and love, all speak of the solidarity of the vulnerable, the finitude that we mere mortals share. When we step beyond personal losses, a similar pattern appears: in the loss of the political transformations we seek, or in Benjaminian terms, with the loss of what has never been realized in history, we discover what binds us to what this history continues to promise, to what we share with other generations.

But the harsher losses of our time take us beyond this pattern. With the thought of the terminus, we lose the entire history of which we are a part, even though we still find ourselves living within it. In this strange era, the death of someone we love has a new resonance, for now the continuity of shared experience within which that singular death matters is also swept away. The ultimate loss of humankind, then, constitutes in part a loss of loss itself. Moreover, if we consider the import of our extinction, the staggering horrors that it will bring to pass, perhaps we might begin to grieve in a thousand ways, except that we will find ourselves grieving *into* the loss we grieve, unable to absorb that loss and move on; we may thus grieve for grief itself, experiencing an emotion without shape and without name.[183]

But will this superlative loss undo all that we feel? Or will it carry us back into the finitude we share with others, accentuating our sense of exposure, sharpening this web of mutual attachment? Confronted with the prospect of losing loss, we may return to it and seize it anew, sensing at last that it is precious, indeed irreplaceable for its capacity to reveal our finitude. We who are about to lose loss may learn at last to cherish and praise it, to find in it a sign of who are and are ceasing to be.

Too deep for tears. – In the final stanza of his "Ode: Intimations of Immortality on Recollections of Early Childhood," William Wordsworth writes of the affective state that comes to one who has lived through the loss of childhood bliss and entered a full adult awareness of human mortality. "The Clouds that gather round the setting sun / Do take a sober colouring from an eye / That hath kept watch o'er man's mortality," he writes; "To me the meanest flower that blows" – the humblest flower that blooms – "can give / Thoughts that do often lie too deep for tears."[184] While regarding a sunset as a metaphor for death is indeed a commonplace of adult life, it is telling that the poet sees the tiniest flower as a sign of shared vulnerability, one that he registers in an emotion "too deep for tears," an affect that flows beneath the threshold of grief, beneath the explicit sense of loss. This affect, it seems, attends to finitude in general, to the stunning fragility that falls on all phenomenal things.

What emotion, then, can register the prospect that such a fragility might give way to disappearance? Would that thought lie "too deep for tears"? Can one weep for an event as immense as the erasure of humankind? Can one grieve for what has not yet taken place? Can an awareness of shared fragility encompass even *this* level of exposure, *this* prospect? Might such a grief be too visible – or too deep? Or would it be so overwhelming that one could not bear to feel it at all? Would such an emotion eventually disappear into numbness or blankness – into a place too deep for the depths themselves?

Such reflections may be relevant when one ponders what seems to be the absence of grief regarding our environmental catastrophe. Nearly everyone, it seems, has perfected the art of turning away from the powerful emotion the situation demands. If one actually *does* grieve for what is to come, one might well feel utterly alone, experiencing a sorrow that nobody else seems to share. Yet the situation may be more complex than it seems. As Kari Marie Norgaard suggests in her book on climate denial, many people evade a full confrontation with the implications of climate change because they feel guilty, helpless, threatened, or overwhelmed. As she points out, speaking about such difficult matters with friends or acquaintances violates cultural norms about what one may discuss in casual conversations; it fits well within accounts of how denial is socially organized.[185] It thus foregrounds how civility can become an obstacle to facing central difficulties of our time. But that reluctance may reveal even more how a certain reluctance may arise from all too vivid an awareness of what is at stake, from an emotional charge too great to bear. Ironically, evasion and avoidance may be signs of recognition.

It may be, then, that those who feel grief intensely but assume that they are alone and those who feel it but evade it share the same emotion, even if they handle it in different ways. For both, however, this emotion is so difficult it cannot even take the form of a grief too deep for tears; it persists on a still deeper level, outside or beyond grief itself, against the very structure of our affective lives. In our time, affect itself buckles under the strain of a thought too heavy to bear. The prospect of human erasure is too much for mere emotion to sustain.

The happiness of thought. – In one of his last essays, "Resignation," Adorno responds to critics who charge that the Frankfurt School practices a form of resignation and thus of political quietism. In reply, he maintains that the demand that every form of thought immediately issue in a call to action is founded on a fear that "[u]ntrammeled thought and the posture that will not let it be bargained away . . . is right." For Adorno, people who are "locked away" should rely on thinking itself to "find an exit": "If the doors are barricaded, then thought more than ever should not stop short." Indeed, the "utopian moment in thinking is stronger the less it . . . objectifies itself into a utopia and hence sabotages its realization." Prior to its content, thinking as such "is actually the force of resistance." Thus thinking is not a form of resignation but of happiness. "Because the thinking person does not need to inflict rage upon himself, he does not wish to inflict it on others. The happiness that dawns in the eye of the thinking person is the happiness of humanity. . . . Thought is happiness, even where it defines unhappiness: by enunciating it. By this alone happiness reaches into the universal unhappiness. Whoever does not let it atrophy has not resigned."[186]

If one takes such a stance seriously today, even terminal thought is happiness. Although it defines an unhappiness without recourse, illuminating what may soon be the absence of an exit, its very capacity to define that unhappiness, to think that imprisonment, resists what it describes. Even where thought speaks of humanity's extinction, its ability to do so, despite all odds, constitutes one last way in which universal humanity may still speak. Now that thought must encounter the prospect of its *own* disappearance, shattering into debris under the sign of the terminus, its very ability to acknowledge that event remains a form of resistance, an instance that evokes what is not to be. Even a terminal thought is happiness.

Trauma of the terminus. – In the pivotal analysis in *Beyond the Pleasure Principle*, Freud argues that trauma befalls the psyche when an event exceeds what it can absorb, when a disturbance breaks through the psyche's protection against stimuli that are too strong. The psyche, finding that breach unbearable, returns to it repeatedly in order to bind that excessive excitation. Thus as Cathy Caruth suggests, what haunts the psyche is not the content of the experience itself but "the shocking and unexpected" intrusion of that event, "the impact of its very incomprehensibility." Because that event traumatized the mind by violating its ways of maintaining itself, it remains beyond what the mind can grasp, exceeding its modes of comprehension.[187]

Can one say that the thought of the terminus constitutes a trauma for thought today? That thought is not an event that imposes itself in a moment of violent bodily experience, nor is it in the past (or not wholly so), nor does it lead to a repetition compulsion of a familiar kind.[188] Yet it befalls a thought that can never prepare for it, invading the mind with something that exceeds what it can understand or know; indeed, the thought of humankind's disappearance cuts through virtually every available mode of comprehension, every practice whereby the mind previously organized its experience, shocking it with an unassimilable, impossible thought. Furthermore, a psychoanalytic approach cannot help one recuperate from the thought of the terminus, for the effort of working through the trauma by bringing it into consciousness cannot lead to recovery; the event in question is still taking place and will continue to take place until the mind itself disappears. In certain respects, then, this thought exceeds even trauma's terms for the unthinkable. An event that does not occur and yet occurs endlessly, that transpires without shattering us in any direct way even as it stuns us beyond all measure, it seems not to occur while at the same time it strikes us with a seemingly infinite force.

If trauma marks the site of unclaimed experience, as Caruth suggests, this thought speaks of a prospect even more dire, a development that will erase human experience *in toto*, and thus an eventuality that no experience could possibly claim; it defeats the very structure of experience itself. As Brassier argues, responding in part to these reflections on trauma, the thought of extinction "is a transcendental trauma: it is the conceptual transposition of a physical phenomenon which undoes the phenomenological resources through which the manifest image would *make sense* of it."[189] That thought undermines the integrity of phenomenological experience itself; as we saw above, it leads to the formation of a nontime in time, an oblivion that operates even in life itself.

Accordingly, insofar as the thought of the terminus does not take place as a corporeal event, the psyche might seem to endure without trauma, in sustaining the familiar habits that protect it from too powerful an intrusion. Yet in doing so, it also sustains itself in relation to

an ongoing horror, palpable beneath ordinary experience, which nothing can help it assimilate. We live in an affective condition at odds
with itself: we are at once protected and vulnerable, secure and devastated; we have already vanished, yet we live on.

12 The vanishing event

Too ordinary to grasp. – The changes to earth's biosphere and its eco-systems, as well as to the status of the world's living species, happen so slowly, in such incremental steps, over such a long period of time, that they never quite constitute an event. Taking place below the threshold of consciousness, causing aspects of noticeable moments without becoming directly evident in their own right, these instances of what Rob Nixon calls "slow violence" slide past nearly every attempt to narrate them, represent them, or make them visible.[190] Like the subconcussions that football players often experience – hard contact that does not cause injuries harsh enough to be recognized as all-out concussions – which over time can do great damage to the brain, these incremental changes seem trivial in themselves until, long afterwards, they are found to have altered everything severely and irreversibly. Even where they do contribute to what seems to be an event, such as a harsher hurricane, one can ignore that crucial background and depict only the extraordinarily violent storm itself, reading it as a freak event, as an exceptional visitation.

This pattern of response confirms the deep bias of the news for reporting *events* – things that *happened*, things that stand out from the background, specific occasions that one can point to, describe, "cover," and photograph. A phenomenon would scarcely be *news* if it constitutes the background itself. At times, then, environmental disasters *do* make the news: the befouling of vast beaches with waste, the record-breaking heat of a summer, the unprecedented loss of polar sea ice – but such coverage cannot quite capture the underlying causes. At other times, the news reports the release of a scientific report about climate change, but then that coverage must emphasize a specific articulation of the problem rather than the problem itself, shifting focus to the question of research, governance, or political reception. As a result, the news seldom covers the primary development of our times, which by its very definition never rises from that background to become something in the foreground.

As a result, one might well wonder why one should think about it, feel something about it, discuss it, or respond to it in any way. Perhaps one knows that it is supremely important, that it cries out for action, that it is an overriding issue of our time, but still . . . there is no video footage of its assault, no image of its injustice, nothing to incite one into a visceral, passionate protest against it and its causes.

But this limitation is not unique to our times, nor is it unique to the news. While Nixon is right to insist that we forge new forms of articulation today – forms that can convey the full dimensions of the problem into the public mind – the inability to speak or comprehend that violence may be intrinsic to the genres and discourses we inherit. It is built into our pictorial genres, which by ancient convention emphasize what emerges into greater visibility in the foreground. It is fundamental as well in our literary genres, which feature how the pressures endemic to shared experience can build toward a culminating conflict, lyrical statement, or narrative resolution. The fact that all these modes share this feature suggests that they derive from an even more basic genre of comprehension, a template of understanding itself.

If all this is so, the terminus in some ways slides by when thought tries to seize it. It, too, is impossible to capture in a single image or represent in a specific death; it eludes any but a counterfactual narrative. It remains too big to grasp, too vague a prospect, too abstract for specific response. Yet it is the overriding development of our time, indeed the most pressing exigency in human history. At once urgent and somehow absent, blank and yet ubiquitous, it demands what is at once impossible and necessary, a thought daring enough to take on what it cannot grasp.

A thought out of place. – Scientists who research aspects of climate science or its effects necessarily accept the conventions of disciplinary knowledge, removing virtually every discernible trace of affect from their writing, any pronouncements about its implications, to focus as much as possible on the research, its methods, its details, and its findings. Although in doing so they remain faithful to one of the few genres available in which one can articulate a knowledge of the incremental, in doing so they set aside any attempt to translate it into the terms of the event. Nevertheless, as they exclude any affective or political reaction to what they chart in order to protect the integrity of the research process itself, they indirectly bring about a severe disassociation between reality and emotion, segregating knowledge and response. While they have been bold enough to trace aspects of climate change, one must nevertheless pause and ask, *for whom* have they done so?

When others speak out about the implications of climate change for our societies, they typically do so within the genres of public policy, economic incentives, or the need for creating or implementing new technologies, relying on the genres of specific disciplines or the rationality of governance, and thus they too evade a fuller response to what they discuss.

But it is not clear that a full-throated voicing of a response would be any better. Should one react as Cassandra does to the future horrors she sees? Should one cry out in absolute pain at the prospect of coming disaster? Her tribulation influences no one; her terrified words reach no hearts, perhaps because no one else has seen what she sees and her knowledge is not theirs. Today, however, one who cries out voices what everyone knows. The scream is redundant; it reaches no one because everyone has already heard it, even if only in a manner they have dismissed or shunted aside. The wild affect falls on ears that, having absorbed enough, have become deaf to further entreaty. The message, it seems, is not *for them.*

Given these conditions, one might well ask, When might an actual response to what we learn take place? When does the knowledge hit home? Or does it forever elude us, disappearing into what is too authoritative, too governmental, too emotional, or too familiar for it to have any effect? Is it fated always to slide by, ungrasped and unknown, like a ghost from the future? Will we ever allow ourselves to be those for whom the message is written, for whom the voice speaks? Perhaps it can never reach us on the levels that remain within social conventions, that accept the partitions of discourse: perhaps it arrives only in a moment of deferred recognition, of Freudian *Nachträglichkeit* or "afterwardsness," when, like the Wolf Man, we unconsciously grasp the significance of what we once saw years ago, of what must have registered on a level of which we were previously unaware.[191] Perhaps it comes to us in a moment of anamorphosis, so that, like those who, turning away from Hans Holbein's *Ambassadors*, can finally see from an odd angle the skull in its foreground, we too, as we step outside normative modes of understanding, can see the outline of our fate.[192] Perhaps this knowledge hits us when we are not our ordinary selves, when in some unpredictable way we move outside the protective mesh of the symbolic and collide with the ghost of the future, that emissary of the Real.

The vanishing event. – Once upon a time, not so long ago, Alain Badiou could speak of *fidelity to the event,* to a singular occasion in politics, love, science, or art through which the subject emerges and through a fidelity to which a subject could gain the potential of a relation to truth. Such an event might be falling in love or experiencing a revolution; in any case, it always takes place on a specific occasion in a way that can seize a person and transform her into a subject.[193]

Today, however, the terminus undoes this scenario; its import greatly exceeds that of any singular occasion, for it erases the preconditions of any such arrival, evacuating in advance the staying power of any given transformation. Yet this cancellation may not entirely efface the logic of the event; one might, for example, sustain a relation to a revolution that will not take place, to an occasion that, even in its absence, may still define one's response to all other aspects of experience. In effect, one might retain a fidelity to the imprint of what will not arrive, the site of a hope that has been undone, partaking of an evental ethics even where that event has not and will not take place.

Such a stance, however, need not maintain itself in the pose of a disappointed expectation, a thwarted hope. On the contrary, it can open up a renewed relation to ordinary time. This prospect is reminiscent of a possibility Blanchot explores in *The Writing of the Disaster*. "Jewish messianic thought," he writes, "suggests the relation between the event and its nonoccurrence." In one account, the Messiah is already present, "at the gates of Rome among the beggars and lepers," in which case "[h]is being there is, then, not the coming." Even further, "it is not even sure that he is a person – that he is someone in particular," for "[a]nyone might be the Messiah – must be he, is not he." All this is so in part because "the coming of the Messiah does not yet signify the end of history, the suppression of time. It announces a time more future."[194] If the future is not literally in the future but in the futural dimension of the present, if justice is not to arrive in a final event but in acts that can take place at any moment, then the event to which one remains faithful is not a singular occasion but its imprint within ordinary time. Such a revision of Badiou might well lead to its own ethics: where we seek to realize the impossible, it takes place; where we hope to enact justice, it appears. Perhaps the event will not arrive *except through* these ordinary acts; the messiah will appear *only* where an ordinary person acts with justice.

But under the sign of the terminus, such an ethics takes on remarkable overtones: in effect, one sustains fidelity to the event even though it has become impossible; one realizes justice in the present without linking it to any consequence or to any promise. This ethics exceeds what we might find in Derrida's reflections on the messianic or on an impossible justice, for through such an act, one realizes a form of redemption that is useless and utterly unredemptive. It is not that in doing the impossible, one overleaps its impossibility and makes it possible; on the contrary, even when one realizes it and makes it palpable, one reveals that it remains impossible, out of reach from within a history defined by the terminus. The messiah appears in his disappearance; the event takes place just as it vanishes.

13 Ethical destitution

The happiness of the damned. – Kant's demand that one comply with the moral law without any pathological motive ironically suggests that *not* complying with it might be satisfying.[195] Moreover, since Bernard de Mandeville, who wrote of how "private vices" lead to "publick [sic] benefits," or Adam Smith, who argued that "it is not from the benevolence of the butcher, the brewer, the baker that we expect our dinner, but from their regard to their own self-interest," the commonplace position has emerged that those who *do* follow their pathological interests may serve the public best. (That reading of Smith, of course, greatly distorts his overall stance, as many scholars have pointed out, yet the received wisdom about the import of his work endures.)[196] Such positions have the merit of refusing the extremity of Kant's argument, which excluded even the feeling of pleasure one might derive from enacting the dictates of the moral law. Nevertheless, by interpreting self-interested actions positively, by elevating pathological motives into a means to the good, these familiar arguments risk taking up the contrary position that pursuing them is superior to enacting justice, that such motives are a better guide. Faced with such a stance, one who still insists on pursuing justice might wonder why this insistence on one's own interest could lead to such prosperity. Such a thought echoes the harsher question that appears in the Hebrew Scriptures: "Why does the way of the wicked prosper?" (Jeremiah 12:1). But such a question already admits that they *do* prosper, that pursuing one's pleasure may well lead to abundance, even happiness. A cursory survey of world history tells one as much: those who indulge in unfettered exploitation of others, in the consumption of goods and services of every kind, reproducing themselves and their cultures without much concern for others or for the future, have typically enjoyed their actions greatly, thriving in the midst of what in retrospect seems to be utterly destructive behavior.

Yet even one who seems immensely comfortable in pursuing one's own pleasure is necessarily, structurally aware of the limits of such pleasure. A life of denial comes at great psychic cost: pleasure of one kind covers up the possibility of a much greater joy. On some level, one who perpetually defers the prospect of such joy cannot help but wish for its arrival, for the coming not necessarily of universal compliance with the moral law, austere as such an event would be, but of a jubilant realization of social justice for all. A version of this insight may be found in Herbert Marcuse, who in writing of the "repressive desublimation" in postwar America suggested that there might be a nonrepressive alternative.[197] Such an argument might well serve as a template for a broader claim that the West lives in a state of repressive abundance, a disastrous happiness – as indeed the thought of the terminus now makes clear. For the happiness of the damned does not erase the reality of damnation, nor does the pleasure of abundance undo the horror that it knowingly denies.

Emma, c'est moi. – Today spectacular environmental crisis – in such instances as oil slicks, the burning of the Amazon rainforest, the bleaching of coral reefs, or massive fires or floods – is so familiar that many people cannot remember a time before it and accordingly cannot imagine a world without it. Even those who lived before the acute phase of this crisis may be unable to reconstruct what that previous era felt like. Nearly everyone now lives with the habit of crisis; it is as ordinary as breathing. Indeed, coverage of this crisis is so familiar it is expected; the public would miss it if it fell silent. It is an essential part of the background noise of this culture, as intrinsic to it as any other feature.

This familiar spectacle finds its echo in our disaster movies, which now take shape across a wide variety of subgenres that will presumably continue to multiply. The scenarios of global devastation are so ubiquitous that actual events merely echo them; on virtually any occasion when a natural disaster strikes with sufficient force, people are heard to comment that it reminds them of a scifi or apocalyptic movie. Such comments reveal that these scenarios are more fundamental to our perception of reality than their realization, that the expectation of universal catastrophe is built into our everyday lives. The world of terminal capitalism knows that it has already outlived its own erasure – and takes pleasure in those entertaining spectacles that aestheticize that awareness.

What makes these familiar horrors endurable? In much the same way that one identifies with one's culture, no matter how deplorable its history, so also today people love the history that includes this endless crisis, however terrifying. This madness is *our* madness; we envy no one else's horror. Indeed, most of those aware of the full contours of climate change who have sufficient incomes still buy large homes, bear several children, take several airplane trips each year, spend their money freely, and enjoy the pleasures of a certain liberty – of a right to destroy – without suffering much more than a twinge of conscience.[198] While they ostensibly deplore this vast crisis, perhaps even imagining for a moment that they might be able to change their behavior and live in symbiosis with other forms of life, in practice they dismiss such moods and return to these deeply familiar pleasures; this passing twinge may thus only inspire them to take a redoubled enjoyment in this turn to those pleasures, this drift from conscience to a share in the madness.[199]

By now it is clear that this disaster is so deeply entrenched in the world we know that it has become ourselves; to bring it to an end would require that we become other than we are. Changing to that degree appalls us; the very prospect strikes us as beyond endurance, well beyond what we might desire. We do not fear the apocalypse; we expect it. To remind our compatriots that our lives will lead to that dire event has no effect, since that fact is not only well known to all but also a part of their very structure of enjoyment. It is thus a vain endeavor to "educate" our fellow citizens out of the lives they lead; such an enterprise only reveals our capacity to talk down to peers who are on some level identified with the catastrophe in which they participate.

Yet few are willing to admit as much, to accept that this disaster is us. In this respect we lack courage. Gustave Flaubert is said to have remarked about Emma Bovary, the protagonist of *Madame Bovary*, "Emma, c'est moi" – Emma is me – thereby suggesting that even as he exposed her great boredom with the world, her insatiable longing to realize the artificial scenarios she encountered in romantic tales, and her love of surfaces and cliches, he recognized that he was not in any essential respect unlike her, that the shallowness he loathed defined him as well. If he did indeed take this step, he dared to affirm that pathology was a fundamental fact of the human condition. Yet it is not the final or determining fact, the only truth; much as this declaration did not cancel Flaubert's ruthless anatomization of Emma's fatal desire, so also our admission does not erase the possibility that we might relinquish our pleasure in this madness, our love for the disaster of our time.

Ignorance of the law. – A well-known principle holds that the ignorance of the law is no excuse; one is bound by the law even if one is unaware of its commands. A similar principle applies, though in another mode, with severe climate change: ignorance of the consequences of one's everyday actions is no excuse for performing them. In both cases, we are bound by what we do not know or do not wish to face; we are guilty of violating limits even if we pretend not to know about them. This is a harsh principle; it holds one responsible even if one claims not to have intended to commit any transgression. But that imposition is consistent with the knowledge that binds us even if it remains mostly unconscious – the knowledge that one cannot breach a limit without consequence. To disclaim this knowledge is merely to deny it, for it holds to the obviously false notion that the nonhuman world is merely a set of resources for human use; it does nothing but inflate the breach into an even more imperious violation.

To recognize the force of the world's reply to human action, then, is to acknowledge a fundamental principle. But taking this step is not enough; that recognition requires that one no longer breach those limits, no longer provoke that reply. The merely physical realities of a changing biosphere can carry ethical weight. Even the thought of the terminus might have a similar edge, serving as an even more devastating reminder. Yet in its annihilating force, it says something more: it reveals that our ignorance has been far deeper than we thought, that a certain breach has taken place for much longer and more systematically than we suspected. Only now, perhaps, are we in a position to learn how profoundly ignorant we have been, how greatly we transgressed that fundamental principle, how many generations ago we departed from what our ecosystems could bear.

Bearing witness. – Those subjected to Nazi policy during the Shoah at times decided to survive so that they might bear witness to the atrocities – to share their personal testimony to what took place, help establish it as a historical fact, make the ultimate import of fascism known to the world, and call humanity's conscience to account. For them, survival was an ethical task. The challenge was not only to remain alive despite all odds but also to remember as much as possible, and in detail, so that some direct knowledge of those events could be given to the world.[200]

Today, however, under the sign of the terminus, that kind of ethical project is no longer possible. Since the horrors befall all of humankind, rather than a specific group of victims, one would no longer bear witness to events in order to share them later with the world; moreover, because of the terminus, one no longer has a future audience for one's testimony. We now live in a world where the memory of this horror will serve no purpose, where the effort to make sure it will never happen again has been cancelled in advance.

But might one bear witness today nevertheless? Might such testimony still have value? Perhaps one might register the import of events today to remain faithful to an ethics of truth – and thus act out of solidarity with any others, all others, who wish to attend to contemporary events with as full a knowledge of their import as possible. In that case, the task would not be to hand our account down to others in the future but to live without blinders, without denial, confronting the significance of the present with as much honesty and courage as we can muster. The task, then, would be to commit ourselves to seeing what is taking place, to pierce through the manifold layers of ideology and obfuscation and seize on what we would otherwise miss – and to tell the truth to ourselves about it. It would have as its purpose no future good but rather a demand actually to live in *this* present, even if, and especially if, this present is sharply divided from itself – and to do so alongside, and in collaboration with, everyone else who seeks to live in the same way.

If such a purpose seems insufficient because it is deprived of a future good, perhaps one should consider the argument Albert Camus provides in the conclusion to *The Myth of Sisyphus*. At the beginning of that book, he ponders "the exact degree to which suicide is a solution to the absurd."[201] How best should one respond to the fact that existence has no meaning? In the final chapter, Camus considers the moment when Sisyphus, having reached the heights, watches the rock fall back down to the plain: "At each of those moments when he leaves the heights and gradually sinks toward the lairs of the gods, he is superior to his fate. He is stronger than his rock." His condition is tragic, writes Camus, because he is "conscious" of his fate, but this very fact allows him to triumph: "Sisyphus, proletarian of the gods, powerless and rebellious, knows the whole extent of his wretched condition: it is what he thinks of during his descent. The lucidity that was to constitute his torture at the same time crowns his victory." As he gazes over his task, Sisyphus "knows himself to be the master of his days." Ultimately, for Camus, "The struggle itself toward the heights is enough to fill a man's heart. One must imagine Sisyphus happy."[202]

The question Camus asks regarding suicide is quite relevant today, for it is not immediately clear how one can go on living with an awareness of the approaching terminus. The solution Camus provides in his conclusion does not apply directly to our condition, for he did not face the question of humanity's disappearance; indeed, the absurd that he confronted is rather mild compared to the far harsher nullities of our time. Nevertheless, his argument can provide a template for what we might pursue. We might cultivate as great a lucidity as possible regarding our condition; we might find value in tarrying with this terminal version of the negative, in abiding alongside the horror of our time. In doing so, we would not need to pretend that we can bear up under its weight, since it is too heavy for the emotions we know, nor that ludicity itself has a redemptive power, for on the contrary it reveals all the more our unredeemed condition. Instead, we would claim only a *weak* mastery – a capacity to sustain a conscious engagement with our condition and by that means take the full

measure of this moment with courage: we would choose against suicide and affirm the ethical project of bearing witness to our fate.

Where It is. – Once upon a time, Freud summed up the aim of analysis
in this way: "Where It was, there I shall be."[203] For Lacan, this statement refers to the fundamental project of psychoanalysis: its attempt
to displace the privilege of consciousness in its confrontation with
the unconscious, to challenge the I's illusions with the It and its base
drives. In effect, then, it challenges one's intentional self to say, with
Flaubert, "Emma, c'est moi."[204]

But today, what would an encounter with the unconscious look
like? Can one acknowledge that the coming terminus reveals one's
unconscious, that this annihilation brings about the full realization
of the drive? Can one say today of *this* version of the It, "Yes, It is I"?
Can the subject of our moment dare to perform an absolutely devastating Act that completes an ethics in the Real?[205] To complete this
ethical project today would require that one enact perhaps the severest
possible version of Lacanian subjective destitution, the Act whereby
one disidentifies with the prestige and integrity of the subject, and
assume responsibility for participating in a mode of the drive that in
its broadest dimensions brings about the disappearance of humankind.

One might be tempted to shrink back from such a prospect and
seek an alternative. Perhaps (one might claim) it is simply impossible to assume that complicity. If so, then the ethical task would be to
assume that very impossibility as one's most defining feature, thereby
acknowledging that the ethical task remains precisely in the form of
its default, in the radical incompletion of that project.

But such an option would condemn the subject to an exile from
the drive; it would abandon the very purpose of analysis. One must
thus turn away from any such alternative and insist that the original
demand holds true, even today – that the I shall be *even where this
version of the It is.* Only in this way can today's subject sustain an
ethical integrity in the face of extinction; only in this way might one
inhabit this vanished world.

No future. – In his stunningly effective critique of heterosexual reproductive culture and its fetishization of the child, Lee Edelman points
out that the queer erotics of the death drive, infesting every subject,
is unacceptable to that culture, which projects it instead onto queer
people, seeing them as a lethal danger to reproductive ideology. In
response, he proposes that queer people identify with that drive and
become figures of the Real, thereby defying that ideology through
and through; in effect, he maps out a version of an ethics of the Real,
an affirmation of the drive so fierce that it cuts through reproductive

ideology. In perhaps his most acute move, when he faces the charge that this stance would cancel reproduction and thus the future of the species, he affirms that prospect, boldly accepting the "no future" that emerges from his stance.[206]

How does this argument fare today under the sign of the terminus? In our time, when the future is on the verge of disappearing in any case, it is no longer defiant to turn against it. Now it is clear that the drive operates in the endless growth of "the economy," the increasing colonization of daily life by the commodity form, and ultimately in severe alterations to the biosphere. The drive has been intrinsic to it all along. Yet it remains true that normative culture has used child-hood and reproductive futurism as a ruse, pulling "the family" over its head to hide this drive from view.[207] It has relied as well on moral arguments for prosperity, growth, and general abundance, justifying the abrogation of any limits on the drive through these apparently cogent rationales despite the obvious consequences of the endless expansion of capitalism for the fate of humankind.

Without question, those who acknowledge their complicity in the erotics of the death drive pierce contemporary ideology, refusing it those false consolations; on this level the template established by Edelman's argument applies. Yet to make such an acknowledgment today does not only mark one out as affirming the resolutely nonnormative nature of desire and the drive or the intrinsically perverse It of the unconscious, for it also acknowledges that one is inhabited by a drive whose unfettered movement is in the process of cancelling a future for humankind. The ethical aspects of this contrast are clear: capitalism never openly affirmed its repudiation of the future, nor has it acknowledged the operation of the drive itself. It has always attempted to disclaim its queer desire. Yet its actual practice reveals that it has been queer all along, a devout practitioner of a purposeless erotics, indeed a jubilant participant in the annihilating *jouissance* of our time. It is thus high time that it cast off its alibis and acknowledge its true shape at last.

Symptoms of crisis. – Although very few historical agents have measured up to the ethical challenges of this moment, acknowledging their participation in practices that may well lead to the disappearance of humanity, many of them nevertheless feel an acute sense of crisis, to which they respond not with an honest engagement but in a mode of belligerent defense, calling on the most retrograde forms of agency available to them in the hope of repudiating that crisis with an equally forceful reply. The longstanding denial of climate change by reactionary political agents in the United States and some other nations; the

drift toward authoritarian politics in many kinds of regimes, including modern democratic nations; the willingness in some states to tolerate the absolute destruction and immiseration of their own populations as they cling to state sovereignty (as in Syria); and the attempt
by stateless organizations to impose their will through international
terrorism, all respond to our current condition with a ferocity that
echoes the radicalism of the Act while doing so for stunningly obtuse
purposes, as if political entities, faced with severe threats, can only
reply through a kind of political atavism, a return to a style of politics that has long since been utterly discredited. Such a response hints
that for some agents, the only conceivable reply to the prospect of the
terminus is to cultivate a politics grounded in a brutal imposition of
a transcendental rationale for the state or for stateless action, as if the
invocation of supreme authority is sufficient to contain the threat.

It is not enough to lament this pattern, to discern within it the
potential demise of what is most valuable in modern regimes. One
must also read it as a symptom – that is, in Lacanian terms, an attempt
to stitch together a social fantasy whereby one can disguise the "lack
in the Other," the incoherence or inconsistency in social reality, or in
the current context, the gap between what modern politics promises
and the disappearance of its preconditions.[208] That symptom – the reliance on an atavistic understanding of political power – reveals that
politics today is undergoing a crisis of its own, confronting the arrival
of its collapse with an attempt to hold together against its increasingly
visible lack of legitimacy. Ironically, however, the emergence of that
symptom only makes all the more evident what it is meant to disguise.
These forms of violence remind us precisely of what they are not, a
politics that would actually confront its new conditions and carry out
a collective version of the Act. Today, the prospect of political transformation may speak loudest in those efforts that most boldly attempt
to destroy it.

The unapproachable law. Under the sign of the terminus, even ethical
thought decays. A number of ethical theories cannot measure up to
the prospect of a world defined by the disappearance of humankind.
At first glance, they do well in making a case for concerted action as
long as there is some chance of avoiding humanity's disappearance.
Utilitarian thought, for example, shaped by the consequentialism
of attempting to bring about the greatest happiness for the greatest
number, as Jeremy Bentham's phrase has it, would argue for doing
whatever it takes to preserve the conditions of happiness for people
all around the world – and for enhancing that happiness as well. In
his ethical theory, Kant proposes a categorical imperative according

to which one should be able to elevate any action one takes into a universal principle – and accordingly insists on the ethical necessity of acting on behalf of all.[209] Virtue theorists such as Alasdair MacIntyre argue, among other things, that the cultivation of virtue takes place within a narrative of one's life as well as of one's position in the long tradition of ethical reflection and practice; accordingly, one might well conclude that today one must act virtuously to safeguard the future of those narratives for oneself and for all, since only by salvaging a future for humankind can one preserve the context necessary for living a virtuous life.[210] In all three cases, one might be able to deduce a second level of the argument, to claim that it is necessary to protect a future for humankind so that the preconditions for ethical action remain in place.

With the prospect of the terminus, however, such theories falter. A consequentialist ethics does not fare well if the preconditions for such consequences wither away. Because the categorical imperative requires one to ponder whether transforming an act into a universal maxim might undermine the maxim itself, it too suffers if the endurance of that universe of others is cast into doubt. For its part, a virtue ethics does not survive well if the narrative context for the virtuous life collapses; without at least an imagined version of the overall narrative arc, one lacks the context for present action. The disappearance of the future leaves all these theories in ruins.

One can overcome this impasse only by finding an ethical principle free of an immanent justification, relieved of any reference to a future or universal good. One recent theory proposes such a principle. In his book on Heidegger, Nazism, and Judaism, Jean-François Lyotard argues that the West has always hated a certain unassimilable thought, a mode that cannot be absorbed or expelled – a thought that Nazism attempted to exterminate. In this thought, God is the name for "an unapproachable law that does not signify itself in nature in figures, but is recounted in a book."[211] Referring to something other than "what the Greco-Christian Occident calls God," in a mode that Levinas describes as "otherwise than Being," thought about this God does not take place in a philosophical discourse but rather in "stories of unpayable debt."[212] It imposes itself as an unassimilable demand that cuts across every myth, every version of the sacred; those who hear it become its hostage, are "[e]xpelled, doomed to exodus."[213] This nameless, unrepresentable law imposes itself without justification, without philosophical grounding, without expository argument.[214] Without calling upon the explanatory resources of immanence, this pure imposition, this absolute exigency, brings no comfort or consolation; on the contrary, it befalls its recipients like a curse, cutting through every possible justification for its demands. For that reason, it avoids the limitations of the theories I sketched above, demanding justice on every occasion no matter what the cost.

This theory of a pure demand is so severe it may not deserve the name of an ethics. In the form that Lyotard gives it, it falls into the precincts neither of religion, philosophy, nor psychoanalysis. It cuts through every such discipline with a rigor of its own. In effect, it exceeds the procedures of thought itself. Moreover, Lyotard emphasizes that the imposition of this law condemns its recipients to exodus; no human community could possibly comply with its demands. That law can become part of no collective, a feature of no polity, an aspect of no regime of positive law. Yet for that very reason, it can impose itself to the bitter end, even after the terminus of ethical theory itself. This notion of an empty, arbitrary, imperious demand applies well to our situation today: because it does not invoke any future good, because it abandons us to history without recourse and without consolation, it commands us to do justice on every occasion, no matter how near the terminus may come. Only this law endures for us today, for only such a law – in its absolute indifference to human flourishing – can withstand the prospect of humanity's utter disappearance, the possibility of thought's own extinction.

Ethical destitution. – Those who carry through on the ethics of psychoanalysis today, who dare to say of the terminus, "Even this It is I," responding to the horror of our time with a stunning form of subjective destitution, do so not only in relation to the drive itself but also to its consequences, in this way accepting that most imperious demand to accept responsibility beyond all rationale and all consequence. In doing so under the sign of the terminus, however, they push past the scenarios outlined in Lacan, Edelman, and Lyotard to assume a more radical stance, working through these versions of the Real to take up the oblivion that lies beyond them.

How, then, can one conceive of an ethics of – and in – oblivion? Can one even outline such a project? Would it borrow on the ethics on view in Levinas or Derrida, enacting a stunningly asymmetric ethics in response to the face of the other or an impossible hospitality that gives without the prospect of return?[215] Such scenarios, however extreme, still invoke the context of gestures toward other human beings; they take for granted the endurance of humankind. But our moment reveals the necessity of responding to humanity's disappearance, to the erasure of the preconditions even for an impossible hospitality. Because Levinas and Derrida both cut through a commonsensical notion of ethical action by revealing its secret complicity with ordinary egotism, attempting to isolate a feature of ethics that refuses self-congratulatory cultural norms, they are oriented to a hyperbolic ethical gesture that becomes its own end. As a result, neither of them considers the implications of an erasure of the preconditions for the scenarios they outline; for them extremity never gives way before even sharper imperatives.

An ethics that takes the measure of the terminus would no longer locate itself within the context of asymmetry or of the impossible. It would cultivate instead the stance of enacting what it could only fail to perform, to remain generous even when it has nothing to give, of loving what it cannot save. It would sustain an ethics even as it admits that it can conceive of no future good that it could serve. It would, in short, perform an ethics after ethics, cultivating a mode of relation after all the promises of relation have fallen away. Accepting that very failure, it would undergo nothing less than the most severe destitution, a catastrophic loss of ethics in the midst of ethics itself.[216]

Who speaks? To whom? – Anyone who sets out to write about the implications of the terminus must ponder these questions: Who can speak a terminal thought? Who can hear it?

One who shares this thought cannot speak within any known category of address: that person does not share a mode of knowledge, a type of wisdom, an instance of command, a genre of narrative or lyric, a confession, a complaint, a prayer, a style of reading, a mode of political advocacy, or an orientation to the good. But its failure in this regard is not due to an oversight or imposture on its part. It does not suffer, for example, from the performative contradiction into which others have fallen. The cynic Diogenes, who contended that human beings are animals and performed his teaching in public (by masturbating in the marketplace, for example), fell into such a contradiction, for he attempted to demonstrate that he was an animal for other people, thereby reaffirming the primacy of human exchange and debate. More recently, Lee Edelman, in affirming a queer renunciation of the future, did so in a medium of address that takes for granted an arena of theoretical dispute which survives over time, well beyond the moment of speech, in effect renouncing the future in a medium of publication, debate, critical response, and theoretical legacy that relies on the perpetual arrival of a future. Ironically, since cynicism and queer critique both argue for a specific thesis, implicitly attempting to persuade others to adopt it, they retain a certain orientation to the public and the future; despite their overt claims, these discourses sustain an optimism of address. Unlike these stances, however, terminal thought speaks of the disappearance of humanity – and thus the forum – as an event that will occur apart from any advocacy on its part, an event that will soon cancel the very conditions within which it will retain any value. Rather than falling into a mode of speech that performatively contradicts itself, speech about the terminus elucidates the contradiction in our time between speech and its own condition, between any intentional project and the dissolution of humanity itself.

Caught within that contradiction, terminal thought cannot take the form of a traditional discourse that promises enlightenment or bestows pleasure. It conveys an alien thought that is unwelcome in any human context. It is utterly indifferent to occasions for philosophical display, the rivalries of articulation, the incitements of literary style, or the contests of critical fashion. On some level it is structurally anonymous, not bound by reference to any particular enunciation, any specific author, or any idiosyncratic mode of critique. Indeed, the terminus defeats in advance any attempt to capture or appropriate it, external as it is to any discourse; all the attempts to articulate it are useless in the face of the actual event.

This mode of speech is thus remarkably unusual, difficult to fit within established conceptions of address. In his essay "What is an Author?," Foucault refers to a category of enunciation, the "initiators of discursive practices," which includes those who, like Marx or Freud, "not only made possible a certain number of analogies that could be adopted by future texts" but also "cleared a space for the introduction of elements other than their own, which, nevertheless, remain within the field of discourse they initiated." They thus remain "heterogeneous" to the "ulterior transformations" of those discourses.[217] One who speaks a terminal thought, however, does the opposite: such a one attempts to grasp how this arriving event *unfounds* discursive practices, how the terminus itself has *already* cleared a space that anyone can explore. In suggesting that we all now inhabit a field of debris, it claims no supremacy over that domain but indicates instead that there can be no such supremacy, that every attempt to outline its significance must fall prey to the terminus as well. Even on this level, then, it remains anonymous, workless, articulating what logically precedes and erases it.

If all this is the case, then how can one enunciate this thought at all? For one to speak a terminal thought, *some* form of articulation on *some* occasion is necessary. Thus someone – anyone – must become the site for this unintended, anonymous thought to speak. Under the pressure of the terminus, authorship itself devolves into nothing more than such a site, the denuded space from which an alien discourse can be spoken.

But who, then, can hear this speech? It is difficult to see how a terminal thought can address the public, for it is not clear that there can be a public without a purpose that its deliberations may serve, and more starkly, without a future in which its discussions might even take place. If one posits that the public survives as a Kantian Idea, an ethical rather than empirical possibility, even that ideal is now in eclipse, overwhelmed by the disappearance of its preconditions. One who listens to such a thought, then, does so not as a member of the public as formerly conceived but rather of its erasure, experiencing the plight of a receptivity without purpose.

By the same token, any book exploring a terminal thought scarcely belongs within a continuing world. Insofar as it participates in the ordinary exchange of ideas, reinforcing the world they help create, in that way obeying the tacit contract every book establishes with its reader, then it betrays itself, undoing its task of considering the terminus. But if it attends to that dire event, it cancels that contract, refusing the norms of address and reception. In doing so, it violates the expectations not only of the one who hears but of the one who speaks as well – for the speaker is always a discourse's first audience, the one whose pulse first takes its measure. Such a book thus interrupts any familiar form of intention and reception; it is unbearable for author and reader alike, even if it somehow is still written and read.

Yet if such a mode of address is still possible, since despite all odds it can be spoken and heard, then it follows that such an articulation is still possible beyond all such expectations. Insofar as such a listening may still take place, one discovers that the collective may persist even after the erasure of the public, in a new, workless, denuded condition. Those sharing this condition may no longer be recognizable: they may not know who speaks or listens, yet their useless receptivity endures, even amidst the ruins.

Truth in the Real. – A terminal thought does not occupy a place within the symbolic order, or the order of language, nor a site within the framework of institutional authority or political mastery that so evidently relies on that order. Nor does it inhabit an imaginary relation to another, formed by an attempt to imitate or mimic the ideal ego, to resemble an image of a stylish or successful mode of thought. Accordingly, if we deploy the three realms outlined by Lacan, this is a speech that transpires in the Real, one that places author and reader alike in that impossible site – and that speaks of a truth that can have no linguistic or imaginary confirmation.

The extraordinary position of this truth is evident from the structural impasses of indexing the moment of humanity's disappearance. As Brassier argues, "Extinction is real yet not empirical, since it is not of the order of experience."[218] Because no person will ever know for sure when the last human being dies, and since even in that moment the declaration of that knowledge could have no audience, the moment of disappearance cannot take place in the symbolic or imaginary, but only in the Real. Even an anticipation of that moment is unassimilable in the rituals of speech, which still tacitly affirm the mutualities of address and language and thus of humanity's continuity over time. Nor can an awareness of that disappearance take the form of knowledge, for no subject will ever be able to call upon it as a mental possession, a discursive or intentional object: it remains in the domain not of knowledge but of truth.

To speak a truth in the Real is to cut through all modes of social relation, all instances of reciprocity, mutuality, generosity, hospitality, or instruction, even if the occasion of its articulation necessarily happens within those domains. It operates beyond the law, even if it cannot evade its location within the law's sphere. Accordingly, it confers no privilege on the author or reader; it consigns them both to that abjected site of a horrific and unassimilable truth, the place of a certain impossible thought.

Who, then, can speak or hear this thought? Only that aspect of the psyche which exceeds a position in the symbolic or imaginary, only a dimension of the subject beyond subjectivity. Yet one can only speak or hear that thought if it enters the domain of articulation, institution, and relation. Although it cuts through that domain with the sharpness of the Real, it can nevertheless be evoked there, registered in some fashion – for otherwise it would dissipate entirely. It is thus a thought that arrives only in the interstices of thought, in what it grasps just as it fails to seize it.

Why, then, should one ever write – or read – a thought of extinction? One can no longer claim to inscribe it as a witness for future others, nor even as someone who will ultimately survive it; one cannot even claim to understand what one attempts to think. Nevertheless, one might write this thought simply to learn how to live under its sign, even if doing so requires one to sort through the debris left behind after the disappearance of virtually every familiar concept (humanity, knowledge, ethics, even writing itself). Although completing such a task is impossible, its import can nevertheless strike an excessive region of subjectivity – an aspect of subjectivity beyond the subject, as Zupančič proposes in a related context – and thus enter us through unanticipated, unknown regions of our experience.[219] The subject, it turns out, is other than, or more than, itself. Thus it is possible even for us, even for apparently finite subjects, to be attuned to this moment despite every difficulty, to haunt the nontime of this time, though in doing so we become as uncanny as humanity itself is fated to be.

The burning book. – Emily Dickinson once sought an audience; eventually she relinquished this hope, writing poems that never left her home. Franz Kafka wrote with fierce intensity, consigning himself utterly to a life of writing, but after having published several works, asked Max Brod to destroy his unpublished writings after his death. Both authors, seeking a place within the world of authorship, focusing intently on a mode of articulation that (thanks to the medium of language) necessarily implies an address to another, at some point turned away from an audience, consigning their work to the paradoxical status of an articulation for no one, a speech in the midst of silence. These gestures, of course, were partial rather than absolute: Dickinson knew that others might assemble and read her poems after her death, just as Kafka had already published some of his work and knew that Brod could fail to honor his request. Nevertheless, in these gestures they conceived of their work at least in part in terms not of the symbolic or imaginary but of the Real, hinting that they sought to evoke a truth that could never find a place where audiences live, where the institutions of discourse hold sway.

One who attempts to write a thought of human extinction similarly straddles a zone between the symbolic and the Real, working at the intersection of what one can and cannot say. In a similar way, one who reads that writing comprehends it within the conventions of discourse yet also apprehends it in another, more elusive mode. Such a writing has no stable status, no clear position in the world. Insofar as it appears from a site in the Real, its content is never quite manifest, its truth not entirely discernible. If the examples of Dickinson and Kafka are any guide, one might say that precisely where this writing appears, it simultaneously disappears; to apprehend what it conveys is to seize what its articulation cannot say. That writing thus burns in the moment it is read, dissolving as it reaches the world.

The hour before dawn. – There are styles of thought that fit the brightness of day; there are ragas for the evening hour; there is a meditation for the night. The thought of the terminus, however, belongs to the hour before dawn, near the end of the long night, in the moment before death. In such a moment comes a desperate clarity, a lucid view of horror free of illusions, when all evasions have disappeared, when all plans for the future have vanished, when one can accept one's place within a heap of ash. This is the hour when truth befalls one at last. One who is condemned now submits to the final blow. Just as in that moment one begins the slide out of the human community into a space beyond it, so also at the terminus the entire collective moves past itself into a domain it cannot know or name. Yet in that moment, the community, already beyond itself, discerns a truth that is meant only for it. In the hour before dawn, humanity at last encounters its own extinction.

15 The solidarity of the fragile

Biopower as thanatopower. – According to Michel Foucault, modern societies are organized around the imperative to preserve life, exercising their most stringent form of power through what is called *biopower*, a form of administrative rationality that treats people not as citizens but as bodies within a population subjected to "the calculated management of life" through statistical inquiry and demographics, the implementation of economic rationality, the adoption of productive machinery, the imposition of disciplinary institutions, the widespread medicalization of life, and the relief from starvation and plague.[220] But those who might wish to dwell entirely on this region of his argument, in part because it reflects his emphasis in other works (on carceral institutions, medicine, and governmentality, for example), would overlook the fact that Foucault's initial argument also states that today "entire populations are mobilized for the purpose of wholesale slaughter in the name of life necessity." Thus the point is not that modern societies perpetually manage the flows of life; it is rather that societies play for the stakes of "the biological existence of a population," so that "the power to expose a whole population to death" – for example, in a nuclear blast – "is the underside of the power to guarantee an individual's continued existence."[221] Thus biopower, the management of life, is *at one and the same time* thanatopower, the power to eradicate life; *bios* goes hand in hand with *thanatos*, the protection with the exposure of life.

It is worth lingering here over the implications of Foucault's initial stance. Can one say, for example, that the emergence of biopolitics might enhance the state's power to preserve life? Mike Davis's analysis in *Late Victorian Holocausts* shows that, on the contrary, the British decision to abide by a laissez-faire economics in the midst of famines in China and India in the late nineteenth century made them far worse, overriding traditional strategies for relieving hunger and abandoning millions to death.[222] That research suggests that modern biopower is far *less* attuned to the concrete demands of bodies than before, for it relies on the claims of political economy rather than the ad hoc but still effective strategies of an earlier polity. Foucault's discussion of war carries forward that account, for it asserts that modern war is potentially much more violent than before, for states now set out not merely to defeat other states but to eradicate entire populations. The very rationality of the modern state, which at times promises to overcome challenges to public health and thus save millions of lives, can also endanger millions of lives through the belligerence of its economic theories, the form of its violence, or the sway of its genocidal racism.

Today modern states impose the logic of biopower all the more. Increasingly insistent on safeguarding their populations from a range of medical, demographic, military, and environmental threats and on alleviating the needs of migrants and refugees, they define themselves ever more openly as instances of biopower, just as certain forms of resistance use forms of violence ever more openly against demographic groups and those intending to protect them (in mass murder, terror, assaults on civilian populations, and attacks on medical and peacekeeping personnel). Yet at the same time these states simultaneously impose the logic of a neoliberal economics on one and all, overriding resistance in the name of growth and efficiency, as if to recapitulate the logic of famine administration in another guise. In seeing human and nonhuman beings as purely material entities, biopower effectively destroys what in them exceeds mere use, what Baudrillard would describe as their *symbolic* value, their capacity to put themselves at stake, regarding them instead as so many items in the indifferent flow of a biological substance.[223] As if determined to put into effect Bentham's dictum to create the greatest happiness for the greatest number, carving up the world to serve the paramount command of general utility, it produces instead the greatest melancholy for the greatest number, for having transformed happiness into a factor within an instrumentalizing calculation, it makes even happiness subservient to its management and thus cancels its independent power. In doing so, it goes far toward reducing all forms of life to a bland and colorless flow, destroying what it pretends to preserve.

Yet even this pattern obscures the underlying momentum whereby the excesses justified by an ideology of life put an intolerable strain on the earth's ecosystems and on the biosphere itself, so that biopower, even where it succeeds in preserving life, becomes *in its own right* a form of thanatopower. For in its very success, biopower has all along enabled humankind to flourish to such a degree that no conceivable material practice could sustain it indefinitely. In ways that Foucault does not address, an excess of life, abrogating the bounds of earth's finitude, becomes a supreme transgression, a defiance of limits so great that it exhausts the prospects for human life itself. In our time, biopower is itself thanatopower, one face of the undoing of the world.

The sovereignty of disaster. – Drawing on Carl Schmitt's contention that every polity relies on a sovereign located at once within and outside the political order, the sole figure empowered to declare a state of exception, Agamben has linked this sovereign to the *homo sacer*, the figure in Roman law who, not worthy of being sacrificed, can be murdered with impunity. In this account, the sovereign and the homo sacer emerge together in the state of emergency, for the sovereign suspension of law corresponds to the expulsion of the homo sacer outside citizenship or legal protection. Such a situation, according to Agamben, defines the modern state in the era of biopower, which reduces the person to a merely biological status, a condition of bare life.[224]

How might sovereignty fare under the sign of the terminus? Although the political situation Agamben summarizes applies broadly, today each state discovers that it is subject to an even more sovereign force, disaster itself. Imposing itself on all life without regard for normative structures, declarations of citizenship, or the drawing of boundaries, disaster abrogates the political at every turn, treating every human being as a moment in a purely biophysical process.[225] It is not only the case that each state manages its population in a cryptic reference to the internment camp, as Agamben suggests; now disaster reduces the entire planet to a single vast camp, coralling all of humanity into a space in which it suffers the threat of an imminent, collective death.[226] At once imitating sovereignty and abrogating it, this power synthesizes the violence of prior political decisions into a single force of ongoing devastation, imposing that ferocity in a new form. Those previous transgressions of all limits intended to produce universal abundance have instead engineered this new agency, which imposes a stunning biological vulnerability on everyone, including agents of the state. One can only conclude that political sovereigns, overriding the tolerance of ecosystems for economic purposes, have been producing this paramount state of emergency all along, one that now imposes itself with exquisite ferocity across the world. What was once a political reduction of the citizen to bare life is now being literalized in the biosphere's imposition on its living creatures; the drift of the political toward biopolitics (and thanatopolitics) has become complete as it gives way to a framework that is truly beyond it.

As a result, humanity now finds itself under the sovereignty of a force that admits of no appeal, that can never undo this state of emergency, that treats all forms of life as instances of the homo sacer, even without any awareness that it is doing so. The political, now suspended in its proper form, takes place in a radically nonhuman mode, abrogating any attempt to contest its impositions. We endure a state more bare than ever before.

The solidarity of the fragile. – In this state of dire emergency, in which the polis is cancelled and even the sovereign overshadowed by a more sinister form, what remains to us who nevertheless endure, who live on in this mode of inexistence? What form of the political might still obtain, even for us?

Only a politics of fragility, a solidarity of the erased and the forgotten, a broken mutuality of those condemned to disappear. Our living together is no longer a matter of population, no longer something to be administered or managed through the instituted knowledges of bio-power, but through direct relations between the condemned – between all those on the verge of dissolution, human and nonhuman alike. In a world without telos, without ground, we share the condition of being utterly exposed – not merely to death or the disorders of embodiment, but also to the finitude of our shared forms of persistence.

In his poem, "September 1, 1939," W. H. Auden captured the somber mood of a world entering war, a scene of mendacity, fear, and defenseless stupor, in which one hope alone remains: "We must love one another or die."[227] Living under the shadow of even greater mendacities today, faced with an even darker prospect, we now must maintain a similar love even without such a hope; we must love one another *and* die. What remains to us is the love of the disappearing for the disappearing, a tenderness that endures even in the shadow of extinction.[228] The justice we enact today has no aim outside itself, no alibi in any other purpose; the love we share does not release us from our fate, does not heal us, but only sustains us in the midst of what cannot be healed. Such love allows suffering to take place in a domain where forms of relationship still hold, even where they are evanescent; it bolsters them with a power so weak it can forestall nothing and contest nothing, yet so strong it allows each to affirm another. In such love there may emerge forms of mutuality that survive even amidst their perfect uselessness. Ours is a truly futile community, a solidarity in oblivion.

Amor fati. – In one of the first discussions of the thought of eternal recurrence, Nietzsche writes that if it "gained possession of you, it would change you as you are or perhaps crush you," lying "upon your actions as the greatest weight."[229] It is "the most abysmal idea," the most daring, the most difficult for any human being to sustain.[230] But would such an idea be able to bear up under the thought of human extinction? Does that idea even require such an extravagant gesture? At times Nietzsche applies radical affirmation primarily to the past, as when he suggests that "to recreate all 'it was' into a 'thus I willed it' – that alone should I call redemption."[231] But elsewhere he extends this affirmation to the future as well: "My formula for greatness in a human being is *amor fati*: that one wants nothing to be different, not forward, not backward, not in all eternity. Not merely bear what is necessary, still less conceal it – all idealism is mendaciousness in the face of what is necessary – but *love* it."[232] Thus it is clear that for Nietzsche this most abysmal thought would include everything that is to come, for if one is to affirm the entire course of events that have led to this moment, one must also affirm all the consequences of those events as well. *Amor fati* applies to past, present, *and* future.

In that case, this most abysmal thought becomes even more so; today, the weight of an absolute affirmation becomes even greater. Yet at first glance, in principle the nature of this thought would not change. On its face, the capacity for absolute, even infinite, affirmation would exclude nothing that could conceivably happen, no matter how dire. To affirm this existence absolutely would also be to say Yes to humanity's disappearance. Indeed, in the mode of *amor fati*, it would not merely bear with it but *love* it. In this account, the sign of Nietzschean greatness today – the sign of a capacity for infinite affirmation – would be the ability to love the entire sequence in which humanity arises and erases itself.

Such an affirmation would not mean endorsement or approval, nor would it indicate a willingness to judge any part of that history as good. It would not suggest that it is better for humanity to disappear than for it to endure, nor would it wish for the reverse. It would simply say Yes to whatever has been and will be, beyond all such judgment. It would thus dare to affirm even the darkest fate, to say Yes to the annihilation of thought itself. Moreover, it would refuse every form of resentment, nostalgia, grief, or lamentation over what has happened or will happen; it would assert a radical acceptance of every loss, every dire extremity, every process that may violate and undo humanity. That thought would not be intimidated by any horrific fate that might befall thought itself: it would dare to affirm and love it all, even to embrace the terminus itself.

But this initial account focuses too narrowly on the idea of the eternal return. For Nietzsche, that thought partakes in a series of interventions meant to bring about a transvaluation of values – to clear a space for free spirits, for those prepared to embark on the great undertaking of becoming philosophers of the future. Ironically, then, inscribed within the effort to affirm all history is the expectation that doing so will produce *another future*, that this affirmation may make possible a transformation of humankind. As a result, even this thought is premised on the endurance of humankind into the future, taking for granted the preconditions for a wholesale alteration in thought. Like other practitioners of the avant-garde, then, Nietzsche relies on the value of the new, of severe alteration, even if in his thought he overleaps much of what counts as modernity: he too is bound up with a certain understanding of history, and as a result *even his thought* is struck down by the terminus. Whatever free spirits have come into existence will survive the terminus no better than the rest of humanity.

This impasse demonstrates that any stance we might concoct to allow us to affirm human extinction would have a similar ambition: it would mark itself out as *absolutely* avant-garde and thus be invested in demonstrating its unique capacity. It would amount to still another attempt to convert this occasion into an opportunity for philosophical sovereignty. A stance of absolute affirmation takes for granted a capacity for humanity to triumph over its conditions precisely by affirming them. Such a gesture, rather than producing any sovereignty, would disappear rapidly without a trace; it would demonstrate only its own vanity, its presumption, its nullity. Under the sign of human extinction, *there can be no possible philosophical victory.* Only one response remains to us today: the gesture whereby thought, confronted with the impossibility of its victory, embraces its failure, accepting the radical nullity of human being.

Endless expenditure. – Premodern thought often posited a telos for history, thought, or action, subordinating itself to a framework that it anchored in a divine limit – in an origin or end, a ground or substance. Modern thought, however, having cancelled this telos, constructed its framework around that mark of erasure – around the internal limit – in such instances as Kant's critical philosophy or Hegel's incorporation of negativity into the movement of Spirit. Both premodern and modern modes, however, are vulnerable to the thought of the terminus, which makes visible the absence of any ground for humanity in the creation and undercuts modernity's concepts of rational autonomy, secular history, or cultural coherence.

The work of Georges Bataille explores an alternative to these two positions, the premodern and the modern, accepting neither a telos nor the inscription of its cancellation within a philosophical system but returning to the moment of cancellation to explore it *in its own right*, to experience what transpires when the very idea of telos, limit, or end disappears, when one undergoes the anguish of the limitless and refuses to absorb it into any mode of knowledge. Such a thought dwells precisely with annihilation, nonbeing, or the impossible – with what destroys any supposed integrity of thought, any form of a *headed* humanity. Inspired by a Nietzschean jubilation, Bataille rejoices in this headless condition, affirming this futile excess, this pure expenditure, this infinity beyond all conceivable purpose – this movement that tears open every closed system of philosophy or theology.[233]

Does it follow that Bataille would celebrate the reckless profusions of capitalism, the burning of fossil fuels to such an extent that they force even the biosphere to alter its patterns? Would he read capitalism as an instance of pure expenditure? But capitalism attempts to harness and control biological profusion, to make a profit out of what it appropriates; it seeks to metabolize the excesses of life, in the process morphing into what Rebekah Sheldon calls "*somatic capitalism –* the intervention into and monetization of life-itself."[234] It is thus a perfect instance of the type of system that wishes to subordinate excess to its own ends, to incorporate the accursed share into systematic growth. The celebration of expenditure, in contrast, affirms a destructive gesture without profit or return; it yearns not for economic expansion but for profusion and loss. Bataille's praise for expenditure, then, constitutes a severe refusal of capitalism. Moreover, as his hatred of fascism makes clear, he also repudiates any attempt by the modern state to harness archaic excess for its purposes, to subordinate myth to the intoxications of a political order. His atheology urges us to overleap the constraints of capitalism or the state and affirm a libidinal life tied to archaic ritual, to forms of expenditure that modernity does not tolerate. His stance, in short, demands that we locate our forms of expenditure in something other than the institutions and practices that surround us.

The devastating consequences of attempting to enclose profusion within a modern economy suggest that adhering to Bataille's alternative would never have produced this environmental crisis. To give the accursed share its due – to refuse to subordinate it to any "head" imposed by these systems – would forestall the sequence that has led to the terminus. Bataille's rejection of the closures of teleology, theology, philosophy, the state, and capitalism make his stance far less damaging to humanity and the nonhuman world alike. His celebration of a headless condition is actually a stance of humility before what exceeds it.

But does it follow that his stance would affirm the terminus itself? In *Inner Experience*, Bataille uses the idea of experience to set aside every external authority, valuing above all "a voyage to the end of the possible of man."[235] Today such an ideal might be read in two ways: it might affirm whatever people might discover on this voyage, tacitly assuming that such a venture would remain possible for human beings indefinitely into the future, but it might also consider the encounter with the erasure of the future as the highest challenge, the very site that marks out "the end of the possible." A similar ambiguity is evident in another remark in that book: "I can bear the weight of the future only on one condition: that others, always others, live in it – and that death washes us, then washes these others without end."[236] Here Bataille finds refuge from the thought of the future in the death of others, but affirms a death that washes those "others without end" – thus evoking the prospect of an *endless* death, a *limitless* cancellation of the ordinary fantasies of the future. But while the terminus seems to offer the prospect of an infinite cancellation, it does so *at once*, rather than without end; in effect, it channels that profusion of death into a punctual and *limited* event, one that ironically eradicates the prospect of an endless death.

Thus Bataille's work foregrounds how human extinction, which might seem to be the highest expenditure possible for humanity, serves as still another instance of constraint. Where Bataille celebrates a form of profusion that in archaic culture takes place across time, in recognized patterns of collective loss, the terminus gathers up that loss into an event that cancels any further prospect for such profusion. It constitutes a form of collective loss that eradicates loss itself. This property of the terminus suggests that the attempt to constrain expenditure creates an infinitely destructive event; to channel excess makes it so violent that it undoes the very context from which it emerges. As it turns out, constraining excess for the purposes of political management or economic growth ultimately produces a terminus that explodes expenditure itself.

One might reply, however, that because Bataille imagines a headless universe that flourishes outside all moral evaluation, he might be able to accept even the terminus. If humanity is not supreme, if the accursed share emerges across all forms of life, then perhaps the loss of humanity – as well as thousands of other species that will disappear over the course of the sixth extinction event we are now causing – will be only one moment within that broader profusion. In this account, nothing in that immense scene of "biological exuberance" would mourn humanity's passing, for it would take place in an amoral universe that cuts through all possible conceptual enclosure.[237] If one goes this far, one might place one's confidence in a resilience beyond the human, in a profusion without reference to human concerns of any kind. In this approach, excess is not to be contained even in ritual expenditure but is to be located on another level entirely, in the sheer excess of life over itself, its inability to stop disrupting itself with an endless series of further expenditures – across timescales far larger than any that are familiar to us.

Such a stance, however appealing, still evades the precise history that has produced the terminus. Rather than being still another instance of biological exuberance, in which species, indulging in a certain excess of life, come and go, this event is generated by the attempt of humanity to subordinate the biosphere to its own ends. It speaks, then, of what *violates* that resilience. Bataille would repudiate such a subordination, as he refuses the cooptation of myth in fascism or the absorption of excess in capitalism; he would attempt to protect every form of nonhuman exuberance as well as the form it takes in human collectives. To affirm the limitless, to embrace excess, is to turn away from the terminus as limit, to rebuke it as the most egregious symptom of the cephalic arrogance of the West. Thus the terminus erases all finalities but also abrogates the atheology that rebukes those finalities as well: it gives us neither a telos nor a mode of the limitless but an event hostile to teleology and expenditure alike.

Impossible arrival. – If these forms of affirmation or expenditure fail in the face of the terminus, is it better to seek a Heideggerian authenticity in the form of being-toward-death, by which one accepts the radical "possibility of the impossibility" of Dasein, recognizing that death is one's "ownmost" fate?[238] Would this existential project, this absorption of one's fate into one's fundamental existential comportment, apply as well to the disappearance of humanity as a whole? But even apart from the question of the terminus, this approach fails on its own ground; as Blanchot points out, death "does not have the solidity which would sustain such a relation. It is that which happens to no one, the uncertainty and the indecision of what never happens."[239] One cannot sustain a relation to something that is not an event, that is not conceivable, that one cannot ultimately anticipate. Yet the question of death does not simply disappear. Instead, Blanchot writes, "There is something I must do to accomplish it; indeed, everything remains for me to do: it must be my work. But this work is beyond me, it is that part of me upon which I shed no light, which I do not attain and of which I am not master."[240] Thus for Blanchot one finds oneself in the midst of an effort without result, without destination, without certainty, without any conceivable mastery – in the midst of a limitless unworking against which one has no refuge.

This position is closely analogous to that of Bataille; here again is a limitless process that occupies one without reprieve and cannot be subsumed into use, knowledge, or mastery of any kind. Like Bataille, Blanchot cuts through both premodern and modern arrangements, situating himself at the site of the cancellation of telos to explore it in its own right, to delineate what transpires when the idea of the limit vanishes. Yet his delineation of that site has an import of its own. Rather than appealing to ritual profusion or biological excess, to forms of expenditure that modernity sought to capture, Blanchot considers the closely related but nevertheless distinct process of dying. Where modernity might attempt to capture this dying in various ways, to put it to use for purposes of power, wealth, or philosophical closure, it eludes such cooptation, sliding away from any such reification.

This parallel between Blanchot and Bataille might suggest that Blanchot's stance also falls prey to the terminus. But Blanchot extends his account of dying to consider disaster as well, showing that embedded even in his initial stance is a perspective from which he might be able to approach the question of the terminus. His work shows that a stance deriving from a consideration of death differs significantly from one grounded in expenditure; even if death might arguably constitute an instance of such expenditure, it takes place in a far more elusive epistemological terrain. The import of that stance for the thought of the terminus becomes clear as soon as Blanchot takes up the question of disaster per se. Contrary to what one might expect, he treats it not as an event within history but rather as one that arrives without arriving and in doing so surreptitiously undermines the entire terrain of seemingly non-disastrous experience. "The disaster ruins everything, all the while leaving everything intact," he writes in the first sentence of *The Writing of the Disaster*. It is "that which does not come, that which has put a stop to every arrival. To think the disaster . . . is to have no longer any future in which to think it."[241] Rather than taking place in time, it displaces and disables time itself, undoing the possibility of arrival, of event. Under its impact, time "is without present," "I without I"; indeed, all that transpires is now "outside being."[242] Disaster is thus not something that constitutes a mode of historical experience; it is what undermines the very possibility of such experience. It disables time, event, history, identity, subject, and experience alike.

In treating disaster in this way, Blanchot does not attempt to undo the significance of the Shoah, for example, nor of the threat of global thermunuclear war, nor of any other historical instance of disaster, all of which remain key references throughout his text. Rather, in following that shift, he attempts to take seriously the import of such events for ordinary life in our time. One can never grasp the import of the Shoah in a purely empirical investigation, any more than one can understand the significance of a nuclear war that would erase any witness: the event thus takes place in another arena, belonging to a more elusive category.[243] This approach is thus virtually unique in its capacity to evoke what I mentioned earlier – the fact that the terminus will never take place in the symbolic or imaginary, but only in the Real, only in what is never communicable in speech or thought. Blanchot's is thus *already* a thought of the terminus, *already* an elucidation of the impossible task of apprehending it.[244]

Yet can it be exemplary in this regard if it is written before the thought of the terminus proper could have come to Blanchot, if it could not register the imminent arrival of what would exceed that thought and become actual? Although nuclear war would have erased humankind, one could not assume that it would necessarily take place; today, however, another event is arriving that may well do so. Perhaps, then, our condition exceeds what he evoked. One might then be tempted to suggest that insofar as the terminus *may actually arrive*, his work accentuates what is scandalous and unique in it: insofar as it arrives, it will constitute *an exceptional event in which the Real as impossible actually takes place.*

Such a question, then, merits a particularly subtle reply. On one level, as I mentioned above, that work refers to an event that no one will witness. As a result, it designates a terminus that must remain a *thought* of the terminus, an event that becomes complete for us in anticipation alone. Perhaps it is only at this phase that one can fully grasp the force of Blanchot's elucidation: once one anticipates an annihilating event, *then* that event arrives in its non-arrival, ruining everything while leaving it intact, erasing even a time in which events might occur. While that argument applies in another way to past disasters (such as the Shoah), it has special force for those that occur without having yet empirically happened. In effect, then, one grasps Blanchot at last when one realizes that the terminus *has already taken place in the Real,* that it has *already* erased the validity of temporality, subjectivity, and historical experience.

Yet such a response risks repudiating the actuality of an event. The displacement from event to non-arrival cannot be absolute, for if it becomes so, then the non-arrival also disappears, and along with it, the entire problematic. Thus even a stance that accentuates its occurrence outside occurrence relies on the occurrence itself. The anticipation can never exhaust what it anticipates, nor the disaster that has already occurred erase the literal occasion to come.

The thought of disaster, then, necessarily occurs on two levels – in that which has already occurred and in doing so has already displaced our entire experience, and that which exceeds our thought of it, takes place beyond any witnessing, and insists outside any conceivable mode of human apprehension. If, as Blanchot argues, disaster (like death) never becomes an event, his claim holds true only within a certain domain: it never becomes an event *for us*, can never be understood in human terms. *Yet it still takes place.*

What one ultimately encounters in these precincts, then, is a disaster beyond that in Blanchot, one that takes place in a zone apart from and beyond us – and as a result reveals the definitive place of what we simply cannot apprehend. Even in thinking the disaster, thought cannot think it: it slips past, unseized and unknown. Here again, but in a still more rigorous register, we must conclude that the thought of the terminus is the terminus of thought.

This abyss of sky. – What then remains to us, we who face the possibility of the extinction of humanity? Stripped of the various strategies whereby thought might respond to that happening, every buffer that theology, philosophy, literature, or thought itself may provide, every gesture proposed even by such exemplars of useless negativity as Nietzsche, Bataille, Blanchot, Derrida, or Edelman, one suffers the ruin of that vast event without reprieve. Here thought, denuded of itself, becomes utter shock in the face of this abyss of sky, enduring a trauma beyond trauma.

But this encounter never becomes a form of ecstatic apprehension, since one never directly faces the terminus itself, never endures absolute nonbeing; something more subtle arrives for us, an oblivion that, having arrived, engulfs a world that is still here. One thus endures a non-encounter, a surreptitious oblivion, in which whatever one can still sense has passed away, much as one's mode of apprehension can no longer seize what it reaches for. Yet the world, in its erasure, is still a form of shelter; this dying, ceaseless and unmasterable, is still a form of living on. Living in this dying, one can still see the sky, fly through its vast space, cavort with infinity – but this is a sky that is also the abyss, a dance that is also oblivion. Such a flight happens only in the Real; it leaves no visible trace; it abandons one to the same field of debris, this same charred landscape under the stars. For if the debris cannot forestall one from a terminal thought – from this leap through oblivion – that thought cannot forestall one's return to the domain of wreckage. In this field, even renunciation falls away, and silence – still an evocation of speech – cracks and collapses. One is left with an unmasterable disquiet, an absolute disarray of spirit, a shattered thought, under this abyss of sky.

Acknowledgments

Over the course of writing and revising this book, I have taken encouragement and support from many students, colleagues, and friends. I wish to thank Jiankun Wu for a pivotal conversation that inspired me to shift from making initial sketches into writing the book; Jack Rodgers and Mollie Eisner for their thoughts in response to early phases of the draft; Alexander Schlutz for several searching conversations regarding this project and its themes; Taylor Schey and Chris Washington for reading the entire manuscript and making astute suggestions for revision; the support of Tilottama Rajan, Rei Terada, Colin Jager, and Nick Halmi for my work on this project and beyond; Soelve Curdts for inviting me to share aspects of this project in an online version of her seminar, "Reading Pasts," in the Department of English and American Studies at Heinrich-Heine-Universität, Düsseldorf, in July 2021, and for the useful comments of the seminar participants; Bob Markley and Lucinda Cole for their savvy advice on strategies for publication; Bowdoin College, for awarding me with a Faculty Leave Supplement toward a sabbatical year in which I completed and revised the book manuscript; Claire Colebrook and Tom Cohen, the editors of the CCC2: Irreversibility series, for their support and their suggestions for revision, as well as to two anonymous reviewers of the manuscript for their comments; the founders at Open Humanities Press for their work in creating and sustaining the press, as well as the splendid colleagues at the press who oversaw the book through the production process; and most of all, Terri Nickel for her useful suggestions for revision, her immense generosity and patience, and the delight of our shared finitude, through which once again, even with this project, radiated the happiness of thought.

Notes

1   Walter Benjamin, "On the Concept of History," in *Selected Writings*, edited by Michael W. Jennings, volume 4: 1938-1940, edited by Howard Eiland and Jennings, translated by Edmund Jephcott and others (Cambridge, MA: Harvard University Press, 2003), 389-400; Theodor Adorno, *Minima Moralia: Reflections from Damaged Life*, translated by E. F. N. Jephcott (London: Verso, 1978).

2   Collings, *Stolen Future, Broken Present: The Human Significance of Climate Change* (Open Humanities Press; Ann Arbor, MI: University of Michigan Library, 2014).

3   Reinhart Koselleck, *Futures Past: On the Semantics of Historical Time*, translated by Keith Tribe (New York: Columbia University Press, 2004), 22.

4   On capitalism's repudiation of those who pointed out its environmental costs, see Christophe Bonneuil and Jean-Baptiste Fressoz, *The Shock of the Anthropocene: The Earth, History, and Us*, translated by David Fernbach (New York: Verso, 2017), 198-221.

5   Benjamin, 392.

6   Benjamin, 392.

7   For a further exploration of the ideas in this essay, see "Toward a Poetics of Disappearance: The Vanishing Commons in Clare's 'The Lament of Swordy Well,'" *Romanticism on the Net* 72, July 2020. https://ronjournal.org/files/sites/140/2020/06/RoN72-73_02.pdf.

8   Jan Zalasiewicz and others, "Stratigraphy of the Anthropocene," *Philosophical Transactions of the Royal Society A*, 369 (March 13, 2011): 1038.

9   Srinavas Aravamudan, "The Catachronism of Climate Change," *Diacritics* 41 (2013): 8. Cf. Claire Colebrook, *The Death of the PostHuman: Essays on Extinction, volume 1* (Open Humanities Press, Ann Arbor, MI: University of Michigan Library, 2014), 24.

10 Günther Anders, "Reflections on the H Bomb," *Dissent* 3 (1956): 149.

11 Alan Weisman, *The World Without Us* (New York: St Martin's, 2007).

12 Eugene Thacker, *In the Dust of This Planet* (Washington, DC: Zero Books, 2011), 5.

13   Marija Grech, "'Where nothing ever was': Anthropomorphic
      Spectrality and the (im)possibility of the post-anthropocene," *New
      Formations* 95 (2019), 34.

14   Claire Colebrook, "The Future in the Anthropocene: Extinction
      and the Imagination," in *Climate and Literature*, edited by Adeline
      Johns-Putra (Cambridge: Cambridge University Press, 2019), 269.

15   Ray Brassier, *Nihil Unbound: Enlightenment and Extinction* (New
      York: Palgrave Macmillan, 2007); see especially 223-39.

16   Apart from Brassier, the key speculative realist I have in mind here
      is Quentin Meillassoux, *After Finitude: An Essay on the Necessity
      of Contingency*, translated by Ray Brassier (New York: Continuum,
      2008), who relies on the "arche-fossil" rather than the death of the
      sun as he examines a world outside of human perception; see es-
      pecially 8-27.

17   See Grech, 35.

18   Thacker, "Notes on Extinction and Existence," *Configurations* 20
      (2012): 137. Brassier, meditating on the implications of humanity's
      eventual extinction, is thus right to ask, *"How does thought think the
      death of thinking?"* See Brassier, 223. However, as noted above, he
      asks this question in response to an event that will take place in due
      course over the far reaches of time, rather than one that might occur
      relatively soon due to human actions.

19   Thacker, *In the Dust of This Planet*, 123. Thacker goes on to explore
      this theme in an analysis of Kant's essay, "The End of All Things,"
      suggesting that Kant theorizes a similar aporia in the thought
      of extinction; see 123-24. See also his discussion of that essay in
      "Notes on Extinction and Existence," 144-46. Both passages refer to
      Immanuel Kant, "The End of All Things," in *Religion and Rational
      Theology*, translated and edited by Allen W. Wood and George Di
      Giovanni (Cambridge: Cambridge University Press, 1996), 217-31.
      But Kant is discussing the absence of alteration in a presumed eter-
      nity to follow the apocalypse; the essay speaks of extinction at best
      only indirectly.

20   Jacques Derrida, *Glas*, translated by John P. Leavey, Jr., and Richard
      Rand (Lincoln: University of Nebraska Press, 1986), 262, 1.

21   For bracing, necessary explorations of how rhetorical reading in
      the de Man tradition, among other critical traditions, bears on a
      host of questions related to climate change and the Anthropocene,
      see Tom Cohen, Claire Colebrook, and J. Hillis Miller, *Theory and
      the Disappearing Future: On de Man, On Benjamin* (New York:
      Routledge, 2012) and *Twilight of the Anthropocene Idols* (London:
      Open Humanities Press, 2016).

22   See Paul de Man, "Textual Allegories by Paul de Man," manuscript transcription by Erin Obodiac, UCIspace@the Libraries, 2010, as quoted in Tom Cohen, "Toxic Assets: De Man's Remains and the Ecocatastropic Imaginary (An American Fable)," in Cohen, Colebrook, and Miller, *Theory and the Disappearing Future*, 109. See ucispace.lib.uci.edu/handle/10575/1092.

23   Martin Hägglund, "Radical Atheist Materialism: A Critique of Meillassoux," in *The Speculative Turn: Continental Materialism and Realism*, edited by Levi Bryant, Nick Srnicek and Graham Harman (Melbourne: re.press, 2011), 114-29.

24   Monique Allewaert, "Toward a Materialist Figuration: A Slight Manifesto," *English Language Notes* 51 (2013): 61-77.

25   Benjamin, 391.

26   Benjamin, 396, 395, 390.

27   Benjamin, 390.

28   Howard Caygill, *Art of Judgment* (Oxford: Basil Blackwell, 1989), 2.

29   Derrida, "The Ends of Man," in *Margins of Philosophy*, translated by Alan Bass (Chicago: University of Chicago Press, 1982), 109-136. The final sentence of this essay is this: "But who, we?" (136).

30   See Jean-Luc Nancy, *Being Singular Plural*, translated by Robert D. Richardson and Anne E. O'Byrne (Stanford: Stanford University Press, 2000), 4, 29, 15-21.

31   If, as Nancy suggests, *"the world is the exposure of humanity,"* then today it exposes humanity in still a further way under the sign of the terminus (18).

32   G. W. F. Hegel, *Phenomenology of Spirit*, translated by A. V. Miller (New York: Oxford University Press, 1977), 10; italics in the original.

33   Hegel, 11, 14, 17, 21.

34   Hegel, 14; italics in the original.

35   Hegel, *Elements of the Philosophy of Right*, translated by H. B. Nisbet (Cambridge: Cambridge University Press, 1991), 20.

36   Hegel, *Phenomenology*, 19.

37   Theodor Adorno, *Negative Dialectics*, translated by E. B. Ashton (New York: Continuum, 1997), 320.

38   Francis Fukuyama, *The End of History and the Last Man* (New York: Free Press, 1992).

39   Compare Brassier, *Nihil Unbound*, 224, who writes, "Unlike the model of death which, at least since Hegel, has functioned as the motor of philosophical speculation, [the extinction of the sun] does not constitute an internal limit for thought, providing the necessary spur for thought to overstep its own bounds and thereby incorporating what was supposed to be exterior to it. . . . The extinction of the sun is not a limit *of* or *for* thought."

40   Vivasvan Soni, *Mourning Happiness: Narrative and the Politics of Modernity* (Ithaca: Cornell University Press, 2010), 6.

41   Soni, 68-69.

42   Benjamin, "Critique of Violence," in *Reflections: Essays, Aphorisms, Autobiographical Writings*, edited by Peter Demetz, translated by Edmund Jephcott (New York: Schocken, 1986), 277-300.

43   George Eliot, *Middlemarch* (New York: Penguin, 1965), 226.

44   Richard Price, *Political Writings*, edited by D. O. Thomas (New York: Cambridge University Press, 1991), 195.

45   Edmund Burke, *Reflections on the Revolution in France, and on the Proceedings in Certain Societies in London Relative to That Event*, edited by Conor Cruise O'Brien (New York: Penguin, 1968), 120. On the extension of the *corpus mysticum* into secular contexts and ultimately to the concept of the body politic, see Steven Blakemore, *Burke and the Fall of Language: The French Revolution as Linguistic Event* (Hanover, NY: University Press of New England, 1988), 15-17.

46   See David Collings, *Monstrous Society: Reciprocity, Discipline, and the Political Uncanny, c. 1780-1848* (Lewisburg, PA: Bucknell University Press, 2009), 74-81.

47   Burke, 193.

48   Elie Wiesel, *Night*, translated by Stella Rodway (New York: Avon, 1960), 44.

49   John Dominic Crossan and Jonathan L. Reed, *In Search of Paul: How Jesus's Apostle Opposed Rome's Empire with God's Kingdom; a New Vision of Paul's Words & World* (New York, HarperCollins, 2004).

50   Bonneuil and Fressoz, 198-221.

51   Benjamin, "On the Concept of History," 390. On Benjamin's reference to Paul here and throughout this text, see Giorgio Agamben, *The Time that Remains: A Commentary on the Letter to the Romans*, translated by Patricia Dailey (Stanford: Stanford University Press, 2005), 138-45.

52   Agamben, *The Time That Remains*, 27, 96, 23.

53 Agamben, *The Time That Remains*, 41.

54 On the contradiction between the nonviolent politics of Percy Bysshe Shelley's *Prometheus Unbound*, Act I, and the transformative effect of Demogorgon's violence in Act III, see Tilottama Rajan, *Romantic Narrative: Shelley, Hays, Godwin, Wollstonecraft* (Baltimore: Johns Hopkins University Press, 2010), 75-76. For a discussion of Benjamin's thinking on violence in relation to Shelley's play, see my *Disastrous Subjectivities: Romanticism, Modernity, and the Real* (Toronto: University of Toronto Press, 2019), 163.

55 Derrida, *Specters of Marx: The State of the Debt, the Work of Mourning, and the New International*, translated by Peggy Kamuf (New York: Routledge, 1994), 27.

56 Compare Derrida, *The Gift of Death* and *Literature in Secret*, translated by David Wills (Chicago: University of Chicago Press, 2008), 69, 71.

57 John Milton, *Paradise Lost*, 1.26. See Milton, *Complete Poems and Major Prose*, edited by Merritt Y. Hughes (Indianapolis, IN: Odyssey Press, 1957).

58 Thomas Pfau, *Minding the Modern: Human Agency, Intellectual Traditions, and Responsible Knowledge* (Notre Dame, IN: Notre Dame University Press, 2015), 149-51.

59 See Stephen Mitchell, "Introduction," in *The Book of Job*, translated by Mitchell (New York: HarperCollins, 1987), vii-xxxii.

60 Here I rely on chapter twelve of my *Stolen Future*, 188-206.

61 Kant, *Critique of Practical Reason*, third edition, translated by Lewis White Beck (Upper Saddle River, NJ: Prentice Hall, 1993), 129.

62 Lewis White Beck, *A Commentary on Kant's "Critique of Practical Reason"* (Chicago: University of Chicago Press, 1960), 270.

63 Alenka Zupančič, *Ethics of the Real: Kant, Lacan* (New York: Verso, 2000), 79-81.

64 See Nancy Yousef, *Isolated Cases: The Anxieties of Autonomy in Enlightenment Philosophy and Romantic Literature* (Ithaca: Cornell University Press, 2004).

65 Gil Anidjar, *Semites: Race, Religion, Literature* (Stanford: Stanford University Press, 2008), 39-63. Of course, one could trace the much longer history of the notion of the sky or the heavens; in this short essay, however, I prefer to focus on how the specifically *secular* use of the sky appears to us under the sign of the terminus.

66   For a recent statement of an antinatalist position within the analytic philosophical tradition, see David Benatar, *Better Never to Have Been: The Harm of Coming into Existence* (Oxford: Clarendon, 2006).

67   For a discussion of the emergence of Tantrism within the context of South Asian religion, see Gavin Flood, *An Introduction to Hinduism* (Cambridge: Cambridge University Press, 1996), 157-172.

68   Thomas Richards, *The Imperial Archive: Knowledge and the Fantasy of Empire* (New York: Verso, 1993).

69   Derrida, *Archive Fever: A Freudian Impression*, translated by Eric Prenowitz (Chicago: University of Chicago Press, 1995), 19.

70   Michel Foucault, *The Order of Things: An Archaeology of the Human Sciences* (New York: Random House, 1970).

71   Joan Copjec, *Imagine There's No Woman: Ethics and Sublimation* (Cambridge, MA: MIT Press, 2002), 94, 95, 96.

72   Claude Lefort, *Democracy and Political Theory*, translated by David Macey (Minneapolis: University of Minnesota Press, 1988), 17-19.

73   Ernesto Laclau, *On Populist Reason* (New York: Verso, 2005).

74   For a more extensive discussion of the internal limit along these lines, see my *Disastrous Subjectivities*, 4-19.

75   See Collings, *Disastrous Subjectivities*.

76   For a more sustained exploration of this shift to a disastrous objectivity, see my *Disastrous Subjectivities*, 171-80.

77   Michel Foucault, *The Foucault Reader*, edited by Paul Rabinow (New York: Pantheon, 1984), 34.

78   Foucault, *The Foucault Reader*, 50.

79   Benjamin, "On the Concept of History," 391-92.

80   Jorge Luis Borges, *Labyrinths: Selected Stories and Other Writings*, edited by Donald A. Yates and James E. Irby (New York: New Directions, 1964), 19-29.

81   Benjamin, "On the Concept of History," 391 (on Leopold von Ranke) and 390 (on how "nothing that has ever happened should be regarded as lost to history").

82   Alfred W. Blumrosen and Ruth G. Blumrosen, *Slave Nation: How Slavery United the Colonies and Sparked the American Revolution* (Naperville, IL: Sourcebooks, 2005), 203-24.

83   Timothy Mitchell, *Carbon Democracy: Political Power in the Age of Oil* (New York: Verso, 2011), 15-18.

84   Douglas A. Blackmon, *Slavery by Another Name: The Re-Enslavement of Black Americans from the Civil War to World War II* (New York: Anchor, 2009); Timothy Mitchell, 12-42.

85   Karl Marx and Friedrich Engels, *Manifesto of the Communist Party*, in *The Marx-Engels Reader*, second edition, edited by Robert C. Tucker (New York: Norton, 1978), 469-500; see especially 482-83.

86   Koselleck, 22.

87   Koselleck, 33, 35.

88   Koselleck, 38.

89   For a pivotal discussion of the history and ideology of the public sphere, see Jürgen Habermas, *The Structural Transformation of the Public Sphere: An Inquiry into a Category of Bourgeois Society*, translated by Thomas Burger with the assistance of Frederick Lawrence (Cambridge, MA: MIT Press, 1991). While Habermas touches on the "basic blueprint," according to which the public sphere is supposed to provide for the regulation of authority according to the public use of reason (27), his analysis overall exposes contradictory elements in the emergence of this domain as well as its place in what he calls "bourgeois ideology."

90   See, for example, the essays and interviews gathered in Foucault, *Power/Knowledge: Selected Interviews and Other Writings, 1972-1977*, edited by Colin Gordon, translated by Gordon and others (New York: Pantheon, 1980); Eve Kosofsky Sedgwick, *Epistemology of the Closet* (Berkeley: University of California Press, 1990), 4-8.

91   Naomi Oreskes and Erik M. Conway, *Merchants of Doubt: How a Handful of Scientists Obscured the Truth on Issues from Tobacco Smoke to Climate Change* (New York: Bloomsbury, 2010).

92   Kant, "An Answer to the Question: 'What Is Enlightenment?'" in *Political Writings*, second edition, edited by Hans Reiss, translated by H. B. Nisbet (Cambridge: Cambridge University Press, 1991), 54-60.

93   See Jacques Lacan, *The Other Side of Psychoanalysis, The Seminar of Jacques Lacan*, Book 17, edited by Jacques-Alain Miller, translated by Russell Grigg (New York: Norton, 2007), 172: "Truth is experienced, this does not at all mean that it thereby knows [*connaît*] any more about the real." Knowledge claims to know something about the real; truth encounters it, experiences it.

94   Albert O. Hirschman, *The Passions and the Interests: Political Arguments for Capitalism Before Its Triumph* (Princeton: Princeton University Press, 1977).

95 John Stuart Mill, *On Liberty and Other Essays*, edited by John Gray (New York: Oxford University Press, 1991), 17.

96 Jacques Derrida, *Rogues: Two Essays on Reason*, translated by Pascale-Anne Brault and Michael Naas (Stanford: Stanford University Press, 2005), 28-41; for an earlier, related argument, see "Autoimmunity: Real and Symbolic Suicides – A Dialogue with Jacques Derrida," in Giovanna Borradori, *Philosophy in a Time of Terror: Dialogues with Jürgen Habermas and Jacques Derrida* (Chicago: University of Chicago Press, 2003), 85-136.

97 Kathryn Yusoff, *A Billion Black Anthropocenes or None* (Minneapolis: University of Minnesota Press, 2018), 96.

98 Andrew Nikiforuk, *The Energy of Slaves: Oil and the New Servitude* (Berkeley: Greystone Books, 2012). The continuity between slavery and the reliance on fossil fuels bears out aspects of Yusoff's argument and reveals that a racial politics permeates the geological knowledge that underpins the modern climate regime; see Yusoff.

99 Chris Washington, *Romantic Revelations: Visions of Post-Apocalyptic Life and Hope in the Anthropocene* (Toronto: University of Toronto Press, 2019), 4.

100 Homi K. Bhabha, "Introduction," in *Nation and Narration*, edited by Bhabha (New York: Routledge, 1990), 4. For a treatment of the central role of the novel in articulating the nation, especially in a postcolonial context, see a key essay in this collection: Timothy Brennan, "The National Longing for Form," 44-70.

101 See Shmuel N. Eisenstadt, editor, *Multiple Modernities* (New Brunswick NJ: Transaction, 2002).

102 For an excellent guide to the response of writer activists to such instances of postcolonial state violence against the environment, see Rob Nixon, *Slow Violence and the Environmentalism of the Poor* (Cambridge, MA: Harvard University Press, 2011).

103 For crucial arguments on the question of modernity, see Bruno Latour, *We Have Never Been Modern*, translated by Catherine Porter (Cambridge, MA: Harvard University Press, 1993), and Fredric Jameson, *A Singular Modernity: Essays on the Ontology of the Present* (New York: Verso, 2002). See also my discussion of a "nonmodern" historiography in *Monstrous Society*, 31-34.

104 Mircea Eliade, *The Myth of the Eternal Return; or, Cosmos and History*, translated by Willard R. Trask (Princeton: Princeton University Press, 1954).

105 Eliade, 102-12.

106 Eliade, 150.

107 Stefan Parmento, "The End of Days: Climate Change, Mythistory, and Cosmological Notions of Regeneration," in Rosalyn Bold, editor, *Indigenous Perceptions of the End of the World: Creating a Cosmopolitics of Change* (Cham, Switzrland: Palgrave Macmillan, 2019), 84, 85.

108 Jonathan Lear, *Radical Hope: Ethics in the Face of Cultural Devastation* (Cambridge, MA: Harvard University Press, 2008), 2, quoting from Frank B. Linderman, *Plenty-Coups: Chief of the Crows* (Lincoln: University of Nebraska Press, 1962), 308-09.

109 Lear, 49, 50.

110 Lear, 52.

111 Here I overleap the remainder of Lear's book, which carefully examines certain ethical possibilities arising from further moments in Plenty Coup's story. Since those reflections, however, pertain to how an indigenous group can call upon its own visionary traditions to imagine how to adjust to its new situation, they ultimately take us into a domain defined by modernity – and thus remain vulnerable to the response I outline here.

112 Alexandra Alter, "'We've Already Survived an Apocalypse': Indigenous Writers are Changing Sci-Fi," *New York Times*, August 4, 2020.

113 David Collings, *Monstrous Society*.

114 Mark Rifkin, *Beyond Settler Time: Temporal Sovereignty and Indigenous Self-Determination* (Durham, NC: Duke University Press, 2017).

115 Jean Baudrillard, *Symbolic Exchange and Death*, translated by Iain Hamilton Grant (Thousand Oaks, CA: Sage, 1993), 39-40. The original French version was published in 1976.

116 Orlando Patterson, *Slavery and Social Death: A Comparative Study* (Cambridge, MA: Harvard University Press, 1982), 5.

117 Frank B. Wilderson III, *Afropessimism* (New York: Liveright, 2020), 227.

118 Wilderson, 205-206.

119 Christina Sharpe, *In the Wake: On Blackness and Being* (Durham, NC: Duke University Press, 2016), 29.

120 Stefano Harvey and Fred Moten, *The Undercommons: Fugitive Planning & Black Study* (New York: Minor Compositions; Brooklyn, NY: Distributed by Autonomedia, 2013), 93.

121 See for example Harvey and Moten, 47-57.

122 Jared Sexton, "The Social Life of Social Death: On Afro-Pessimism and Black Optimism," In*Tensions* 5 (2011): 36-37.

123 Achille Mbembe, *Critique of Black Reason*, translated by Laurent Dubois (Durham, NC: Duke University Press, 2017), 167-69. For his further, extended meditation on these and related themes, see *Necropolitics*, translated by Steven Corcoran (Durham, NC: Duke University Press, 2019).

124 Frantz Fanon, *The Wretched of the Earth*, translated by Richard Philcox (New York: Grove, 2004), 2, 5-6. Fanon's reflections on these themes inspire this strand in Afropessimist thought. On the idea of "end of the world," see also Calvin Warren, "Black Nihilism and the Politics of Hope," *The New Centennial Review* 15 (2015): 239. But where Fanon conceives of the end of the colonizing regime, Warren refers to the wholesale destruction of the world – "something like *death* for the world," an event that "would destroy the field of all possible solutions."

125 For a meditation on the possibility of violent action in response to the environmental crisis, see Andreas Malm, *How to Blow Up a Pipeline: Learning to Fight in a World on Fire* (New York: Verso, 2021).

126 T. S. Eliot, "Tradition and the Individual Talent," in *Selected Essays: New Edition* (New York: Harcourt, Brace, 1950), 5.

127 Milton, *Paradise Lost*, 7.31.

128 William Shakespeare, sonnet 18, in *The Complete Works of Shakespeare*, third edition, edited by David Bevington (Glenview, IL: Scott, Foresman, 1980), 1587.

129 Walt Whitman, *Song of Myself: The First (1855) Edition* (New York: Penguin, 1976), 29.

130 Levi R. Bryant, *The Democracy of Objects* (Open Humanities Press; Ann Arbor: University of Michigan Library, 2011).

131 For an exploration of the radical erasure of human concern, see my "Blank Oblivion, Condemned Life: John Clare's 'Obscurity,'" in *Romanticism and Speculative Realism*, edited by Chris Washington and Anne C. McCarthy (New York: Bloomsbury, 2019), 75-91.

132 Jacques Lacan, *Anxiety. The Seminar of Jacques Lacan*, Book 10, edited by Jacques-Alain Miller, translated by A. R. Price (Maldon, MA: Polity, 2014), 332.

133 On the *pharmakon*, see Derrida, "Plato's Pharmacy," in *Dissemination*, translated by Barbara Johnson (Chicago: University of Chicago Press, 1981), 95-117; on the *pharmakos*, see René Girard, *Violence and the Sacred*, translated by Patrick Gregory (Baltimore: Johns Hopkins University Press, 1977), 94-98.

134 William Wycherley, *The Country Wife*, edited by Thomas H. Fujimara (Lincoln, NB: University of Nebraska Press, 1965), 139.

135 Peter Burke, *Popular Culture in Early Modern Europe* (New York: Harper and Row, 1978), 178-204.

136 Amitav Ghosh, *The Great Derangement: Climate Change and the Unthinkable* (Chicago: University of Chicago Press, 2016), 11-24.

137 Cf. Ghosh, 63-73.

138 See, for example, Thacker, *In the Dust of This Planet.*

139 For an exemplary story in that mode, see H. P. Lovecraft, "At the Mountains of Madness," in *Tales* (New York: Penguin Putnam, 2005), 481-586.

140 Kant, *Critique of the Power of Judgment*, translated by Paul Guyer (Cambridge: Cambridge University Press, 2000), 131-40. This discussion of the fate of the sublime in our time is based on the Coda to my *Disastrous Subjectivities*, 171-80.

141 Shelley, "Mont Blanc," in *Shelley's Poetry and Prose*, second edition, edited by Donald H. Reiman and Neil Fraistat (New York: Norton, 2002), 97-101, lines 107, 103, 113.

142 T. S. Eliot, "The Waste Land," in *The Complete Poems and Plays, 1909-1950* (New York: Harcourt, Brace, and World, 1971), 37-55.

143 Roland Barthes, *Critical Essays*, translated by Richard Howard (Evanston, IL: Northwestern University Press, 1972), 98.

144 Slavoj Žižek, *The Sublime Object of Ideology* (New York: Verso, 1989), 44-45.

145 Žižek, 31.

146 Baudrillard, *Simulations*, translated by Paul Foss, Paul Patton and Philip Beitchman (New York: Semiotext(e), 1983).

147 For a useful guide to the relation between the Real and the symbolic, see Bruce Fink, *The Lacanian Subject: Between Language and Jouissance* (Princeton: Princeton University Press, 1995), 24-31. For a searching, speculative account of the Real, see Žižek, *Interrogating the Real*, edited by Rex Butler and Scott Stephens (New York: Continuum, 2005).

148 For a representative statement of this argument, see Bernard Stiegler, *The Decadence of Industrial Democracies*, translated by Daniel Ross and Suzanne Arnold (Malden, MA: Polity Press, 2011); see especially 42-3, 101, 150-51. See also *The Lost Spirit of Capitalism*, translated by Ross (Malden, MA: Polity Press, 2014), 19-21. These books respectively constitute volumes 1 and 3 of the series *Disbelief*

and Discredit, one of the crucial series in which Stiegler articulates this argument.

149 This is the thesis of Stiegler's foundational book, *The Fault of Epimetheus*, volume 1 of *Technics and Time*, translated by Richard Beardsworth and George Collins (Stanford: Stanford University Press, 1998); see especially 29-81 and 134-79.

150 For a representative argument along these lines, see *Uncontrollable Societies of Disaffected Individuals*, volume 2 of *Disbelief and Discredit*, translated by Daniel Ross (Malden, MA: Polity Press, 2013), especially 50-79, 103-26. In his final years Stiegler touches on the implications of his thesis for our condition in the Anthropocene, seeing the latter as a further and more ominous development of the trajectories he analyzed earlier in his work. Although at times he mentions the potentially dire consequences of the current environmental crisis, referring for example to the prospect of an "entropic catastrophe," he does not go so far as to theorize the terminus or its implications for thought. See Stiegler, *The Neganthropocene*, edited and translated by Daniel Ross (London: Open Humanities Press, 2018), 238.

151 On capitalism's attempt to incorporate nature into its own processes, see Jason W. Moore, *Capitalism in the Web of Life: Ecology and the Accumulation of Capital* (New York: Verso, 2015).

152 Friedrich Nietzsche, *Beyond Good and Evil: Prelude to a Philosophy of the Future*, translated by Walter Kaufmann (New York: Vintage, 1966), 49.

153 Jacques Lacan, *The Psychoses, The Seminar of Jacques Lacan*, Book 3, edited by Jacques-Alain Miller, translated by Russell Grigg (New York: Norton, 1993), 13.

154 Adorno, *Aesthetic Theory*, edited by Gretel Adorno and Rolf Tiedemann (New York: Routledge and Kegan Paul, 1984).

155 Slavoj Žižek, *Interrogating the Real*, 312-13.

156 See Adorno, *The Culture Industry: Selected Essays on Mass Culture*, edited by J. M. Bernstein (New York: Verso, 1991).

157 Peter Sloterdijk, *Terror from the Air*, translated by Amy Patton and Steve Corcoran (Los Angeles: Semiotext(e), 2009), 60-61.

158 Sloterdijk, 109.

159 See Elizabeth Kolbert, *The Sixth Extinction: An Unnatural History* (New York: Henry Holt, 2014). Dipesh Chakrabarty, "The Climate of History: Four Theses," *Critical Inquiry* 35 (2009): 197-222 argues that anthropogenic climate change undoes the traditional separation of natural and social history, placing the idea of humanity as a

species within a historical framework, undermining basic assumptions of the discipline of history. But as I am suggesting here, humanity's place within history troubles its status as a species, so that it belongs at least in part in the category of an antispecies.

160 See Martin Heidegger, *Being and Time*, translated by John Macquarrie and Edward Robinson (New York: HarperPerennial, 1962), 32: Dasein is "distinguished by the fact that, in its very Being, that Being is an *issue* for it."

161 For a relevant discussion of the constitutive instabilities of Derridean hospitality, see Martin Hägglund, *Radical Atheism: Derrida and the Time of Life* (Stanford: Stanford University Press, 2008), 103-6.

162 Mark Twain, *Adventures of Huckleberry Finn,* second edition, edited by Sculley Bradley and others (New York: Norton, 1977), 229.

163 Octavia Butler, *Parable of the Talents* (New York: Warner, 1998), 65.

164 Kant, *Critique of Practical Reason,* 169.

165 Kant, *Critique of the Power of Judgment,* 318-22.

166 Seth Shostak, "Scanning the Skies," SETI institute website, August 2023: https://laserseti.net/

167 Anders, 146-47.

168 Konrad Paul Leissmann, "Hiroshima and the 'Auschwitz Principle': Günther Anders' Theory of Industrial Killing," in *The Genocidal Temptation: Auschwitz, Hiroshima, Rwanda, and Beyond,* edited by Robert S. Fry (Lanham, MD: University Press of America, 2004), 200; Anders, *Die atomare Drohung* (Munich: Radikale Überlegungen, 1981), 200, as translated and quoted in Leissmann, 202.

169 Anders, 147-48.

170 Edward Thompson, "Exterminism, the Last Stage of Civilization," in *Exterminism and Cold War,* edited by New Left Review (London: Verso, 1982), 20.

171 Derrida, "Différance," in *Margins of Philosophy,* translated by Alan Bass (Chicago: University of Chicago Press, 1981), 1-27; Hägglund, *Radical Atheism.*

172 Jacques Khalip, "Contretemps: Of Extinction and Romanticism," *Literature Compass* 13 (2016): 634.

173 Giorgio Agamben, "What Is the Contemporary?," in *What is an Apparatus?,* translated by David Kishik and Stefan Pedatella (Stanford: Stanford University Press, 2009), 44, 47.

174 Aaron Schuster, *The Trouble with Pleasure: Deleuze and Psychoanalysis* (Cambridge, MA: MIT Press, 2016), 7, 38. My argument throughout this section responds to that of Brassier, *Nihil Unbound*, who suggests that the eventual extinction of the sun is also *"the extinction of space-time"* (230) and that to find a philosophical adequation to this thought, or "acknowledge" the "truth" of extinction, one must "also recognize that he or she is already dead" (239).

175 Justin Gillis and Kenneth Chang, "Scientists Warn of Rising Oceans from Polar Melt," *New York Times*, May 12, 2014.

176 Important instances of potential tipping points include the absorption of heat into the Arctic Sea as the northern icecap melts, the increasing release of methane from Arctic permafrost, and the release of carbon dioxide from the drought-ridden, drying rainforest of the Amazon region. See my *Stolen Future*, 7-11, 26-28; Fred Pearce, *With Speed and Violence: Why Scientists Fear Tipping Points in Climate Change* (Boston: Beacon Press, 2007); and Nikolas Kozloff, *No Rain in the Amazon: How South America's Climate Change Affects the Entire Planet* (New York: Palgrave Macmillan, 2010).

177 Calvin Warren, "Black Nihilism and the Politics of Hope," *The New Centennial Review* 15 (2015): 218. I thank Taylor Schey for this reference.

178 Here I allude to the signal stance of Maurice Blanchot, who articulates his sense of refusal most directly in "Refusal," in *Friendship*, translated by Elizabeth Rottenberg (Stanford: Stanford University Press, 1997), 111-12.

179 Renato Rosaldo, "Imperialist Nostalgia," *Representations* 26 (1989): 107-22.

180 Emily Dickinson, *The Complete Poems of Emily Dickinson*, edited by Thomas H. Johnson (Boston: Little, Brown, 1960), 116.

181 *The Holy Bible*, Revised Standard Version (New York: Thomas Nelson, 1946, 1952). I thank Taylor Schey for reminding me of this passage.

182 Shelley, *Prometheus Unbound* 4.573-74, in *Shelley's Poetry and Prose*, 286.

183 On grief for grief itself, see my *Stolen Future*, 151.

184 William Wordsworth, "Ode," later given the title "Ode: Intimations of Immortality on Recollections of Early Childhood," in *Major Writings*, edited by Stephen Gill (New York: Oxford University Press, 1984), 297-302, lines 199-201, 205-6.

185 Kari Marie Norgaard, *Living in Denial: Climate Change, Emotions, and Everyday Life* (Cambridge: MIT Press, 2011), 80, 105, 132-4.

186 Adorno, "Resignation," in *Critical Models: Interventions and Catchwords*, translated by Henry W. Pickford (New York: Columbia University Press, 1998), 289-93.

187 Sigmund Freud, *Beyond the Pleasure Principle*, translated by James Strachey (New York: Norton, 1961); Cathy Caruth, *Unclaimed Experience: Trauma, Narrative, and History* (Baltimore: Johns Hopkins University Press, 1996), 6.

188 For an account that draws on the current psychiatric understanding of trauma as Post-Traumatic Stress Syndrome to posit a "Pretraumatic Stress Syndrome" that registers the impact of a future-oriented anxiety and to theorize its presence in contemporary culture, see E. Ann Kaplan, *Climate Trauma: Foreseeing the Future in Dystopian Film and Fiction* (New Brunswick, NJ: Rutgers University Press, 2016).

189 Brassier, *Nihil Unbound*, 230. Brassier goes on to complete this argument in his final paragraph, holding that philosophy can achieve a "binding of extinction, through which the will to know is finally rendered commensurate with the in-itself" (239).

190 Nixon, *Slow Violence.*

191 See Freud, "From the History of an Infantile Neurosis," in *Three Case Histories* (New York: Collier, 1963), 196, 202.

192 Lacan, *The Four Fundamental Concepts of Psychoanalysis*, edited by Jacques-Alain Miller, translated by Alan Sheridan (New York: Norton, 1981), 88-89.

193 Alain Badiou, *Being and Event*, translated by Oliver Feltham (New York: Bloomsbury, 2013), 245-53, 412-30.

194 Blanchot, *The Writing of the Disaster*, translated by Ann Smock (Lincoln: University of Nebraska Press, 1986), 141-2.

195 Kant, *Critique of Practical Reason.*

196 Bernard de Mandeville, *The Fable of the Bees* (New York: Penguin, 1989). Originally entitled *The Fable of the Bees: Or, Private Vices, Publick Benefits.* Adam Smith, *An Inquiry into the Nature and Causes of the Wealth of Nations*, Volume I (Indianapolis, IN: Liberty Fund, 1981), 26-27. For useful guides to the overall complexity of Smith's argument, see David McNally, *Political Economy and the Rise of Capitalism: A Reinterpretation* (Berkeley: University of California Press, 1988), 152-257; Vivenne Brown, *Adam Smith's Discourse: Canonicity, Commerce, Conscience* (New York: Routledge, 1994); and Athol Fitzgibbons, *Adam Smith's System of Liberty, Wealth and Virtue: The Moral and Political Foundations of* The Wealth of Nations (Oxford: Clarendon Press, 1995). On the process whereby

Smith's work achieved canonic status, see Salim Rashid, *The Myth of Adam Smith* (Northampton, MA: Edward Elgar, 1988), 135-81.

197 Herbert Marcuse, *One-Dimensional Man: Studies in the Ideology of Advanced Industrial Society* (Boston: Beacon Press, 1964), 72.

198 On the right to destroy, see my *Stolen Future*, 139-40.

199 For a related point, see Colebrook, "Not Symbiosis, Not Now: Why Anthropogenic Change is Not Really Human," *Oxford Literary Review* 34 (2012): 199, who argues that the recent "post-theoretical turns to affect, vitality, embodiment or living systems" deny "the two faces of the Anthropocene era – both the irrevocable infraction of the bounds of the earth by 'man', and the ongoing myopia of the human species' inability to think its detachment, disconnectedness, malevolence and stupidity in relation to a planet that it continues to imagine as environment, *oikos,* cosmos or *Gaia.*" The insistence on symbiosis, in short, denies humanity's status as an antispecies, those features of it that potentially cut against its contexts and its own future flourishing. But insisting too strongly on this dimension overrides a possible ethical response to this "stupidity"; one must be careful not to naturalize this dimension and thus make this antivitality into an aspect of an essential human nature.

200 For a useful discussion of this theme, see Terrence Des Pres, *The Survivor: An Anatomy of Life in the Death Camps* (New York: Oxford University Press, 1976), 27-50.

201 Albert Camus, *The Myth of Sisyphus, and Other Essays,* translated by Justin O'Brien (New York: Vintage, 1955), 5.

202 Camus, 89-91.

203 Freud, *New Introductory Lectures in Psychoanalysis,* translated by James Strachey (New York: Norton, 1964), 71. In the James Strachey translation, this sentence read, "Where id was, there ego shall be." But Freud used the ordinary German pronouns to name these agencies of the psyche, and I will follow his usage here, though I will capitalize It for clarity. Freud followed up this sentence with the reflection, "It is a work of culture – not unlike the draining of the Zuider Zee," implying that psychoanalysis in effect drains the It, making it accessible to the I; his ethics participated, one might say, in the appropriation of the psychic landscape for the purposes of culture, making psychoanalysis complicit in certain anti-ecological practices. The Lacanian reading of this sentence, which I follow here, moves in the opposite direction, insiting on the ethical project whereby the I encounters what it cannot drain, accepting the limits of its cultural impositions.

204 Lacan, *The Ethics of Psychoanalysis, The Seminar of Jacques Lacan*, Book 7, edited by Jacques-Alain Miller, translated by Dennis Porter (New York: Norton, 1992), 7.

205 For a study of themes relevant in this context, see Zupančič, *Ethics of the Real*.

206 Lee Edelman, *No Future: Queer Theory and the Death Drive* (Durham, NC: Duke University Press, 2004), 1-31; see especially 29.

207 For a related discussion of how capitalism relies on an ideology of the family and scapegoats gay people to disguise the fact that it actually loosens traditional family structures, see John D'Emilio, "Capitalism and Gay Identity," in *The Lesbian and Gay Studies Reader*, edited by Henry Abelove and others (New York: Routledge, 1993), 467-76.

208 For a discussion of the lack in the Other useful in the present context, see Žižek, *Sublime Object*, 118-128.

209 For example, Kant provides the example of one with a deposit in his possession belonging to another who has just died, arguing that he must go ahead and fulfill his duty, for if one took the money for oneself one would act on a principle that would, due to the consequences of elevating it to a universal principle, "annihilate itself." See Kant, *Critique of Practical Reason*, 27.

210 Alasdair MacIntyre, *After Virtue: A Study in Moral Theory*, third edition (Notre Dame: University of Notre Dame Press, 2007), 204-25.

211 Jean-François Lyotard, *Heidegger and "the jews,"* translated by Andreas Michel (Minneapolis: University of Minnesota Press, 1990), 80.

212 Lyotard, 81, 84. See Immanuel Lévinas, *Otherwise than Being; or, Beyond Essence*, translated by Alphonso Lingis (Pittsburgh: Duquesne University Press, 1998).

213 Lyotard, 93.

214 Lyotard, 94.

215 For pivotal statements in this regard see Levinas, *Totality and Infinity: An Essay on Exteriority*, translated by Alphonso Lingis (Pittsburgh: Duquesne University Press, 1969), and Derrida, *Given Time: I. Counterfeit Money*, translated by Peggy Kamuf (Chicago: University of Chicago Press, 1992).

216 Here I shift from my earlier thoughts on an impossible ethics in *Stolen Future*, 136-58, to take into account the new context of ethical reflection under the sign of the terminus, drawing in

part on my argument regarding ethical destitution in *Disastrous Subjectivities*, 160-69.

217 Foucault, *Language, Counter-Memory, Practice: Selected Essays and Interviews*, translated by Donald F. Bouchard and Sherry Simon (Ithaca, NY: Cornell University Press, 1977), 131, 132-3.

218 Brassier, *Nihil Unbound*, 238. In a similar vein, Thacker argues that the thought of extinction is "opposed to the idea that extinction describes an event (actual or virtual), or that extinction is the experience (or impossibility of experience) of death-as-perishing on a mass scale, or that extinction is a measurable scientific datum"; it "can only be thought . . . can only be said to exist, as a *speculative annihilation*." See Thacker, *In the Dust of this Planet*, 125.

219 Zupančič, 96-104.

220 Foucault, *The History of Sexuality: Volume I, An Introduction*, translated by Robert Hurley (New York: Vintage, 1990), 140, 138-45.

221 Foucault, *The History of Sexuality*, 137.

222 Mike Davis, *Late Victorian Holocausts: El Niño Famines and the Making of the Third World* (New York: Verso, 2001).

223 Jean Baudrillard, *Symbolic Exchange and Death*. For an extensive treatment of the contest between this reductive treatment of human beings and Baudrillardian symbolic exchange in the era of the industrial revolution, see my *Monstrous Society*.

224 Carl Schmitt, *Political Theology: Four Chapters on the Concept of Sovereignty*, translated by George Schwab (Chicago: University of Chicago Press, 2005); Agamben, *Homo Sacer: Sovereign Power and Bare Life*, translated by Daniel Heller-Roazen (Stanford: Stanford University Press, 1998).

225 Colebrook hints at a similar rereading of Agamben in "Not Symbiosis, Not Now," 187.

226 Agamben, *Homo Sacer*, 166-80. For an argument that in the nuclear era, Earth becomes a vast concentration camp, see Anders, "Theses for the Atomic Age," *The Massachusetts Review* 3 (1962), 495.

227 W. H. Auden, "September 1, 1939," *Selected Poems: New Edition*, edited by Edward Mendelson (New York: Vintage, 1979), 86-89.

228 For an earlier meditation on a form of love that endures in the midst of this disaster, see my *Stolen Future*, 152-53.

229 Friedrich Nietzsche, *The Gay Science, With a Prelude in Rhymes and an Appendix of Songs*, translated by Walter Kaufmann (New York: Vintage, 1974), 274.

230 Nietzsche, *On the Genealogy of Morals* and *Ecce Homo*, translated by Walter Kaufmann (New York: Vintage, 1967), 306.

231 Nietzsche, *Thus Spoke Zarathustra: A Book for None and All*, translated by Walter Kaufmann (New York: Penguin, 1966), 139.

232 Nietzsche, *Ecce Homo*, 258.

233 For a pivotal statement of his position, see Georges Bataille, "The Notion of Expenditure," in *Visions of Excess: Selected Writings, 1927-1939*, edited by Allan Stoekl, translated by Stoekl, Carl R. Lovitt and Donald M. Leslie, Jr. (Minneapolis: University of Minnesota Press, 1985), 116-29. For useful treatments of Bataille's work, see Derrida, "From Restricted to General Economy: A Hegelianism without Reserve," in *Writing and Difference*, translated by Alan Bass (Chicago: University of Chicago, 1978), 251-77, and Denis Hollier, *Against Architecture: The Writings of Georges Bataille*, translated by Betsy Wing (Cambridge, MA: MIT Press, 1992).

234 Rebekah Sheldon, *The Child to Come: Life after the Human Catastrophe* (Minneapolis: University of Minnesota Press, 2016), 118.

235 Georges Bataille, *Inner Experience*, translated by Leslie Anne Boldt (Albany, NY: SUNY Press, 1988), 7.

236 Bataille, *Inner Experience*, 21.

237 In his attempt to explain widespread non-reproductive sexual activities in mammals and birds, as well as non-binary gender attributes in the natural world, through concepts that go well beyond normative appropriations of Darwin's theory of evolution, Bruce Bagemihl eventually argues for what he calls "biological exuberance," drawing especially on Bataille's heterodox teaching on biological waste and extravagance. See Bagemihl, *Biological Exuberance: Animal Homosexuality and Natural Diversity* (New York: St Martin's, 1999), 252-55. Bagemihl thus foregrounds in another context the sharp corrective Bataille's thought can bring to key intellectual traditions of the modern West.

238 Heidegger, *Being and Time*, 304-11, 307.

239 Blanchot, *The Space of Literature*, translated by Ann Smock (Lincoln, NB: University of Nebraska Press, 1982), 155.

240 Blanchot, *The Space of Literature*, 126. Blanchot elaborates on the absence of the event of death, the associated impossibility of anticipating it, and the shift to a radical passivity in the face of dying at several points in his work, including *The Space of Literature*, 120-59; *The Step Not Beyond*, translated by Lycette Nelson (Albany, NY: SUNY Press, 1992), 93-100, 106-10, 123-25; and, from a slightly

different angle, *The Writing of the Disaster*, 3, 13-33, 39-40, 65-72, 117-18, 121.

241 Blanchot, *The Writing of the Disaster*, 1.

242 Blanchot, *The Writing of the Disaster*, 15, 5.

243 On the non-empirical status of the nuclear event, see Derrida, "No Apocalypse, Not Now (Full Speed Ahead, Seven Missiles, Seven Missives)," *Diacritics* 14 (1984), 20-31. For Blanchot's meditation specifically on what thinking a nuclear event may entail, see *Friendship*, 101-8.

244 Blanchot acknowledges the link between his thought of disaster and the Lacanian Real in *The Writing of the Disaster*, 38: "[W]rite in the thrall of the impossible real, that share of disaster wherein every reality, safe and sound, sinks."

Bibliography

Adorno, Theodor. *Aesthetic Theory.* Edited by Gretel Adorno and Rolf Tiedemann. Translated by C. Lenhardt. New York: Routledge and Kegan Paul, 1984.

---. *The Culture Industry: Selected Essays on Mass Culture.* Edited by J. M. Bernstein. New York: Verso, 1991.

---. *Minima Moralia: Reflections from Damaged Life.* Translated by E. F. N. Jephcott. London: Verso, 1978.

---. *Negative Dialectics.* Translated by E. B. Ashton. New York: Continuum, 1997.

---. "Resignation." In *Critical Models: Interventions and Catchwords.* Translated by Henry W. Pickford. New York: Columbia University Press, 1998. 289-93.

Agamben, Giorgio. *Homo Sacer: Sovereign Power and Bare Life.* Translated by Daniel Heller-Roazen. Stanford: Stanford University Press, 1998.

---. *The Time that Remains: A Commentary on the Letter to the Romans.* Translated by Patricia Dailey. Stanford: Stanford University Press, 2005.

---. "What Is the Contemporary?" In *What is an Apparatus?* Translated by David Kishik and Stefan Pedatella. Stanford: Stanford University Press, 2009. 39-54.

Allewaert, Monique. "Toward a Materialist Figuration: A Slight Manifesto." *English Language Notes* 51 (2013): 61-77.

Alter, Alexandra. "'We've Already Survived an Apocalypse': Indigenous Writers are Changing Sci-Fi." *New York Times*, August 4, 2020.

Anders, Günther. *Die atomare Drohung.* Munich: Radikale Überlegungen, 1981.

---. "Reflections on the H Bomb." *Dissent* 3 (1956): 146-55.

---. "Theses for the Atomic Age." *The Massachusetts Review* 3 (1962): 493-505.

Anidjar, Gil. *Semites: Race, Religion, Literature.* Stanford: Stanford University Press, 2008.

Aravamudan, Srinavas. "The Catachronism of Climate Change." *Diacritics* 41 (2013): 6-30.

Auden, W. H. *Selected Poems: New Edition.* Edited by Edward Mendelson. New York: Vintage, 1979.

Badiou, Alain. *Being and Event.* Translated by Oliver Feltham. New York: Bloomsbury, 2013.

Bagemihl, Bruce. *Biological Exuberance: Animal Homosexuality and Natural Diversity.* New York: St Martin's, 1999.

Barthes, Roland. *Critical Essays.* Translated by Richard Howard. Evanston, IL: Northwestern University Press, 1972.

Bataille, Georges. *Inner Experience.* Translated by Leslie Anne Boldt. Albany, NY: SUNY Press, 1988.

---. "The Notion of Expenditure." In *Visions of Excess: Selected Writings, 1927-1939.* Edited by Allan Stoekl. Translated by Stoekl, Carl R. Lovitt and Donald M. Leslie, Jr. Minneapolis: University of Minnesota Press, 1985. 116-29.

Baudrillard, Jean. *Simulations.* Translated by Paul Foss, Paul Patton and Philip Beitchman. New York: Semiotext(e), 1983.

---. *Symbolic Exchange and Death.* Translated by Iain Hamilton Grant. Thousand Oaks, CA: Sage, 1993.

Beck, Lewis White. *A Commentary on Kant's "Critique of Practical Reason."* Chicago: University of Chicago Press, 1960.

Benatar, David. *Better Never to Have Been: The Harm of Coming into Existence.* Oxford: Clarendon, 2006.

Benjamin, Walter. "Critique of Violence." In *Reflections: Essays, Aphorisms, Autobiographical Writings.* Edited by Peter Demetz. Translated by Edmund Jephcott. New York: Schocken, 1986. 277-300.

---. "On the Concept of History." In *Selected Writings*, Volume 4: 1938-1940. Edited by Howard Eiland and Michael W. Jennings. Translated by Edmund Jephcott and others. Cambridge, MA: Harvard University Press, 2003. 389-400.

Bhabha, Homi K. "Introduction." In *Nation and Narration.* Edited by Bhabha. New York: Routledge, 1990.

Blackmon, Douglas A. *Slavery by Another Name: The Re-Enslavement of Black Americans from the Civil War to World War II.* New York: Anchor, 2009.

Blakemore, Steven. *Burke and the Fall of Language: The French Revolution as Linguistic Event.* Hanover, NY: University Press of New England, 1988.

Blanchot, Maurice. *Friendship.* Translated by Elizabeth Rottenberg. Stanford: Stanford University Press, 1997.

---. *The Space of Literature.* Translated by Ann Smock. Lincoln, NB: University of Nebraska Press, 1982.

---. *The Step Not Beyond.* Translated by Lycette Nelson. Albany, NY: SUNY Press, 1992.

---. *The Writing of the Disaster.* Translated by Ann Smock. Lincoln, NB: University of Nebraska Press, 1986.

Blumrosen, Alfred W. and Ruth G. Blumrosen. *Slave Nation: How Slavery United the Colonies and Sparked the American Revolution.* Naperville, IL: Sourcebooks, 2005.

Bonneuil, Christophe and Jean-Baptiste Fressoz. *The Shock of the Anthropocene: The Earth, History, and Us.* Translated by David Fernbach. New York: Verso, 2017.

Borges, Jorge Luis. *Labyrinths: Selected Stories and Other Writings.* Edited by Donald A. Yates and James E. Irby. New York: New Directions, 1964.

Borradori, Giovanna. *Philosophy in a Time of Terror: Dialogues with Jürgen Habermas and Jacques Derrida.* Chicago: University of Chicago Press, 2003.

Brassier, Ray. *Nihil Unbound: Enlightenment and Extinction.* New York: Palgrave Macmillan, 2007.

Brennan, Timothy. "The National Longing for Form." In *Nation and Narration.* Edited by Homi K. Bhabha. New York: Routledge, 1990. 44-70.

Brown, Vivenne. *Adam Smith's Discourse: Canonicity, Commerce, Conscience.* New York: Routledge, 1994.

Bryant, Levi R. *The Democracy of Objects.* Open Humanities Press; Ann Arbor: University of Michigan Library, 2011. http://www.openhumanitiespress.org/books/titles/the-democracy-of-objects/.

Burke, Edmund. *Reflections on the Revolution in France, and on the Proceedings in Certain Societies in London Relative to That Event.* Edited by Conor Cruise O'Brien. New York: Penguin, 1968.

Burke, Peter. *Popular Culture in Early Modern Europe.* New York: Harper and Row, 1978.

Butler, Octavia. *Parable of the Talents.* New York: Warner, 1998.

Camus, Albert. *The Myth of Sisyphus, and Other Essays.* Translated by Justin O'Brien. New York: Vintage, 1955.

Caruth, Cathy. *Unclaimed Experience: Trauma, Narrative, and History.* Baltimore: Johns Hopkins University Press, 1996.

Caygill, Howard. *Art of Judgment.* Oxford: Basil Blackwell, 1989.

Chakrabarty, Dipesh. "The Climate of History: Four Theses." *Critical Inquiry* 35 (2009): 197-222.

Cohen, Tom, Claire Colebrook, and J. Hillis Miller. *Theory and the Disappearing Future: On de Man, On Benjamin.* New York: Routledge, 2012.

Cohen, Tom. "Toxic Assets: De Man's Remains and the Ecocatastropic Imaginary (An American Fable)." Cohen, Claire Colebrook, and J. Hillis Miller. *Theory and the Disappearing Future: On de Man, On Benjamin.* New York: Routledge, 2012. 89-129.

Colebrook, Claire. *The Death of the PostHuman: Essays on Extinction, volume 1.* Open Humanities Press; Ann Arbor, MI: University of Michigan Library, 2014.

---. "The Future in the Anthropocene: Extinction and the Imagination." In *Climate and Literature.* Edited by Adeline Johns-Putra. Cambridge: Cambridge University Press, 2019. 263-80.

---. "Not Symbiosis, Not Now: Why Anthropogenic Change is Not Really Human." *Oxford Literary Review* 34 (2012): 185-209.

Collings, David. "Blank Oblivion, Condemned Life: John Clare's 'Obscurity.'" In *Romanticism and Speculative Realism.* Edited by Chris Washington and Anne C. McCarthy. New York: Bloomsbury, 2019. 75-91.

---. *Disastrous Subjectivities: Romanticism, Modernity, and the Real.* Toronto: University of Toronto Press, 2019.

---. *Monstrous Society: Reciprocity, Discipline, and the Political Uncanny, c. 1780-1848*. Lewisburg, PA: Bucknell University Press, 2009.

---. *Stolen Future, Broken Present: The Human Significance of Climate Change*. Open Humanities Press; Ann Arbor, MI: University of Michigan Library, 2014.

---. "Toward a Poetics of Disappearance: The Vanishing Commons in Clare's 'The Lament of Swordy Well.'" *Romanticism on the Net* 72 (July 2020).

Copjec, Joan. *Imagine There's No Woman: Ethics and Sublimation*. Cambridge, MA: MIT Press, 2002.

Crossan, John Dominic and Jonathan L. Reed. *In Search of Paul: How Jesus's Apostle Opposed Rome's Empire with God's Kingdom; a New Vision of Paul's Words & World*. New York, HarperCollins, 2004.

Davis, Mike. *Late Victorian Holocausts: El Niño Famines and the Making of the Third World*. New York: Verso, 2001.

de Man, Paul. "Textual Allegories by Paul de Man." Manuscript transcription by Erin Obodiac. UCIspace@the Libraries, 2010. ucispace.lib.uci.edu/handle/10575/1092.

D'Emilio, John. "Capitalism and Gay Identity." In *The Lesbian and Gay Studies Reader*. Edited by Henry Abelove and others. New York: Routledge, 1993. 467-76.

Derrida, Jacques. *Archive Fever: A Freudian Impression*. Translated by Eric Prenowitz. Chicago: University of Chicago Press, 1995.

---. "Différance." In Derrida, *Margins of Philosophy*. Translated by Alan Bass. Chicago: University of Chicago Press, 1981. 1-27.

---. "The Ends of Man." In Derrida, *Margins of Philosophy*. Translated by Alan Bass. Chicago: University of Chicago Press, 1982. 109-136.

---. "From Restricted to General Economy: A Hegelianism without Reserve." In *Writing and Difference*. Translated by Alan Bass. Chicago: University of Chicago, 1978. 251-77.

---. *The Gift of Death* and *Literature in Secret*. Translated by David Wills. Chicago: University of Chicago Press, 2008.

---. *Given Time: I. Counterfeit Money.* Translated by Peggy Kamuf. Chicago: University of Chicago Press, 1992.

---. *Glas.* Translated by John P. Leavey, Jr. and Richard Rand. Lincoln: University of Nebraska Press, 1986.

---. "No Apocalypse, Not Now (Full Speed Ahead, Seven Missiles, Seven Missives)." Translated by Catherine Porter and Philip Lewis. *Diacritics* 14 (1984): 20-31.

---. "Plato's Pharmacy." In Derrida, *Dissemination.* Translated by Barbara Johnson. Chicago: University of Chicago Press, 1981. 61-171.

---. *Rogues: Two Essays on Reason.* Translated by Pascale-Anne Brault and Michael Naas. Stanford: Stanford University Press, 2005.

---. *Specters of Marx: The State of the Debt, the Work of Mourning, and the New International.* Translated by Peggy Kamuf. New York: Routledge, 1994.

Des Pres, Terrence. *The Survivor: An Anatomy of Life in the Death Camps.* New York: Oxford University Press, 1976.

Dickinson, Emily. *The Complete Poems of Emily Dickinson.* Edited by Thomas H. Johnson. Boston: Little, Brown, 1960.

Edelman, Lee. *No Future: Queer Theory and the Death Drive.* Durham, NC: Duke University Press, 2004.

Eisenstadt, Shmuel N., editor. *Multiple Modernities.* New Brunswick NJ: Transaction, 2002.

Eliade, Mircea. *The Myth of the Eternal Return; or, Cosmos and History.* Translated by Willard R. Trask. Princeton: Princeton University Press, 1954.

Eliot, George. *Middlemarch.* New York: Penguin, 1965.

Eliot, T. S. "The Waste Land." In *The Complete Poems and Plays, 1909-1950.* New York: Harcourt, Brace, and World, 1971. 37-55.

---. "Tradition and the Individual Talent." In *Selected Essays: New Edition.* New York: Harcourt, Brace, 1950. 3-11.

Fanon, Frantz. *The Wretched of the Earth.* Translated by Richard Philcox. New York: Grove, 2004.

Fink, Bruce. *The Lacanian Subject: Between Language and Jouissance.* Princeton: Princeton University Press, 1995.

Fitzgibbons, Athol. *Adam Smith's System of Liberty, Wealth and Virtue: The Moral and Political Foundations of* The Wealth of Nations. Oxford: Clarendon Press, 1995.

Flood, Gavin. *An Introduction to Hinduism.* Cambridge: Cambridge University Press, 1996.

Foucault, Michel. *The Foucault Reader.* Edited by Paul Rabinow. New York: Pantheon, 1984.

---. *The History of Sexuality: Volume I, An Introduction.* Translated by Robert Hurley. New York: Vintage, 1990.

---. *Language, Counter-Memory, Practice: Selected Essays and Interviews.* Translated by Donald F. Bouchard and Sherry Simon. Ithaca, NY: Cornell University Press, 1977.

---. *The Order of Things: An Archaeology of the Human Sciences.* New York: Random House, 1970.

---. *Power/Knowledge: Selected Interviews and Other Writings, 1972-1977.* Edited by Colin Gordon. Translated by Gordon and others. New York: Pantheon, 1980.

Freud, Sigmund. *Beyond the Pleasure Principle.* Translated by James Strachey. New York: Norton, 1961.

---. *New Introductory Lectures in Psychoanalysis.* Translated by James Strachey. New York: Norton, 1964.

---. *Three Case Histories.* New York: Collier, 1963.

Fukuyama, Francis. *The End of History and the Last Man.* New York: Free Press, 1992.

Ghosh, Amitav. *The Great Derangement: Climate Change and the Unthinkable.* Chicago: University of Chicago Press, 2016.

Gillis, Justin and Kenneth Chang. "Scientists Warn of Rising Oceans from Polar Melt." *New York Times,* May 12, 2014.

Girard, René. *Violence and the Sacred.* Translated by Patrick Gregory. Baltimore: Johns Hopkins University Press, 1977.

Grech, Marija. "'Where nothing ever was': Anthropomorphic Spectrality and the (im)possibility of the post-anthropocene." *New Formations* 95 (2019): 22-36.

Habermas, Jürgen. *The Structural Transformation of the Public Sphere: An Inquiry into a Category of Bourgeois Society.* Translated by Thomas Burger with the assistance of Frederick Lawrence. Cambridge, MA: MIT Press, 1991.

Hägglund, Martin. *Radical Atheism: Derrida and the Time of Life.* Stanford: Stanford University Press, 2008.

---. "Radical Atheist Materialism: A Critique of Meillassoux." In *The Speculative Turn: Continental Materialism and Realism.* Edited by Levi Bryant, Nick Srnicek and Graham Harman. Melbourne: re.press, 2011. 114-29.

Harvey, Stefano and Fred Moten. *The Undercommons: Fugitive Planning & Black Study.* New York: Minor Compositions; Brooklyn, NY: Distributed by Autonomedia, 2013.

Hegel, G. W. F. *Elements of the Philosophy of Right.* Translated by H. B. Nisbet. Cambridge: Cambridge University Press, 1991.

---. *Phenomenology of Spirit.* Translated by A. V. Miller. New York: Oxford University Press, 1977.

Heidegger, Martin. *Being and Time.* Translated by John Macquarrie and Edward Robinson. London: SCM Press, 1962.

Hirschman, Albert O. *The Passions and the Interests: Political Arguments for Capitalism Before Its Triumph.* Princeton: Princeton University Press, 1977.

Hollier, Denis. *Against Architecture: The Writings of Georges Bataille.* Translated by Betsy Wing. Cambridge, MA: MIT Press, 1992.

The Holy Bible. Revised Standard Version. New York: Thomas Nelson, 1946, 1952.

Jameson, Fredric. *A Singular Modernity: Essays on the Ontology of the Present.* New York: Verso, 2002.

Kant, Immanuel. "An Answer to the Question: 'What Is Enlightenment?'" In *Political Writings.* Second edition. Edited by Hans Reiss. Translated by H. B. Nisbet. Cambridge: Cambridge University Press, 1991. 54-60.

---. *Critique of Practical Reason.* Third edition. Translated by Lewis White Beck. Upper Saddle River, NJ: Prentice Hall, 1993.

---. *Critique of the Power of Judgment.* Translated by Paul Guyer. Cambridge: Cambridge University Press, 2000.

---. "The End of All Things." In *Religion and Rational Theology.* Translated and edited by Allen W. Wood and George Di Giovanni. Cambridge: Cambridge University Press, 1996. 217-31.

Kaplan, E. Ann. *Climate Trauma: Foreseeing the Future in Dystopian Film and Fiction.* New Brunswick, NJ: Rutgers University Press, 2016.

Khalip, Jacques. "Contretemps: Of Extinction and Romanticism." *Literature Compass* 13 (2016): 628-636.

Kolbert, Elizabeth. *The Sixth Extinction: An Unnatural History.* New York: Henry Holt, 2014.

Koselleck, Reinhart. *Futures Past: On the Semantics of Historical Time.* Translated by Keith Tribe. New York: Columbia University Press, 2004.

Kozloff, Nikolas. *No Rain in the Amazon: How South America's Climate Change Affects the Entire Planet.* New York: Palgrave Macmillan, 2010.

Lacan, Jacques. *Anxiety. The Seminar of Jacques Lacan,* Book 10. Edited by Jacques-Alain Miller. Translated by A. R. Price. Maldon, MA: Polity, 2014.

---. *The Ethics of Psychoanalysis. The Seminar of Jacques Lacan,* Book 7. Edited by Jacques-Alain Miller. Translated by Dennis Porter. New York: Norton, 1992.

---. *The Four Fundamental Concepts of Psychoanalysis.* Edited by Jacques-Alain Miller. Translated by Alan Sheridan. New York: Norton, 1981.

---. *The Other Side of Psychoanalysis. The Seminar of Jacques Lacan,* Book 17. Edited by Jacques-Alain Miller. Translated by Russell Grigg. New York: Norton, 2007.

---. *The Psychoses. The Seminar of Jacques Lacan,* Book 3. Edited by Jacques-Alain Miller. Translated by Russell Grigg. New York: Norton, 1993.

Laclau, Ernesto. *On Populist Reason.* New York: Verso, 2005.

Latour, Bruno. *We Have Never Been Modern.* Translated by Catherine Porter. Cambridge, MA: Harvard University Press, 1993.

Lear, Jonathan. *Radical Hope: Ethics in the Face of Cultural Devastation.* Cambridge, MA: Harvard University Press, 2008.

Lefort, Claude. *Democracy and Political Theory.* Translated by David Macey. Minneapolis: University of Minnesota Press, 1988.

Leissmann, Konrad Paul. "Hiroshima and the 'Auschwitz Principle': Günther Anders' Theory of Industrial Killing." In *The Genocidal Temptation: Auschwitz, Hiroshima, Rwanda, and Beyond.* Edited by Robert S. Fry. Lanham, MD: University Press of America, 2004. 193-206.

Lévinas, Immanuel. *Otherwise than Being; or, Beyond Essence.* Translated by Alphonso Lingis. Pittsburgh: Duquesne University Press, 1998.

---. *Totality and Infinity: An Essay on Exteriority.* Translated by Alphonso Lingis. Pittsburgh: Duquesne University Press, 1969.

Linderman, Frank B. *Plenty-Coups: Chief of the Crows.* Lincoln: University of Nebraska Press, 1962.

Lovecraft, H. P. *Tales.* New York: Penguin Putnam, 2005.

Lyotard, Jean-François. *Heidegger and "the jews."* Translated by Andreas Michel. Minneapolis: University of Minnesota Press, 1990.

MacIntyre, Alasdair. *After Virtue: A Study in Moral Theory.* Third edition. Notre Dame: University of Notre Dame Press, 2007.

Malm, Andreas. *How to Blow Up a Pipeline: Learning to Fight in a World on Fire.* New York: Verso, 2021.

Mandeville, Bernard de. *The Fable of the Bees.* New York: Penguin, 1989.

Marcuse, Herbert. *One-Dimensional Man: Studies in the Ideology of Advanced Industrial Society.* Boston: Beacon Press, 1964.

Marx, Karl and Friedrich Engels. *Manifesto of the Communist Party.* In *The Marx-Engels Reader.* Second edition. Edited by Robert C. Tucker. New York: Norton, 1978. 469-500.

Mbembe, Achille. *Critique of Black Reason.* Translated by Laurent Dubois. Durham, NC: Duke University Press, 2017.

---. *Necropolitics.* Translated by Steven Corcoran. Durham, NC: Duke University Press, 2019.

McNally, David. *Political Economy and the Rise of Capitalism: A Reinterpretation.* Berkeley: University of California Press, 1988.

Meillassoux, Quentin. *After Finitude: An Essay on the Necessity of Contingency.* Translated by Ray Brassier. New York: Continuum, 2008.

Mill, John Stuart. *On Liberty and Other Essays.* Edited by John Gray. New York: Oxford University Press, 1991.

Milton, John. *Complete Poems and Major Prose.* Edited by Merritt Y. Hughes. Indianapolis, IN: Odyssey Press, 1957.

Mitchell, Stephen. "Introduction." In *The Book of Job.* Translated by Mitchell. New York: HarperCollins, 1987. vii-xxxii.

Mitchell, Timothy. *Carbon Democracy: Political Power in the Age of Oil.* New York: Verso, 2011.

Moore, Jason W. *Capitalism in the Web of Life: Ecology and the Accumulation of Capital.* New York: Verso, 2015.

Nancy, Jean-Luc. *Being Singular Plural.* Translated by Robert D. Richardson and Anne E. O'Byrne. Stanford: Stanford University Press, 2000.

Nietzsche, Friedrich. *Beyond Good and Evil: Prelude to a Philosophy of the Future.* Translated by Walter Kaufmann. New York: Vintage, 1966.

---. *The Gay Science, With a Prelude in Rhymes and an Appendix of Songs.* Translated by Walter Kaufmann. New York: Vintage, 1974.

---. *On the Genealogy of Morals* and *Ecce Homo.* Translated by Walter Kaufmann. New York: Vintage, 1967.

---. *Thus Spoke Zarathustra: A Book for None and All.* Translated by Walter Kaufmann. New York: Penguin, 1966.

Nikiforuk, Andrew. *The Energy of Slaves: Oil and the New Servitude.* Berkeley: Greystone Books, 2012.

Nixon, Rob. *Slow Violence and the Environmentalism of the Poor.* Cambridge, MA: Harvard University Press, 2011.

Norgaard, Kari Marie. *Living in Denial: Climate Change, Emotions, and Everyday Life.* Cambridge: MIT Press, 2011.

Oreskes, Naomi and Erik M. Conway. *Merchants of Doubt: How a Handful of Scientists Obscured the Truth on Issues from Tobacco Smoke to Climate Change.* New York: Bloomsbury, 2010.

Parmento, Stefan. "The End of Days: Climate Change, Mythistory, and Cosmological Notions of Regeneration." In Rosalyn Bold, editor. *Indigenous Perceptions of the End of the World: Creating a Cosmopolitics of Change.* Cham, Switzerland: Palgrave Macmillan, 2019. 71-90.

Patterson, Orlando. *Slavery and Social Death: A Comparative Study.* Cambridge, MA: Harvard University Press, 1982.

Pearce, Fred. *With Speed and Violence: Why Scientists Fear Tipping Points in Climate Change.* Boston: Beacon Press, 2007.

Pfau, Thomas. *Minding the Modern: Human Agency, Intellectual Traditions, and Responsible Knowledge.* Notre Dame, IN: Notre Dame University Press, 2015.

Price, Richard. *Political Writings.* Edited by D. O. Thomas. New York: Cambridge University Press, 1991.

Rajan, Tilottama. *Romantic Narrative: Shelley, Hays, Godwin, Wollstonecraft.* Baltimore: Johns Hopkins University Press, 2010.

Rashid, Salim. *The Myth of Adam Smith.* Northampton, MA: Edward Elgar, 1988.

Richards, Thomas. *The Imperial Archive: Knowledge and the Fantasy of Empire.* New York: Verso, 1993.

Rifkin, Mark. *Beyond Settler Time: Temporal Sovereignty and Indigenous Self-Determination.* Durham, NC: Duke University Press, 2017.

Rosaldo, Renato. "Imperialist Nostalgia." *Representations* 26 (1989): 107-22.

Schmitt, Carl. *Political Theology: Four Chapters on the Concept of Sovereignty.* Translated by George Schwab. Chicago: University of Chicago Press, 2005.

Schuster, Aaron. *The Trouble with Pleasure: Deleuze and Psychoanalysis.* Cambridge, MA: MIT Press, 2016.

Sedgwick, Eve Kosofsky. *Epistemology of the Closet.* Berkeley: University of California Press, 1990.

Sexton, Jared. "The Social Life of Social Death: On Afro-Pessimism and Black Optimism." In *Tensions* 5 (2011): 1-47.

Shakespeare, William. *The Complete Works of Shakespeare.* Third edition. Edited by David Bevington. Glenview, IL: Scott, Foresman, 1980.

Sharpe, Christina. *In the Wake: On Blackness and Being.* Durham, NC: Duke University Press, 2016.

Sheldon, Rebekah. *The Child to Come: Life after the Human Catastrophe.* Minneapolis: University of Minnesota Press, 2016.

Shelley, Percy Bysshe. *Shelley's Poetry and Prose.* Second edition. Edited by Donald H. Reiman and Neil Fraistat. New York: Norton, 2002.

Shostak, Seth. "Scanning the Skies." SETI institute website. August 2023. https://laserseti.net/

Sloterdijk, Peter. *Terror from the Air.* Translated by Amy Patton and Steve Corcoran. Los Angeles: Semiotext(e), 2009.

Smith, Adam. *An Inquiry into the Nature and Causes of the Wealth of Nations.* Indianapolis, IN: Liberty Fund, 1981.

Soni, Vivasvan. *Mourning Happiness: Narrative and the Politics of Modernity.* Ithaca: Cornell University Press, 2010.

Stiegler, Bernard. *The Decadence of Industrial Democracies.* Translated by Daniel Ross and Suzanne Arnold. Malden, MA: Polity Press, 2011.

---. *The Fault of Epimetheus.* Translated by Richard Beardsworth and George Collins. Stanford: Stanford University Press, 1998.

---. *The Lost Spirit of Capitalism.* Translated by Daniel Ross. Malden, MA: Polity Press, 2014.

---. *The Neganthropocene.* Edited and translated by Daniel Ross. London: Open Humanities Press, 2018.

---. *Uncontrollable Societies of Disaffected Individuals.* Translated by Daniel Ross. Malden, MA: Polity Press, 2013.

Thacker, Eugene. *In the Dust of This Planet.* Washington, DC: Zero Books, 2011.

---. "Notes on Extinction and Existence." *Configurations* 20 (2012): 137-48.

Thompson, Edward. "Exterminism, the Last Stage of Civilization." In *Exterminism and Cold War*. Edited by New Left Review. London: Verso, 1982. 1-33.

Turner, Victor. *The Ritual Process: Structure and Anti-Structure*. New York: Aldine, 1969.

Twain, Mark. *Adventures of Huckleberry Finn*. Second edition. Edited by Sculley Bradley and others. New York: Norton, 1977.

Warren, Calvin. "Black Nihilism and the Politics of Hope." *The New Centennial Review* 15 (2015): 215-248.

Washington, Chris. *Romantic Revelations: Visions of Post-Apocalyptic Life and Hope in the Anthropocene*. Toronto: University of Toronto Press, 2019.

Weisman, Alan. *The World Without Us*. New York: St Martin's, 2007.

Whitman, Walt. *Song of Myself: The First (1855) Edition*. New York: Penguin, 1976.

Wiesel, Elie. *Night*. Translated by Stella Rodway. New York: Avon, 1960.

Wilderson, Frank B. III. *Afropessimism*. New York: Liveright, 2020.

Wordsworth, William. *Major Writings*. Edited by Stephen Gill. New York: Oxford University Press, 1984.

Wycherley, William. *The Country Wife*. Edited by Thomas H. Fujimara. Lincoln, NB: University of Nebraska Press, 1965.

Yousef, Nancy. *Isolated Cases: The Anxieties of Autonomy in Enlightenment Philosophy and Romantic Literature*. Ithaca: Cornell University Press, 2004.

Yusoff, Kathryn. *A Billion Black Anthropocenes or None*. Minneapolis: University of Minnesota Press, 2018.

Zalasiewicz, Jan, and others. "Stratigraphy of the Anthropocene." *Philosophical Transactions of the Royal Society A* 369 (March 13, 2011): 1036-55.

Žižek, Slavoj. *Interrogating the Real*. Edited by Rex Butler and Scott Stephens. New York: Continuum, 2005.

---. *The Sublime Object of Ideology*. New York: Verso, 1989.

Zupančič, Alenka, *Ethics of the Real: Kant, Lacan*. New York: Verso, 2000.

www.ingramcontent.com/pod-product-compliance
Lightning Source LLC
Chambersburg PA
CBHW020159090426
42734CB00008B/871